Regulating the Financial Sector in the Era of Globalization

Also by Zuhayr Mikdashi

FINANCIAL INTERMEDIATION IN THE 21st CENTURY

INTERNATIONAL BANKING: Innovations and New Policies

BANKERS' AND PUBLIC AUTHORITIES' MANAGEMENT OF RISKS

FINANCIAL STRATEGIES AND PUBLIC POLICIES: Banking, Insurance and Industry

TRANSNATIONAL OIL ISSUES: Policies and Perspectives

THE INTERNATIONAL POLITICS OF NATURAL RESOURCES

THE COMMUNITY OF OIL-EXPORTING COUNTRIES: A Study in Governmental Cooperation

CONTINUITY AND CHANGE IN THE WORLD OIL INDUSTRY

A FINANCIAL ANALYSIS OF MIDDLE EAST OIL CONCESSIONS: 1901–1965

LES BANQUES À L'ÈRE DE LA MONDIALISATION

Regulating the Financial Sector in the Era of Globalization

Perspectives from Political Economy and Management

Zuhayr Mikdashi
Honorary Professor and Founder, Institute of Banking and Finance
University of Lausanne, Switzerland

Foreword by
William C. Hunter
Senior Vice President and Director of Research
Federal Reserve Bank of Chicago, USA

First published 2003 by
PALGRAVE MACMILLAN
Houndmills, Basingstoke, Hampshire RG21 6XS and
175 Fifth Avenue, New York, N. Y. 10010
Companies and representatives throughout the world

PALGRAVE MACMILLAN is the global academic imprint of the Palgrave Macmillan division of St. Martin's Press, LLC and of Palgrave Macmillan Ltd. Macmillan® is a registered trademark in the United States, United Kingdom and other countries. Palgrave is a registered trademark in the European Union and other countries.

ISBN 1–4039–0626–2 hardback
ISBN 1–4039–1638–1 paperback

This book is printed on paper suitable for recycling and made from fully managed and sustained forest sources.

A catalogue record for this book is available from the British Library.

Library of Congress Cataloging-in-Publication Data
Mikdashi, Zuhayr M.
    Regulating the financial sector in the era of globalization : perspectives from political economy and management / Zuhayr Mikdashi ; foreword by William C. Hunter..
        p. cm.
    ISBN 1–4039–0626–2 – ISBN 1–4039–1638–1 (pbk.)
        1. Banks and banking–State supervision. 2. Financial institutions–State supervision. 3. Financial crises. 4. Banking law. 5. Financial institutions–Law and legislation. I. Title.
HG1725.M55 2003
354.8–dc21   2003042974

10   9   8   7   6   5   4   3   2   1
12   11   10   09   08   07   06   05   04   03

Printed and bound in Great Britain by
Antony Rowe Ltd, Chippenham and Eastbourne

Contents

List of Tables and Figures

Notes on the Contributors

William C. Hunter, who holds a BSc from Hampton University, and an MBA and Ph.D. from Northwestern University, USA, is Senior Vice President and Director of Research at the Federal Reserve Bank of Chicago. He is a member of the bank's management committee, serves as Chief Economic Adviser to the bank's president, and is an associate economist on the Federal Open Market Committee, the Federal Reserve System's key monetary policy committee. In April 2002 he organized the Chicago Fed Asset Price Bubble Conference.

Prior to joining the Chicago Federal Reserve Bank, he was Vice President in charge of basic research at the Federal Reserve Bank of Atlanta, where he also managed the financial markets group. He has held faculty positions in many well-known American universities, and has consulted with numerous government agencies and private corporations. In 1982 he was Visiting Professor at the Board of Governors of the Federal Reserve System in Washington, and in 1983 lectured at the NATO Advance Study Institute, Anacapri, Italy. He has served as the US Treasury Adviser to several monetary authorities in Europe and Asia.

He is currently co-editor of *Research in Banking and Finance* and an associate director of several important academic journals having published more than seventy articles in leading finance and economic journals and edited five books. Among his recent contributions is, 'The Internet and Commercial Banking Industry: Strategic Implications from a US Perspective' in Zuhayr Mikdashi *et al.* (ed.), *Financial Intermediation in the 21st Century* (Basingstoke: Palgrave, 2001). He is also co-editor and co-author of the treatise, 'Risk Management in the Global Economy: Measurement and Macroeconomic Implications', *Journal of Banking and Finance*, Special Issue, vol. 26, nos 2/3 (2002), pp. 205–620.

Zuhayr Mikdashi (D. Phil. in Economics and International Relations, University of Oxford) was a Professor of Banking and Finance at the University of Lausanne during the years 1976–2003.

Previously, he was Research Fellow at the Harvard University Centre for International Affairs, Resources for the Future in Washington, DC, and the Japanese Institute for Developing Economies in Tokyo; Visiting Professor at the Indiana University Graduate School of

Business Administration; Professor at the American University of Beirut, Consultant at the World Bank Group, and at other national/regional organizations; Expert-Adviser at the United Nations Centre on Transnational Corporations, New York.

He has organized several international colloquia in finance at the Graduate School of Management and Economics of the University of Lausanne, where he founded the Institute of Banking and Finance in 1989 and served as its first Director for a four-year term. He is the author of several books and articles on finance and development.

List of Abbreviations and Glossary

AMC	asset management company
BCBS	Basel Committee on Banking Supervision, Basel, Switzerland established in 1974; members: Belgium, Canada, France, Germany, Italy, Luxembourg*, Japan, The Netherlands, Spain*, Sweden, Switzerland*, United Kingdom,United States of America (*subsequently became full members)
BIS	Bank for International Settlements, Basel, Switzerland
BRA	bank restructuring agency
CAMELS	Capital adequacy, Asset quality, Management competence, Earnings strength, Liquidity sufficiency, Sensitivity to market risks
CCL	Contingent Credit Line, IMF
CCC	crisis control cycles
CD	certificate of deposit
CEO	chief executive officer
CFO	chief financial officer
CLS	continuous linked settlement
DvP	delivery versus payment
ECB	European Central Bank, Frankfurt, Germany
EEA	European Economic Area (European Union plus Norway, Liechtenstein and Iceland)
EU	European Union
FDIC	Federal Deposit Insurance Corporation, USA
FDICIA	Federal Deposit Insurance Corporation Improvement Act (1991), USA
FDIs	foreign direct investments
FHLB	Federal Home Loan Bank (System), USA
FSA	Financial Services Authority, UK
FSAP	Financial Sector Assessment Programme, IMF
FSCS	Financial Services Compensation Scheme, UK
FSF	Financial Stability Forum, BIS-Basel, Switzerland
FSI	financial soundness indicators
G-7	Regular meetings of finance ministers and central bank governors; members: Canada, France, Germany, Italy, Japan, United Kingdom, United States of America

G-8	G-7 plus Russia. Until 1998, G-8 foreign ministers and G-7 finance ministers met in conjunction with G-8 Summits. At the Birmingham Summit in 1998, the G-8 introduced the 'leaders only' format, with foreign ministers and finance ministers meeting separately in advance of the Summit; members: Canada, France, Germany, Italy, Japan, Russia, United Kingdom, United States of America
G-10	Eleven industrial countries' ministers of finance and central bank governors meet on a semi-annual basis; members: Belgium, Canada, France, Germany, Italy, Japan, The Netherlands, Sweden, Switzerland, United Kingdom, United States of America
G-24	Intergovernmental group of twenty-four on international monetary affairs; members: Algeria, Argentina, Brazil, Colombia, Democratic Republic of Congo, Côte d'Ivoire, Egypt, Ethiopia, Gabon, Ghana, Guatemala, India, Iran, Lebanon, Mexico, Nigeria, Pakistan, Peru, Philippines, South Africa, Sri Lanka, Syria, Trinidad and Tobago, Venezuela. China has the status of 'special invitee'
GAO	General Accounting Office, USA
GDP	gross domestic product
GNP	gross national product
Fed	Federal Reserve System, the US central bank
HLI	highly leveraged institution
IADI	International Association of Deposit Insurers
IAIS	International Association of Insurance Supervisors
IASB	International Accounting Standards Board, London
IBRD	International Bank for Reconstruction and Development
ICSID	International Centre for the Settlement of Investment Disputes
IDA	International Development Association
IFC	International Finance Corporation
IIF	Institute of International Finance, Washington, DC
IMF or Fund	International Monetary Fund, Washington, DC
IOSCO	International Organization of Securities Commissions
IPO	initial public offering
IRS	Internal Revenue Service, USA
IT	information technology

LLR	lender of last resort
London Club	Private-sector creditor institutions that collectively negotiate the restructuring of their loans with a country in default
LTCM	Long-Term Capital Management (HLI hedge fund)
M&A	mergers and acquisitions
MDBs	multilateral development banks
MIGA	Multilateral Investment Guarantee Agency, Washington, DC; 157 member countries
NAFTA	North American Free Trade Agreement
NASD	National Association of Securities Dealers
NASDAQ	National Association of Securities Dealers Automated Quotations system
NYSE	New York Stock Exchange
OCC	Office of the Comptroller of the Currency – US Department of the Treasury
OECD	Organization for Economic Cooperation and Development, Paris; members: Australia, Austria, Belgium, Canada, Czech Republic, Denmark, European Union, Finland, France, Germany, Greece, Hungary, Iceland, Republic of Ireland, Italy, Japan, Korea, Luxembourg, Mexico, The Netherlands, New Zealand, Norway, Poland, Portugal, Spain, Sweden, Switzerland, Turkey, United Kingdom, United States of America
OPEC	Organisation of Petroleum Exporting Countries – Vienna; members: Algeria, Indonesia, Iran, Iraq, Kuwait, Libya, Nigeria, Qatar, Saudi Arabia, United Arab Emirates, Venezuela
OPIC	Overseas Private Investment Corporation, USA
OTC	over-the-counter
OTS	Office of Thrift Supervision, US Department of the Treasury
Paris Club	Governmental creditor agencies that negotiate collectively the restructuring of their loans with a country in default – hosted by the French Treasury
P/E	price/earnings ratio
Repo	Financial instrument which serves to exchange cash temporarily for securities for a predetermined period. Various legal arrangements exist to perform that function (repurchase agreements, reverse repurchase agreements, sell/buy backs, and securities lending)

ROSC	Report on the Observance of Standards and Codes, IMF
RTGS	real-time gross settlement
SBA	Swiss Bankers' Association
SDR	Special Drawing Right, an international reserve asset created by the IMF in 1969 and valued dayly on the basis of a basket of key currencies, currently four whose weights in per cent are: US dollar 45; euro 29; Japanese yen 15; and pound sterling 11.
SEC	Securities and Exchange Commission, USA
SFBC	Swiss Federal Banking Commission
SIPA	Securities Investor Protection Act (1970), USA
SIPC	Securities Investor Protection Commission, USA
SME	small/medium-size enterprises
SNDs	subordinated notes and debentures
SPEs	special purpose entities
SRF	Supplemental Reserve Facility, IMF
TBTF	too big to fail (financial institution)
TBTR	too big to rescue (financial institution)
TMT	technology, media and telecommunications
VaR	Value at Risk
WBG	World Bank Group (IBRD, IFC, IDA and MIGA ICSID), Washington, DC
WTO	World Trade Organization, Geneva

Acknowledgements

William C. Hunter introduces this book with the quintessence of his rich expertise and experience in the field of financial regulation. Thanks to strategic vantage positions in central banking, research forums and academia – in the United States of America and internationally – he offers insightful ideas and thoughtful recommendations of particular interest to a wide spectrum of concerned readers. I am grateful for his notable contribution.

In relation to certain issues examined in this book, gratitude is also owed, without implication, to Andrew Crockett and William R. White (Bank for International Settlements – BIS), Michel Habib (University of Zurich), Sarkis Khoury (University of California), François Leroux (Graduate School of Management – HEC, Montreal), Philip Lowe (now Reserve Bank of Australia – previously at BIS), Claude Poppe (Citigroup), Bernhard Speyer (Deutsche Bank AG), Harry Stordel (Crédit Suisse Group), Grant B. Taplin (formerly of the International Monetary Fund), and David Walker (Canada Deposit Insurance Corporation). Their remarks are personal and are not necessarily those of the above-mentioned institutions.

Amanda Watkins, senior commissioning editor for this book, has been of great value in steering judiciously its publication, with the efficient help of the Palgrave/Macmillan's staff. Essential logistical and research work have been, diligently and conscientiously, provided by my graduate assistants Reda Gherbi and Johanna Keller.

Copy-editing, control of proofs, preparation of the index, and general supervision throughout the production process have been most competently and scrupulously performed thanks to Keith Povey's expertise, aided by his colleagues Elaine Towns and A. V. M. Horton.

Finally, I would be amiss not to mention my family's wonderful support.

ZUHAYR MIKDASHI

Purpose and Organization of the Book

Regulation in this volume refers to the body of policies, methods, principles, techniques and procedures that are designed to influence the behaviour and results of economic agents or participants in a market economy. Guided by the goal of enhancing and protecting public welfare, regulatory frameworks often resort to incentives or sanctions. Such instruments are intended to promote, over the longer term, higher levels of innovation, efficiency and fairness – compatible with reasonable risk-taking and stability.

Within the context of the ongoing complex transformation in the world's financial landscape characterized by increasingly interdependent and interconnected economies, this book examines the role of public authorities and of business executives in the prevention, moderation, containment and resolution of financial problems.

Chapter 1 is an introductory review of major micro and macro factors of *risk*, which, if not properly controlled, could blow up into crises of various types or importance. To reduce the eventuality of crises, the role of *governance* (Chapter 2) and of *prudential regulation* (Chapter 3) are examined. The implementation of the principles and rules of safety and soundness through effective *supervision* and *enforcement* is probed in Chapter 4. Chapter 5 examines major categories of governmental *safety nets*. Chapter 6 reflects on *financial stabilization* and the role of international organizations or forums, notably the International Monetary Fund (IMF). Chapter 7 concludes with an overview on the significance of *judgement* in the assessment and control of risks, and the prevention of crises.

The analysis is non-mathematical, with a focus on the identification and evaluation of major economic, socio-political and managerial factors of critical importance to an optimal regulation of financial intermediation. It also highlights key challenges of financial regulation in a dynamic environment calling for new developments aimed at strengthening further the resilience of financial intermediation in the service of the public good. Conceptual frameworks presented in this book are deduced from significant empirical evidence and key research studies – some of which are cited succinctly, or referred to.

The book seeks to advance the understanding of the multifaced reality of modern finance for the benefit of specialists and generalists – be they students, researchers or professionals.

Foreword: Incentive-based Supervision and Regulation of Financial Institutions

William C. Hunter

The regulation and supervision of financial firms

Banks and other financial institutions are generally considered to require regulation. One reason is that these institutions tend to be highly leveraged; that is, they have low ratios of capital to assets and cash to assets compared to other types of firms. These institutions also have assets that tend to be opaque. This is especially true in the case of commercial banks. Investors do not have as much information on a bank's condition as does the bank's management. This asymmetry of information between banks and investors – a form of capital market imperfection – makes it difficult to determine whether banks are healthy (or solvent but temporarily illiquid) during periods of economic stress.

History has shown that, during a banking or financial crisis, the potential for negative spillover to the larger economy is higher than in crises occurring in other industries, because banks typically are closely intertwined with interbank borrowings, and balances and payments clearing arrangements. This potential for systemic risk – the fear that the whole process could multiply until there is a fully-fledged banking or financial panic – is one of the major reasons that central bankers are expected to maintain the stability of the financial system in addition to their primary objective of price stability.

Effective supervision of banks and financial institutions is important, because they are important to the functioning of the economy. But regulations meant to address market failure are sometimes the root cause of banking industry problems. The problems of moral hazard, regulatory forbearance and distortions in incentives are known to result from the mispricing of the so-called safety net. These problems have been shown in numerous countries to be the underlying cause of industry problems and to have cost taxpayers enormous sums of money.

Inadequate supervision can also have obvious impacts. Institutions that engage in excessively speculative lending generally do not allocate capital to its best use. The rapid increase in US real estate prices in the 1980s is a case in point. Fuelled by imprudent bank lending, the rapid increase in real estate values was one of the primary reasons for the so-called credit crunch in the USA. It contributed to the problems at many large US commercial banks and to the US economic recession of the early 1990s.

Financial crises

In general, financial crises have their root causes in macroeconomic or microeconomic problems or shocks, and the major cause by far of most financial crises is an unstable macro economy. For example, deteriorating asset quality, asset price bubbles and wide swings in asset prices and exchange rates all obviously strain the fundamental business of banking and can lead to system-wide problems. A banking crisis is generally triggered by macroeconomic shocks, but it can be made significantly worse by microeconomic structural problems. These include poor corporate governance; distorted incentives generated by poorly structured regulatory arrangements; illegal activities such as insider lending and fraud; and general ineptness caused by factors such as poor internal controls. These shortcomings can allow a relatively minor problem to grow into a major one, as the recent Asian financial crisis reminded us.

Despite recent turmoil in world financial markets, we must remember that financial crises are nothing new. Since the 1970s alone, more than 125 countries, including the USA, have experienced at least one serious financial or banking crisis. In more than half of these episodes, a developing country's entire banking system became insolvent, and in more than forty cases the cost of resolving the crises averaged about 13 per cent of gross domestic product (GDP).

The initial lessons to be learnt from recent experiences are, first, that no single country should consider itself immune to financial crisis, and second, the cost of resolving a crisis once it has occurred is almost certain to be very high. The countries suffering financial crises typically exhibited many similar characteristics: government directed and connected lending; poor supervision of the financial system; an inadequate legal infrastructure; absence of a credit culture in which lenders and investors make judgements based on independent credit assessments and sound financial analysis; underdeveloped bond and long-term capital markets; lack of adequate accounting disclosure and transparency; ineffective systems of corporate governance; and excessive and imprudent risk-taking by financial institutions operating with explicit or implicit governmental guarantees, among others. However, the crisis countries also had unique elements that contributed, and in many cases, set off, their particular episodes: weak fixed exchange rate regimes often pegged to the US dollar, significant debt and asset price deflation, and persistent current account deficits, most often financed by short-term unstable foreign capital inflows. Thus, while most crises have much in common, they nevertheless can have unique precipitating elements.

The above list of common characteristics observed in the crisis countries suggests lessons in and of themselves. Stated differently, the third and perhaps most important lesson to be learnt from these events is that infrastructure, broadly defined to include most of these common characteristics, matters. Countries with a strong financial infrastructure, including good operational (and not just theoretical systems of supervision and regulation), legal frameworks and private property rights have tended to be more immune to financial shocks and have tended to enjoy more stable rates of growth. Such stability in the financial system breeds the necessary trust that the Federal Reserve considers essential to a well-functioning competitive financial system. Weak legal institutions for corporate governance are known to have had an important effect on the extent of currency depreciations and stock market declines in the Asia crisis countries. Measures of legal protections, enforceability of contracts, corruption and judicial efficiency were all shown to be important in determining the depth of the crisis.

Mitigating financial crises

The need for sound macroeconomic policy to protect against financial crisis is fairly self-evident. In fact, many economists and policy-makers would argue that creating the environment for stable growth is the single most important solution. It's also typically the major responsibility of central banks around the world. Nevertheless, macroeconomic instability continues to be the major cause of financial crises.

As noted above, it is absolutely essential that a minimally effective infrastructure be put in place. Localized to the banking industry, the most important components are:

- a system of laws and rules for corporate governance and property rights. This includes laws covering bankruptcy and the rights of creditors in seizing or disposing of assets;

- a uniform set of transparent accounting standards, statements and supporting schedules and reports;
- a facility providing for external bank auditors and examiners; and
- rules for public disclosure of non-proprietary financial information.

Clearly, most of these elements are outside the direct control of banks and bank supervisors. However, they are vital to the work of bank supervisors and to the ability of the market to evaluate the performance of banks. For developing economies and those in transition, it is imperative that these elements be in place before the banking system is privatized. For developed countries, it is important to realize that having some, but not all, of these elements is a recipe for trouble.

As has been made clear from the recent accounting and corporate governance scandals in the USA, the accounting system is a very basic ingredient of an efficient financial market. The rules for preparing financial statements must be clearly specified and adhered to, as these statements communicate vital information to creditors, investors, commercial counterparts and regulators alike. The need for public disclosure is closely related to the standardization of accounting principles. The question is not whether financial statements *should* be available to the public; it is *how often* they should be provided and the appropriate amount of information they should include.

There is a limited role for (heavy-handed) regulation if markets have *both* the relevant information *and* the capability to discipline banks adequately. If markets have the ability to discipline, but lack complete information, the role of regulations should be to provide the market with adequate disclosure.

The general level of public disclosure has increased as financial markets have demanded more and better information from all firms. This is particularly true in banking, where there is a need for better information on hidden reserves, loan loss provisions and non-performing loans.

The benefits of disclosure are included among the lessons policymakers have learnt as a result of derivatives' debacles of the last several years. Regulations requiring firms to disclose both their *ex ante* rationale for their derivatives' positions as well as the *ex post* performance would have resulted in many derivatives' positions being unwound much sooner and prevented the large losses that occurred. More disclosure is generally preferred to less. Disclosure and market discipline are powerful complements to the direct regulation of institutions and are an important part of the regulator's arsenal. The BIS *Core Principles for*

Effective Banking Supervision notes that disclosure is a complement to effective bank supervision.

The incentive compatible approach to supervision and regulation

Effective regulation must, first and foremost, be goal-orientated, not process-orientated. It should not discourage appropriate changes in technology and market structure. Regulation should be constructed to be self-evolving, if possible. Regulatory change that is dependent on the actions of cumbersome political bodies – national or international – is generally difficult to implement. It is better to have a structure that is designed to evolve with the industry. Regulatory goals should also be accomplished in the most efficient way possible. A regulatory approach is efficient if it accomplishes the desired goal with the least amount of negative spillover to the industry's activity. That is, supervisors should use the least intrusive approach to achieve regulatory goals. Efficient regulation should rely on market mechanisms; that is, be incentive-compatible. However, it is essential to have the appropriate infrastructure in place before relying on market-driven mechanisms.

Under the 'command and control approach' to regulation, the government simply states which actions are permitted and which are prohibited. As is well known, there are a number of problems with this approach. First, there is the problem of informational asymmetry. Regulations cannot be enforced effectively if they require credible information about a firm that is either not readily available or is overly costly to obtain. This leads to a second problem – the law of unintended consequences. In a command and control regulatory regime, pure command regulations may induce unintended behaviour by regulated firms. For example, deposit insurance is intended to safeguard the depository system. However, it is argued widely that deposit insurance contributed to the savings and loan debacle in the USA, and that explicit and implicit government guarantees in the financial sector played an important role in recent global financial crises. In the US case, it has been argued that deposit insurance in fact gave weak thrifts an incentive to increase the risk of loan portfolios. If the risk paid off, they were essentially out of financial trouble; but if it did not, the thrift insurance fund absorbed the loss. A third problem with the command approach is implementation. Because of the previous two problems, command and control regulations require significant and sometimes intrusive monitoring. This can also lead to command regulations becoming more 'complicated' than the activity they regulate. What sometimes result are 'one-size-fits-all' rules that tend to be overly restrictive and limit a firm's ability to capitalize on its competencies and comparative advantage. As regulators seek to mandate regulation that controls the behaviour of financial firms, these firms will almost simultaneously take account of by these regulations as they seek to optimize their performance. Thus, the regulations – if they are to be remotely effective – need to be set at precisely the right levels if they are to induce the desired behaviour. As is well known, this is a difficult mechanism design problem for bank regulators and one that will become increasingly difficult to solve as a result of banks' increased use of complex new financial instruments, the advance of information technology, and global consolidation, among other reasons.

The alternative to command and control regulation is the incentive compatible approach. Incentive compatible regulation has developed in direct response to the problems noted above. This approach seeks to align the incentives of the firm's owners and operators with social goals. It makes it, in the firm's *own self-interest*, to achieve regulatory objectives efficiently. It spells out desired outcomes and then allows the firm to determine how to best achieve the results. Although incentive compatible regulation is a preferred approach over the long term, it should be noted that banking and financial sector regulators in virtually all countries rely heavily on the command and control regulatory approach. Fortunately, there is a well-established trend among regulators in the developed economies to improve this type of regulation diligently, and to move effectively towards more 'performance-based' regulation.

Clearly, banking supervisors have learned the importance of ensuring that incentives induced by capital regulations are compatible with supervisory objectives. In this regard, efforts to enhance public disclosures of the scale and scope, results and risks of bank trading activities have been motivated by a desire to bring greater market discipline to bear on banks. In addition, supervisors have begun to attempt to build better financial incentives into regulatory capital requirements. The recent proposed amendments to the Basel Capital Accord are designed to provide incentives for accurate risk measurement by allowing banks to select the approach that best reflects underlying risks and associated capital levels.

As the complexity of institutions, instruments, and markets – highlighted by increased interconnectedness driven by advances in technology (both information processing technology and financial technology, or financial engineering) increases, the probability of market surprises and the need for co-ordinated supervision and regulation will almost certainly increase. In this regard, another lesson regulators and supervisors have learnt is that direct measures of risk-taking can provide misleading assessments of overall exposure in an environment characterized by complex interconnections among policies, institutions, instruments and markets. These interactions almost always produce non-normally distributed outcomes (the so-called 'fat tails' problem) or surprise correlations in situations where outcomes were thought to be *ex ante* independent. For example, direct lending exposure of global depository financial institutions to Thailand, Malaysia and South Korea were limited at the time of the crisis. However, proxy hedging of these risks in other, more liquid and deeper, markets – including those in Hong Kong, Australia, Brazil and Mexico, proved costly when these markets were affected adversely by evolving events and their spillover effects.

The possibility of the need for increased regulatory and supervisory co-ordination has been understood by some as grounds for supporting the case for a single global financial regulator. It is my belief that this growing desire for centralized regulation must be tempered with caution, given the inherent difficulties associated with the design and implementation of socially optimal regulation. As is well known, inappropriate implementation of even well-designed regulation tends to create more problems than it solves. This is because regulation does not occur in a vacuum. Firms and agents react to changes in regulation in ways that affect the effectiveness of the regulation. In essence, regulators must know exactly how economic agents will react in order to implement optimal regulatory rules. However, given that regulators are generally looking from the outside in, such understanding is difficult and elusive. This is why enhancing market discipline is so important to the overall process of international harmonization of regulation. Market discipline complements regulators' efforts, thus allowing more effective supervision. Certainly, regulators have learnt that there is no way to ensure a fail-safe financial system. Supervisors need help, and market discipline provides a partial solution. Enhancing market discipline through dynamic incentive compatible approaches is the next challenge confronting regulators more generally. Supervisors must pursue regulations that are adaptive. This is especially the case in emerging markets and economies in transition. That is, regulation must be dynamic and adaptive, since these markets/economies are in fact emerging and/or in transition.

The Federal Reserve Bank of Chicago has long pushed for more market discipline through increased disclosure and transparency, and through such schemes as mandatory issuance of subordinated debt by large and complex banking organizations. In our view, mandatory subordinated debt is incentive compatible in that it aligns the incentives and risk preferences of bondholders with those of bank supervisors. Being subordinated to other liabilities, the debt holders would be risk sensitive and would monitor and discipline bank behaviour. They would demand higher rates from riskier banks (a direct effect) and have stronger incentives to resolve problems quickly, and avoid forbearance and its associated costs. In addition, increases in interest rate spreads provide signals to supervisors that risk is increasing (an indirect effect).

The political economy of regulating the financial sector

There appears to be a growing consensus among economists and analysts that while we may know how to resolve most ongoing bank problems, there remain serious political problems in implementing the necessary solutions. This is especially the case with respect to gaining agreement to use public funds to resolve insolvencies. Governments and regulators are under political pressure to delay taking what they know to be correct but likely to be painful and unpopular actions. By reducing the threat of runs on banks, the safety-net permits regulators to avoid taking these actions. The world-wide evidence demonstrates clearly that the many regulators have become poor and unfaithful agents for their healthy bank and taxpayer principals, and have, albeit unintentionally, exacerbated the frequency of banking crises. The regulators' poor agent problem has been as costly as the banks' moral hazard problem.

The issue of moral hazard was at the root of much of the recent financial crisis in East Asia, as banks avoided due diligence in the belief that governments would cover their mistakes. Foreign lenders compounded this problem by substituting implicit sovereign guarantees for their own financial due diligence and failing to discriminate among borrowers. Failures of corporate governance were compounded by supervisory failures, and systematically weak segments of the financial sector precipitated system-wide bank failures. Financial liberalization was not accompanied by proper supervision and regulation. Procedures for failure resolution were lacking, allowing one sphere of the financial sector's weaknesses to jeopardize the entire banking system in a number of countries.

In this book, Professor Mikdashi presents a comprehensive, pragmatic and masterful examination of the complexities of financial regulation, and the role of public authorities and business executives in the prevention, moderation, containment and resolution of financial crises. The analysis presented in this volume explores the micro- and macroeconomic causes of problems in financial institutions and markets, along with their resolution processes. The book contains a strong set of observations by a knowledgeable contributor to the field as well as novel recommendations to improve banking sector resiliency and recuperative abilities. By highlighting the causes and consequences of crises, and what it takes to prevent them, it should contribute to keeping these issues at the forefront of the policy debate. The timely publication of this volume, combined with a remarkable breadth of analysis, represents a fine addition to this important field, and supervisors and financial institution executives alike should benefit greatly from its contents.

1
Introduction: Risks and Protagonists

Free trade – albeit conducted within different institutional frameworks of varying degrees of openness – have existed over various stretches of human civilization, and have spanned more or less extensive realms. In antiquity, for example, the period of *Pax Romana* (Roman peace) allowed commerce to flourish within the Roman empire, its provinces and dependencies, and beyond to non-Roman trading partners. This era is broadly defined as covering the two-century period extending from the reign of Augustus (27BC–AD14) to that of Marcus Aurelius (AD161–180). In more recent times, over long periods of the nineteenth and twentieth centuries, several countries espoused free trade and adopted the gold standard, with little or no regulation on cross-border capital movements.

The last quarter of the twentieth century witnessed the inception of a trend of economic globalization. This modern phenomenon is the outcome of protracted negotiations by the world's major economic nations, which agreed to dismantle gradually or to reduce substantially their protectionist barriers. The World Trade Organization (WTO), the International Monetary Fund (IMF), and other international institutions currently underpin the process of global multilateral freeing of trade in goods, services and capital. The WTO focuses on freeing cross-border trade, while the IMF is concerned primarily with promoting an open and stable multilateral payment system among its member countries (see Chapter 6). Cross-border financial transactions have, since the 1970s, grown considerably faster than world gross domestic product (GDP) in an environment of financial innovation and spectacular advances in information technology (IT) allowing for the instantaneous treatment, communication and diffusion of information.

Proponents of 'free capital movements' have highlighted this phenomenon's contribution to the efficient allocation of resources, based

1

on comparative advantage and international division of labour. The foregoing benefits have not been without risk to institutions or national/regional economies, however. The risks in question are identified hereafter.

1.1   Risks of a financial institution

Risk is simply defined as a 'measurable possibility of losing or not gaining value,'[1] whereas uncertainty lacks the attributes of being conceptually identifiable and/or being empirically measurable.[2] At the level of a financial enterprise, risk can be classified into four categories: (i) managerial, organizational, strategic and model-related; (ii) customers'/counter-parties' credit worthiness; (iii) concentration of exposures; and (iv) legal/operational factors. At the country or macro level, risk factors include *inter alia* business turbulences, socio-political upheavals, natural catastrophes or disasters with a human cause.

Figure 1.1 proposes a paradigm for risk management comprising two interrelated major domains. The first domain consists of risk categories (A, B, C and D in the shaded area) that are largely within the direct control of management. They cover (i) credit worthiness of customers and counter-parties; (ii) exposure or concentration of portfolios; (iii) legal/operational risks; and (iv) quality of management – judged notably by reference to its judicious strategies, efficient organization, and sound models.

The second domain covers categories of risk (E and F) that are generated mainly by external forces. These risks pertain to the socio-political and macroeconomic environment, as well as to the volatility of markets (namely, interests, yields, currencies, indices and so on). Several elements of risk can be insured totally or partially, mitigated or transferred through appropriate techniques.

The overriding goal of a private enterprise in a market economy is to create value for its stakeholders, and notably for those risking their capital. In striving for that goal, a financial institution – prompted by prudence – has access to an arsenal of risk mitigation techniques. The cost of these techniques could be more or less onerous, and their ready supply would depend on prevailing conditions. Certain risks are uninsurable: this is notable in the case of reputational and strategic risks – which affect the franchise value of an enterprise. Indeed, reputation is an intangible and precious asset often built up over many years by a visionary management and dedicated quality service. It can be compromised instantly by ignorance or greed, leading to the ruin of the enterprise.

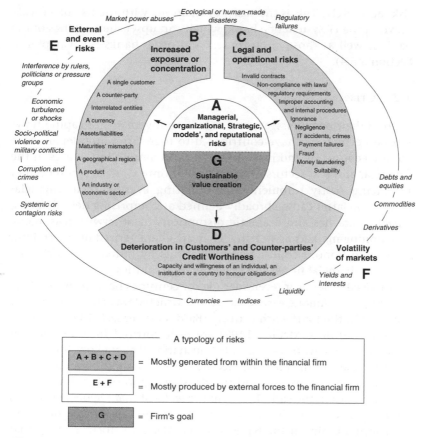

Figure 1.1 A financial institution's universe of risks: a paradigm for risk management

While management in a financial institution focuses on value creation through retaining the risks it can competently and profitably manage within the enterprise, governmental policy in an open-market economy seeks first and foremost to master system-wide risks consistent with optimal stability and sustainable growth. Judicious management pre-requires from the parties concerned to identify clearly and measure accurately all risks and their relationships. However, the analytical unravelling of the knot of risks into its separate elements is not an easy process. Indeed, conceptually distinct elements of risk are in reality difficult to disentangle and assess individually. It is accordingly difficult *ex ante* to estimate the cumulative impact of a spectrum of risks accurately. This is the case, for example, with the risk of a break-down of the IT system of a bank, which can upset the activities of the bank as well as those of customers and other banks (see Chapter 3, Section 3.5.4).

1.2   Crises

Beyond their benefits, freer and speedier movements of capital flows in open economies have contributed to increasing interdependence among economies and institutions, and to amplifying swings in the financial and real sectors of modern economies – with a potential of producing costly turbulences culminating eventually in financial crises. The latter can be broadly defined as comprising debt defaults, currency crashes and dramatic disruptions in otherwise reasonably functioning markets or systems. They are characterized by generalized failures to honour contractual obligations by individuals, financial and non-financial firms, and governmental entities.

Financial crises over recent decades or centuries have been variously documented.[3] Among early crises, those which devastated the banks of Florence in the fourteenth century (Bardi and Peruzzi, 1348), and the fifteenth century (Medici, 1492) are noteworthy.[4] In more modern times, one crisis with considerable transnational contagious impact can be traced back to the post-Napoleonic Wars' economic boom in Britain fuelled by new industries, and the massive export of British capital to Latin America in the early 1820s, in the wake of that region's liberation from Spanish rule. Britain's growing trade imbalance, however, provoked a drain on the Bank of England's gold stock. To stop that drain, the Bank of England raised its discount rate substantially in the summer of 1825. The London Stock Exchange (which had been experiencing a speculative mania) crashed in October, triggering a bank run that spread to the Continent. The Bank of England failed to stem the banking panic, and its passive attitude led to widespread bankruptcies and a recession. Lending to Latin America was suspended, hurting that region's export industry and the tax proceeds of the debtor governments concerned. This led to generalized defaults on sovereign debt. After this, it took three decades to solve the debt crisis of the region.[5]

The origins of financial crises hitting a given economy can be traced to acute domestic problems or external shocks in various areas. These areas belong to changes in financial conditions, or in real activities. They comprise, notably: the failure of important financial intermediaries, the collapse of confidence in financial markets, the surge in the price of one or more basic commodities, competitive currency devaluations, public policy blunders, default of a sizeable country on its financial obligations, cataclysms, psychological factors (such as herding behaviour, irrational exuberance or panics), speculative attacks, natural catastrophes and wars.

A foreign exchange or currency crisis can be defined as a substantial shift over a given short period by reference to an index which takes into consideration (i) a large devaluation or depreciation in a currency *vis-à-vis* one leading currency or a basket of major currencies used in international trade; and/or (ii) the central bank's intervention to defend the exchange rate by selling large amounts of international reserves or by raising substantially interest rates that absorb pressure on the said exchange rate.

Banking crises can be defined by reference to (a) grave difficulties on the liabilities side of the banking sector which could ultimately lead to a run by depositors on their banks, or to the failure to roll-over interbank deposits; and/or (b) severe problems relating to bank exposures to risk – leading to sharp declines in the value of loans, trading portfolios, real estate, and various other assets or collaterals belonging to banks.[6]

Shocks can happen concomitantly or sequentially, and can reinforce the frequency, depth, breadth or duration of crises. Thus, a banking crisis can trigger a currency crisis – and vice versa. Bank intermediation typically accounts for a larger share of the financial sector in developing countries – in comparison with developed economies, where financial markets have a prominent role.

Systemic risk refers to the situation that one or more of the above-mentioned shocks could cause serious damage to the financial system's capacity to function. For example, the financial intermediation and payment system in a country, and eventually beyond,[7] could be disrupted, with significant adverse effects on the real economy. In every financial system where institutions are interlinked through an active interbank market, there is a potential for systemic risk (see Chapter 3).

Systemic risk's negative externalities have a substantial effect on the real economy – namely by contracting national output and destroying employment. This is likely to occur through one or more of these inter-related channels: (i) payment system disruptions (including bank runs) causing the failure of enterprises; (ii) disruption of credit flows to profitable projects; (iii) collapses in asset prices leading to the contraction of wealth and of spending, and to an increase in uncertainty; and (iv) an unexpected sharp fall in consumer confidence and/or investor confidence and spending.[8]

Public policy failures – if left uncorrected – can eventually generate financial crises. Major problems in this field include: (i) unsound macroeconomic policies – for example inflationary policies, excessive public deficits, market distortions, foreign exchange overvaluation *vis-à-vis* major trading partners; (ii) deficiencies in regulatory frameworks – relating to such issues as inadequate capital rules favouring foreign borrowing regardless of risk, unsound credit policies and practices, excessive concentrations of exposures and so on; (iii) widespread deliberate condoning of managers' misconduct – in violation of known rules of prudence and accountability; and (iv) absence of rigorous controls, honest supervision and efficient enforcement systems.[9]

An economic shock with a systemic risk potential can spread beyond a national economy, and 'contaminate' other systems and countries. The most vulnerable countries are those that have fundamental intertwined links (through monetary/financial, trade, or political relationships) with the troubled source, or those that have similar socio-economic conditions. Contagion can be further fanned in an environment of opacity and uncertainty, by irrational or unfounded fears – that is, not related to economic fundamentals. The latter fears provoke increases in risk aversion, loss of confidence, herd behaviour and financial panic, in which expectations of a deterioration become self-fulfilling.

Country risk refers to the probability that the economic agents (of the private and public sector) in a given country cannot or will not service or repay their external obligations as contracted. This probability is based on key economic, social and political conditions and events affecting that country[10] (see also Chapter 6). *Sovereign risk* refers to the risk that a particular sovereign government or a sovereign-supported institution is unable or unwilling to honour its repayment obligations (foreign, as well as domestic). Country and sovereign risks are not likely to have a significant spillover impact on other economies, especially if the distressed economy is relatively small, with limited regional or international trading and financial relations. One cannot rule out, however, a herd-like non-rational behaviour of creditors and investors who lump together several emerging economies without objective differentiation of their fundamentals.

The measurement of country and sovereign risks has been clarified after the default of Mexico on its international debt in August 1982, which spread to Latin American and other developing countries world-wide. Before August 1982, US regulators accepted that 'a single US bank may have loans outstanding to 20 different public enterprises in Brazil, none of which exceeds 10 per cent of the bank's capital, but which taken together may far exceed the limit, and still not be in violation of the rule'.[11] Nowadays, all risk exposures of a financial intermediary to a foreign country are agregated, and have together not to exceed the prudential ceiling (10 per cent in the above case).

In analysing recent balance of payments'[12] crises in emerging economies, one can identify conceptually two sources of difficulties:

(i) *Liquidity*: negative changes in sentiment among creditors and investors are not justified by the fundamentals in the country concerned. Financial institutions and investors would ask for reimbursement, and stop new funding. Such an attitude is generally prompted by reasons of increased risk aversion, loss of confidence, contagion from another market, or herd behaviour.

(ii) *Solvency*: this problem results from the deterioration in the earning capacity (and consequently in the value) of the country's productive assets. A liquidity crisis can provoke a solvency crisis – in so far as the drying-up of finance impairs the normal debt-servicing capacity of the entities concerned, and jeopardizes their productive capacity and net cash flow. This situation would lead eventually to the deterioration in the value of the economy's assets, and ultimately to the insolvency and default of borrowers.[13]

A commonly used sovereign risk indicator is the differential of the yields between a hard currency Treasury Bond (for example, that of the USA) and an equal maturity debtor government's bond denominated in the same currency. The reliability of that indicator is conditional on market participants having access to timely, accurate and complete information on debtor creditworthiness – which is unfortunately not invariably the case. Moreover, investors could assign to a sovereign bond a lower risk premium, in the expectation that the debtor government in question would have the support of major creditor nations or multilateral institutions in troubled periods.[14]

Following the capital account liberalization in several economies since the 1970s, several international investment funds manage financial volatility[15] and return by allocating predetermined specified percentages of their assets across different countries and sectors. Should the market value of a fund's investment in a given country fall in the aftermath of a crisis, the manager of that fund would be induced to rebalance the fund's composition by liquidating a portion of the fund's assets in other countries – notably those with similar risk profiles in favour of safer havens. The countries encountering disinvestments would have their stock prices and currencies put under pressure – especially when liquidity in these countries is strained. This phenomenon of transmission could well be called systemic risk by indirect contagion.[16]

The threat of generalized runs on banks and total collapse of the global financial sector, is remote. It presupposes (i) the existence of open and fully integrated financial markets; and (ii) the absence of governmental actions to check that collapse. The USA, the European Union (EU)[17] and other governments have various tools to control the spread of financial problems, and co-operate to halt or moderate the transnational propagation of systemic risk (see Chapter 6).

Financial crises have cost national economies dear – in both direct resolution costs to the government and other broader costs to society – since the early 1980s. Governmental bail-out costs to financial institutions for Nordic countries (Norway, Sweden and Finland) ranged from 4 per cent to 11 per cent of their gross domestic product (GDP) in the early 1990s. Mexico's financial crisis in the mid-1990s cost its taxpayers 20 per cent of GDP. East Asian countries suffered in 1997–8 even more, with an estimated domestic cost for cleaning the Indonesian financial sector of 50–60 per cent of GDP, compared with about 40 per cent in Thailand, 15 per cent in Korea and 12 per cent in Malaysia.[18]

The foregoing figures exclude the other heavy costs encountered by distressed countries – recession, stagnation or depression, destruction of know-how and of business relations (for example, between defaulting financial institutions and their customers), drastic falls in standards of living, and the ensuing socio-political turmoil – that characterize financial crises.[19] Furthermore, indicated figures exclude forgone opportunities, anarchy and the loss of life. A country crisis can rebound on creditors and trading partners, with a substantial negative impact on the latter.

An empirical study covering a sample of forty-seven banking crises since the mid-1970s found that output losses associated with the crises had been in the range of 15 per cent to 20 per cent of annual GDP. These crises, it is worth noting, could last longer and be costlier in a developed country (for example, Japan) than in some emerging economies.[20]

Financial liberalization has allowed market forces to play a major role in setting the pattern of financial flows. It brought higher levels of growth to several countries.[21] Those with legal–regulatory systems that protect the rights of national and foreign investors are most likely to benefit.[22]

Figure 1.2 presents a sketch of the principal parties in global financial markets of interest to this book. They include governmental
entities, private firms and multilateral institutions. Parties that can
readily access international private financial markets on competitive
terms belong to credit-worthy developed and emerging economies.

Some countries (the shaded area in Figure 1.2) may not be able to tap
private international markets directly on the basis of their own

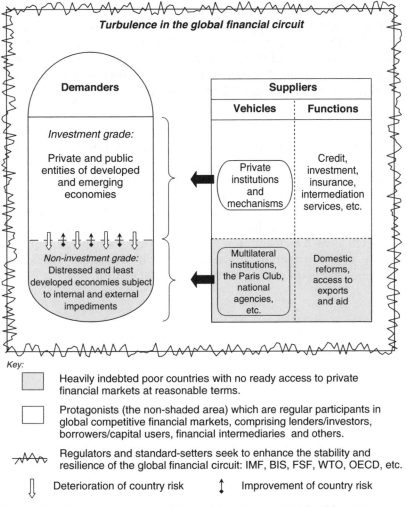

Figure 1.2 Protagonists in global financial markets: a sketch of functions and
flows

credit-rating merits. These countries can obtain limited international funding through multilateral development banks (MDBs). The latter's capital is mainly owned by the governments of developed economies. Given their superior credit ratings, MDBs (the largest is the World Bank Group) are able to borrow from world capital markets on more attractive terms than their developing member countries could otherwise obtain directly on the basis of their own credit rating. Nevertheless, the capacity for MDBs' borrowing is constrained by the size of their authorized statutory capital.[23]

Trade and financial openness has, on average, contributed to higher productivity and income per capita.[24] To participate in international financial markets, countries encountering economic problems generally require appropriate domestic reforms and easier access to export markets[25] (see also section 6.1.2 in Chapter 6).

* * *

The universe of risk is vast and dynamic. Continuous research is needed to refine definitions, measures and assessments of risk components, and to identify their interdependencies. As stated by the president of the Risk Management Association, 'risk management is not pure science; rather, it's a finely intertwined helix of analysis, economics, behaviour, chance and experience. And the helix continues to fatten as each element grows in complexity.'[26] Chapter 2 will focus on the role of corporate governance and self-regulation, with special reference to the risk management of financial institutions.

2
Challenges of Corporate Governance

This chapter analyses the important interests of key participants in the financial sector: both private stakeholders and the public authorities. Certain business practices are then examined in the light of the fundamental principles of good governance and self-regulation.

2.1 Stakeholders' risk-reward sharing

A firm's principal stakeholders comprise: its board of directors and senior management; its shareholders, employees, customers; and various suppliers or subcontractors. Their objectives should, in principle, converge in expanding the wealth of their enterprise, though they would compete in the sharing out of that wealth. Stakeholders' individual interests, which can be a source of rivalry, are outlined in Figure 2.1.

Guided by a sustainable steady growth of gross national product (GNP), the public authorities' objectives for the financial sector cover a wide spectrum. They include those relating to ensuring financial stability, efficient mobilization and allocation of financial resources, general availability of financial services, implementation of monetary policy, safety and soundness of the financial system, optimization of fiscal revenues, respect for the rules of competition, disclosure of a wide range of pertinent and truthful information, and the observance of social and ethical codes, among others.

The principles, rules, processes and structures adopted by the board of directors in monitoring and overseeing management stand for corporate governance (see Figure 2.2). The latter's aim is to replace conflicts of interest with synergy – thereby raising the wealth created by the firm – and to apportion that wealth appropriately among stakeholders. The board of directors needs to ensure that the firm is

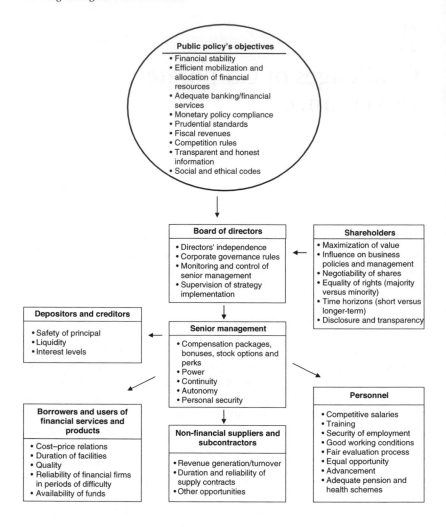

Figure 2.1 Public policy and the bargaining among a financial firm's stakeholders: converging, neutral or competing interests?

run in the interests of its shareholders and investors, and that its chief executive officer (CEO) and top management have adequate incentives to operate the company efficiently, with the aim of creating wealth for its owners and other stakeholders. Good and honest governance could have better chance of being successfully designed and implemented

The corporate governance framework should ensure the strategic guidance of the company, the effective monitoring of management by the board, and the board's accountability to the company and the shareholders.

A. Board members should act on a fully informed basis, in good faith, with due diligence and care, and in the best interests of the company and the shareholders.
B. Where board decisions may affect different shareholder groups differently, the board should treat all shareholders fairly.
C. The board should ensure compliance with applicable law and take into account the interests of stakeholders.
D. The Board should fulfil certain key functions, including:

   (1) Reviewing and guiding corporate strategy, major plans of actions, risk policy, annual budgets and busines plans, setting performance objectives, monitoring implementation and corporate performance; and overseeing major capital expenditures, acquisitions and divestitures.
   (2) Selecting, compensating, monitoring and when necessary, replacing key executives and overseeing succession planning.
   (3) Reviewing key executive and board remuneration, and ensuring a formal and transparent board nominations process.
   (4) Monitoring and managing potential conflicts of interest of management, board members and shareholders, including misuse of corporate assets and abuse in related party transactions.
   (5) Ensuring the integrity of the corporation's accounting and financial reporting systems, including the independent audit, and that appropriate systems of control are in place, in particular, systems for monitoring risk, financial control, and compliance with the law.
   (6) Monitoring the effectiveness of the governance practices under which it operates and making changes as needed.
   (7) Overseeing the process of disclosure and communications.

E. The board should be able to exercise objective judgement on corporate affairs independent, in particular, from management.

   (1) Boards should consider assigning a sufficient number of non-executive board members capable of exercising independent judgement to tasks where there is a potential for conflict of interest. Examples of such key responsibilities are financial reporting, nomination and executive and board remuneration.
   (2) Board members should devote sufficient time to their responsibilities.

F. In order to fulfil their responsibilities, board members should have access to accurate, relevant and timely information.

Source: OECD, *Principles of Corporate Governance*, Paris, 16 April 1999.

Figure 2.2 The responsibilities of the board of directors

with the active participation of genuinely independent and competent directors prompted by the longer-term interests of their company.

2.1.1   Corporate boards

Boards of directors' responsibilities are often decided by tradition and law.[1] For an effective oversight over management, having 'outsiders' (that is, people not employed by the company) on the board of directors is not sufficient. These people should be chosen by shareholders and need to have the stamina to question the CEO on his management. In reality, directors are generally chosen by a nominating committee of existing board members in which the CEO is often a key participant. The committee nominates one person for each vacancy to 'vote' on – with no choice for shareholders. It is theoretically possible for shareholders in the USA and a few other jurisdictions to nominate their own candidates. The process, however, is fraught with pitfalls, since the incumbent board and management will fight such candidates – often called 'rebels' – using all possible legal/financial means, paid for by the shareholders' money.

Three factors facilitate the election of a truly independent board: (i) the selection process should be outside the control of management; (ii) more candidates should be proposed than the vacancies available – to provide a real choice to shareholders; and (iii) the inclusion in the list of proposed candidates of any person nominated by a significant group of shareholders.

For a veteran of corporate boards of directors, the Board of Overseers of Harvard University could be used as a model. Its basic requirements are that (a) at least one-and-a-half times as many candidates should be running for the board as there are vacancies; (b) the nomination committee does not comprise any member of the existing board; (c) nominations can be made through the signatures of 0.75 per cent or more of the number of voters registered at the last election; and (d) each nomination will carry with it a sufficiently long description of each candidate's background, qualifications and plans. Voting participation is high. The commitment of elected overseers has thus proved exemplary, compared to most business boards. Emulating the Harvard model would prompt elected board members to be devoted to their constituency of shareholders, and not to the CEO, as is often the case.[2]

The independence of the board of directors can be further enhanced if it is not chaired by the CEO who – in the capacity of chairperson – is likely to influence board members. In the USA, 75 per cent of the major Standard & Poor's (S&P) 500 companies had in 2002 a single person serving as both chairperson and CEO. A survey of some 200 US corporate directors in the same year, sitting between them on approximately 500 boards, indicated that 69 per cent support splitting the CEO/chairperson role, and the appointment of a non-executive chairperson.[3]

Germany's corporate responsibilities' model is based on a two-tier system with separate membership: the non-executive supervisory board and the executive managing board. The separation, confirmed by law, gives oversight authority to the first entity over strategic decisions made by the second. For companies with more than 500 employees, trade union representatives have been part of supervisory boards since 1954. For companies with more than 2000 employees, trade unions have had parity with shareholders in these boards since 1976. Investors and employees increasingly have obtained (i) more transparency from management – subject to strict confidentiality rules – and (ii) more clout in sanctioning top executives, eventually forcing their resignation once it is deemed that they have failed in performing their responsibilities successfully.[4]

The board of directors' independence, competence and authority are crucial to the prosperity of the firm, and to rewarding properly shareholders and other stakeholders. This is fully recognized by all codes of corporate governance. According to that of the OECD – which benefited from inputs of the IMF, the World Bank and various professional groups – the board's responsibilities should be guided by the principles outlined in Figure 2.2.

2.1.2 Management's compensation

Corporate governance is concerned increasingly with the wealth distribution and control rights of investors. Shareholders, in particular, should be able to exercise their right to participate in governing their corporations. This should enable them to monitor top management and eventually to remove self-serving, crony-pone, nepotistic, unaccountable and incompetent executives.[5] The ultimate objective of shareholders is to maximize their wealth – through dividends and/or capital appreciation of their investments. Though they differ with respect to their time horizons, a significant portion of shareholders focus increasingly on near-term results.

Executives generally seek to maximize their compensation through high salaries, stock options, retirement packages and various other bonuses and perks. Evidence revealed over 2001–03 showed that a few executives of large or medium/small publicly-quoted companies enriched themselves, while their enterprises and their shareholders sustained considerable losses.[6] One source reckoned that, in 2000, 99 per cent of the S&P 500 companies distributed stock options to top executives and senior management, with only two companies showing expenses for such allocations in their annual reports. It was estimated that this practice led to overstating earnings by about 12 per cent – in comparison to a full expensing of stock options as advocated in several quarters.[7]

Companies' top executives have also sought to maximize their retirement benefits. In so doing, a few have paid little attention to the potentially adverse impact of the pursuit of self-centered interests on shareholder wealth. Reference could be made here to a European-based multinational conglomerate, ABB, which was held in iconic deference in the 1990s when it built a vast global industrial empire, including an in-house bank. Two former CEOs in that period (Percy Barnevik and Göran Lindhall) missed presenting their 'pension packages' of 148 million (€100.3 million) and 85 million (€57.6 million) Swiss francs, respectively, for the information of, and formal approval by, the company's full board of directors. These CEOs had nevertheless ostensibly championed corporate governance and transparency.

The first of these former CEOs had reportedly admitted partial responsibility for the company's poor results,[8] just before his retirement – while pocketing a performance-based 'pension' deemed to be extravagant by European standards. Indeed, in transforming the company, certain strategic decisions made by Barnevik, as CEO of ABB, proved later to have been unwise. Among these is the acquisition in the USA of the Connecticut-based Combustion Engineering, Inc. in 1990 – bought for US$1.3 billion. This firm's acquisition was based on grossly underestimated liabilities for asbestos insulation in boilers it had sold in the 1970s – though ABB knew at that time about the health risks (notably, lung cancer) related to asbestos.[9] ABB had already paid to claimants US$865 million over 1990–2001.[10] After the public uproar that occurred once details of these pension packages were disclosed to the full board, the shareholders and the general public, both of the former CEOs of ABB agreed to return 137 (Barnevik 90 and Lindhall 47) million Swiss francs (totaling €92.9 million)[11].

In another case that attracted wide public attention in 2002, a US-based multinational conglomerate, General Electric (GE) (also with important financial affiliates), offered an overly generous retirement agreement to a former chairman and CEO (agreement signed in December 1996). The said retirement covered, beyond pension plans, multi-million-dollars-worth of apartments, private-jet usage, home-entertainment systems, and other perks. The agreement stated 'the Company [GE] shall provide Mr Welch, for the remainder of his life, continued access to Company facilities and services comparable to those provided to him prior to his retirement, including to Company aircraft, cars, office, apartments, and financial planning services'.[12] In mid-September 2002, he agreed with GE's board of directors to forgo the retirement privileges.[13] Other peer CEOs have also had lavish employment and retirement packages, and occasionally egregious practices have been encouraged – such as granting and subsequently writing-off loans to executives.[14]

One of the major challenges of capitalism is to ensure that risks and rewards are shared appropriately among the stakeholders of a firm. In particular, managers need to be motivated adequately through their compensation packages (salaries, bonuses, perks, pensions and so on) in order to perform reliably in the best interest of their shareholders. This implies that the latter should know about compensation packages obtained by their executives, to be able to assess them in the light of shareholders' interests. Equally, the employees need to be fully apprised, especially when their jobs – and often their pension fund – are tied to the performance of the company for which they work.

An important function for the corporate board of directors in market economies is to align the interests of managers (known as 'agents') with the interests of owners (the 'principals') who employ these managers. The alignment of interests is optimal when incentives built into managers' contracts are compatible with market efficiency and maximum shareholder value. Managers' incentives are mainly material, consisting primarily of pay packages that cover – besides salaries – stock options and other bonuses or perks. To reach an optimal arrangement, and to avoid rent being taken by managers at the expense of shareholders, arm's-length negotiations need to be conducted by a committee of independent board members (representing genuinely shareholders interest) vis-à-vis senior management.

Shareholders are often fragmented into diffuse groups of individuals or entities. In the corporate structure, logically, they should be properly represented by a duly elected board of directors whose prerogatives include setting the executives' pay levels. Empirical evidence has shown that the majority of board members are not genuinely independent and do not operate at arm's-length *vis-à-vis* management, as is ideally required: they are often directed or influenced by top executives. The effective constraint on managers' power to extract rent to the detriment of shareholders is public opinion and improved regulation – in the absence of a major owner capable of providing discipline. Market forces are reckoned to be weak or ineffective in reaching optimal executive compensation arrangements.[15]

2.2   Controversial practices

Influential managers seek to raise their benefits by a variety of forms, and their temptation to excesses is likely to increase in periods of euphoric expectations. This can be illustrated, for example, by reference to certain unseemly business practices which have become public knowledge. For example, managers of mutual funds inflated the value of their portfolios of stocks in order to attract new and unsuspecting investors and/or keep existing ones. Their objective was to sustain the generation of attractive commission fees for themselves.[16]

Certain investment bankers are reckoned to have derived high profits during the IT or 'dotcom' bubble of 1999–2000, when underwriting the initial public offerings (IPO) of client companies. Thus Credit Suisse First Boston (CSFB) was charged by the SEC with allocating larger shares in IPOs at underpriced levels to selected favoured investors – mainly some hundred hedge funds. These investors' benefits arose from the difference between the underpriced IPO shares and the much higher price they obtained on the first trading day, when allocated shares were sold. Outsiders – usually small investors – could not access these IPOs, and would only be able to pick up shares after their price had jumped.

In the above-mentioned episode, CSFB reportedly derived its benefits through inflated commissions, and the commitment of privileged investors to paying unusually high commissions (up to US\$3 per share in lieu of 5 cents) on routine trades (other than those of the IPOs concerned) of liquid stocks – such as those of International Business Machines Corporation. The SEC estimated that the favoured investors were pressured to pay between 35 per cent and 65 per cent of their IPO profits to CSFB.[17]

An 'efficiency rationale' could ostensibly be made for the above-mentioned arrangements for splitting IPO profits with customers, namely that regular investors implicitly commit to subscribing to IPOs in slack times in qui pro quo for being favoured in good times.

Other securities firms have also been involved in unseemly conduct. One hitherto common practice among investment banking/securities firms has been to induce their financial analysts to recommend dud securities knowingly to gullible investors. These analysts would thus generate large fees for their firms, and relatively big bonus rewards for themselves. The real victims of such practices were small and unsophisticated investors who bought in the aftermarket at the height of the IT bubble in 1999–2000, only to see prices collapse soon thereafter.[18]

In May 2002, the SEC sought to address such conflicts of interest regarding financial analysts. In particular, its new rules aim at controlling 'favourable' research, by insulating analysts from influences that could impair their objectivity and independence: prohibiting compensation from specific investment banking transactions; disclosing compensation from investment banking clients; barring analysts and members of their households from investing in a company's securities prior to its initial public offering if the company is in the business sector that the analyst covers; disclosing information on equity securities owned by each analyst in the recommended companies or owned by the securities firm (1 per cent or more); among others.[19]

Some financial analysts and brokers have often – at least until the year 2002 – functioned as salesmen of their financial institutions, recommending the purchase of the securities of client firms. In so doing, they were prompted by the raising of their remuneration – the latter being linked to transaction fees and/or investment banking deals (IPOs, M&A and so on). By serving as marketing tools to attract corporate clients, securities' analysts became the pawns of investment bankers in their group, and instead of making objective recommendations based on the genuine quality of client firms, their recommendations became tainted.[20] Investors acting on their recommendations have thus unwittingly been misled.[21]

Malpractices by investment bankers, brokers, analysts or managers – when detected – have been sanctioned by the authorities representing the public interest. This was the case with Merrill Lynch, whose star analyst (Henry Blodget) had recommended during 1999–2001 that the public should purchase stocks he disparaged in private. The New York State Attorney General, Eliot Spitzer, charged that Merrill misled small investors on purpose, with overly optimistic research on companies that were also its investment banking clients.[22] Some of these investors, who suffered major losses on the basis of advice offered by securities' firms, filed 'class action' suits against financial analysts and their institutions – for example, against Henry Blodget and Merrill Lynch in relation to the common stock of Interliant, Inc., and against Jack Grubman and Citigroup's Salomon Smith Barney in relation to Global Crossing, Inc.[23]

Specifically, these complaints allege that defendants violated sections 10(b) and 20(a) of the Securities Exchange Act of 1934, and SEC Rule 10b-5, by the issuance of analyst reports regarding investee companies which recommended the purchase of their common stocks, and which set price targets without any reasonable factual basis. Furthermore, when issuing their reports, investors claim that defendants failed to disclose significant material conflicts of interest they had, in light of their use of financial analysts' reputation and reports, to obtain investment banking business. Investors contend, furthermore, that the said analysts issued their reports in which they were recommending the purchase of stocks while failing to disclose material, private and adverse information which they possessed, as well as their true opinion about the investee companies.

Merrill Lynch settled with the regulatory authorities for the wrongdoing of its employees. Yet beyond its direct pecuniary payment, the reputation of the said financial firm has suffered, thereby losing some customers, as well as talented executives to rival companies. As part of the settlement, Merrill Lynch agreed, *inter alia*, to separate the evaluation of research analyst compensation from the investment-banking business, and to make additional disclosures on relations with client firms.[24]

In the case of Citigroup's Salomon telecom star analyst, Jack Grubman, it was widely reported that he continuously rated highly in his research WorldCom as a 'buy', only to downgrade it to 'neutral' belatedly on 21 April 2002 when the stock had already lost 90 per cent of its peak value. He admitted that he had already known at '[the] beginning [of] March of this year [that] WorldCom disclosed the existence of an SEC [fraud] accounting inquiry, reduced its earnings estimates, changed CEOs, suffered multiple rating agency downgrades, and drew closer to a restructuring that would likely have diluted the equity of existing shareholders.'[25] The above-mentioned telecommunications company ended up filing for bankruptcy by September 2002.[26]

The resignation of the Salomon trader in mid-August 2002 brought him US$32 million, appoved by Citigroup's top management. He had at that time a yearly compensation package of US$20 million. Such corporate rewards were deemed to be outrageous, as the House Financial Committee Chairman, Michael Oxley, noted 'In his pursuit of riches, he has failed in his fiduciary obligations and has deceived investors for too long.'[27] He also disclosed information obtained from Citigroup thanks to the Committee's subpoena about millions of dollars of gains made by WorldCom insiders on shares of initial public offerings underwritten by Citigroup/Salomon Smith Barney. Former WorldCom Chairman, Bernard Ebbers, alone made over US$11 million.[28] Nearly all major US-based investment banks have been under investigation by the US Congress, regulators and the judiciary. Public authorities have been keen to find out the extent to which the 'spinning' of 'hot' IPO shares (those producing high capital gains over very short periods) had been a practice of favouritism to corporate executives who rewarded these banks with lucrative business.[29]

To the extent that the managers of investment banks are prompted by underwriting fees, they seek to influence their research analysts through compensation; thus these analysts are not able to provide independent appraisals. Evidence shows that analysts who attempt to be independent are harassed and ostracized. One academic researcher testified that

> securities analysts report that they are frequently pressured to make positive buy recommendations or at least to temper negative opinions. According to one survey, 61% of all analysts have experienced retaliation – threat of dismissal, salary reductions, etc. – as the result of negative research reports. Clearly, negative research reports (and ratings reductions) are hazardous to an analyst's career. Congress could either adopt, or instruct the NASD to adopt, an anti-retaliation rule: no analyst should be fired, demoted, or economically penalised for issuing a negative report, downgrading a rating, or reducing earnings, price, or similar target.

The above-mentioned researcher also cited studies demonstrating that truly 'independent' analysts have given superior quality recommendations to investors, compared with analysts associated with underwriters.[30]

Leading investment firms operating in the US market recognized in 2001–3 the responsibility of some of their executives or employees in deluding unsuspecting investors, and that malpractices (such as biased ratings on stocks), were aimed at winning investment banking business, to generate large revenues for their firms and substantial bonuses for themselves. Following on a wave of public criticisms and investigations by public regulators, the firms under scrutiny committed in 2002–3 to reform their practices. In particular, they agreed to address conflicts of interests within their firms by (a) insulating research analysts from investment banking pressure to obtain investment banking fees, (b) imposing a complete ban on the spinning of IPOs to corporate executives and directors who are in the position to 'greatly influence'

investment banking decisions, and (c) disclosing analysts' recommendations to allow the comparison and evaluation of their performance.
They furthermore agreed to a monetary settlement totalling close to
$1.4 billion, split into (i) penalties, (ii) restituting funds to investors,
(iii) committing over a five-year period to contract with at least three
independent research firms, and (iv) carrying out 'investor education'
programs. The largest payer was Citigroup ($400 million), followed by
Merrill Lynch and Credit Suisse ($200 million for each), Morgan Stanley
($125 million), Goldman Sachs ($110 million), Bear Stearns, Deutsche
Bank, J. P. Morgan Chase, Lehman Brothers, and UBS ($80 million
each), and US Bancorp's Piper Jaffray ($32.5 million). Negotiated sums
have apparently been apportioned in relation to the size and involvement of individual firms. US regulators, however, chose not to emulate
their Japanese counterparts, who have – in similar circumstances –
severely sanctioned their culprit investment firms by banning them
from securities' underwriting and related business for specified periods
of time. Some deem the above-mentioned settlement a palliative falling
short of an effective administration of justice (refer to *The Economist* in
the note).[31]

Conglomerates of financial services often give scope to conflicts of
interest. The latter arise from the absence of effective separations
(dubbed 'Chinese walls') between different functions and lines of business. Competition and transparency could be enhanced through the
development of independent institutions focused on a particular activity – for example, local or regional banking, research analysis, underwriting, securities trading, brokerage, insurance, asset management and
so on. This assumes that those working with such focussed financial
institutions will refrain from exploiting privileged foreknowledge or
other advantages at the expense of their customers to obtain personal
gain.

To require financial activities to be conducted by separately-owned
enterprises would be objected to by executives who seek diversification
and conglomerization. They would argue that their financial institution
and their customers would be denied various potential advantages of
combining several lines of financial activities, namely: (i) economies of
size and scope which allow for the spreading of fixed costs – such as the
infrastructure of technology – over a larger number of customers and
transactions; (ii) the mitigation of risks through the diversification of
operations across different geographic regions, different lines of business,
and different customers; (iii) the synergy of cross-selling a variety of
financial products and services; and (iv) the convenience of one-stop

shopping for customers, especially when the latter need complementary products or services, or when they choose to have a single agent to cater for most or all of their financial requirements.[32]

2.3 Self-interest and self-regulation

After a few scandals which injured investors and pulled down the reputation of the financial services industry, several financial and business groups sought to refine their Corporate Governance rules. One investment banker proposed a ten-point plan that he considered reflected best practices in 2002:

> First, public companies should describe to shareholders, either in the Annual Report or the Proxy Statement, how its system of corporate governance works to ensure their interests.
>
> Second, all listed companies should have a majority of independent directors, both in substance and appearance.
>
> Third, the Board of Directors should be required to determine that no 'independent' director has any relationship that the Board believes may impair or appear to impair, the exercise of that director's independent judgement. Additionally, the nature of that director's relationship should be fully disclosed to shareholders.
>
> Fourth, non-management, independent directors should be required to meet periodically without the 'insiders', including the CEO, being present.
>
> Fifth, both Audit Committees and Compensation Committees should consist entirely of independent directors.
>
> Sixth, executive officer compensation should be aligned closely with shareholders' interests by making equity a very material portion of such compensation, and compensation committees should be encouraged to develop guidelines that require that equity be held for significant periods of time.
>
> Seventh, all compensation plans granting stock options or other company securities to directors or executive officers should be approved by both the Compensation Committee and by shareholders.
>
> Eighth, all 'compensation' or other financial relationship with the company and its executive officers or directors should be fully, fairly and promptly disclosed.
>
> Ninth, all transactions in company securities by executive officers or directors should be disclosed within 48 hours.

Tenth, while 'insider' selling in advance of bad news is already illegal, in the case of CEOs, we should mandate a one-year 'claw back' in the case of bankruptcy, regardless of the reason.[33]

To restore public confidence, the world's leading financial market – the New York Stock Exchange Board – moved to tighten its corporate accountability and listing standards.[34]

Well-governed companies, have outperformed their peers. They are judged using the following criteria of governance:

(i)   *accountability of board members*, who are chosen on merit and are focused primarily on their company – with the majority of members being independent of the company's management (that is, with non-executive positions);

(ii) *shareholders' equality*, giving all shareholders the same rights (in voting, distribution of profits, freedom to dispose of their shares without blockages from management and so on);

(iii) *honest disclosure* and transparency of financial and operational data, which are communicated promptly using internationally recognized accounting standards; and

(iv) *effective independent audit*, and credible oversight by the board of directors of the top management whose compensation packages are negotiated by committees of independent board members.[35]

Human behaviour is generally driven by perceived self-interest. Allowing for unbridled self-centred interest could, however, lead some parties to interfere unduly with the rights of other parties, and could fan greed and abuse. This, in turn, would create a favourable environment for problems that have an adverse effect on the economy and society at large. Two diametrically opposed scenarios of business conduct are proposed in Figure 2.3: the one on the left leads to *prosperity*, while the other leads to *breakdowns*. Various possibilities exist, depending on the importance of certain factors, notably the power of 'good' governance and the effectiveness of self-regulation.

The failure to observe corporate governance rules is likely to exist in an environment where opacity prevails. Moreover, during the rising phase of economic cycles, executives have a propensity to neglect the principles of professionalism, prudence, vigilance and ethics. Equally, one might expect corporate scandals to be uncovered on the downturn of economic activity, as deceived and injured parties resort to courts and the media to discuss their problems and seek redress.

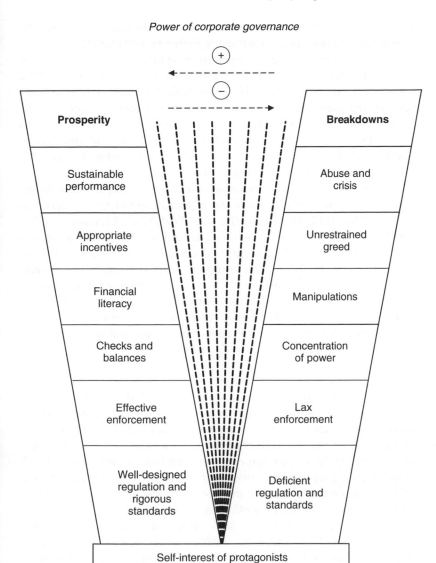

Figure 2.3   Virtuous versus vicious leadership

To gear self-interest to higher levels of sustainable growth, decision-makers need well-planned incentives, and rigorous standards. The latter require effective enforcement, supported by 'checks and balances' to avoid abuses. Balanced incentives for various stakeholders in an enterprise – as well as for various social groups – should normally favour the conjugation of effort towards achieving higher benefits for all.

One could argue that the long-term enlightened self-interest of an individual would lead him or her to avoid the traps of misconduct. One could also argue that responsible professional groups could rationally espouse self-regulation based on rigorous standards acceptable to various stakeholders. In reality, those who are self-regulated often fail to enforce the standards they agreed upon, or to apply the appropriate sanctions. This was the case in the auditing profession in the USA before 2002 (see section 4.2 of Chapter 4).[36]

The perennial challenge is whether one can be both party and judge. This can be shown, for example, by reference to failings observed in the late 1990s till 2002 within the New York Stock Exchange (NYSE) Board. The Board has the authority to enforce its rules by annual examination of its trading members (some 1366 people working for 365 firms) and its 2800 listed companies. Its self-regulatory powers enable it to resort, *inter alia*, to the taping of telephone conversations, and the monitoring of postal or electronic mail. A few of its board members were, however, CEOs of companies which came under official investigation for problems of governance and dubious practices. Indeed some quarters query the effectiveness of NYSE's self-regulatory mechanism.[37]

Self-regulation could also favour financial firms at the expense of consumers. One empirical analysis has shown that 'self-regulation of financial markets is not necessarily first-best efficient because (1) the interests of exchange members are sometimes not well aligned with the interests of the consumers of their services or (2) intra-exchange distributive conflicts can impede the adoption of efficient rules'.[38] Well-designed governmental oversight regulations – allowing for competition among financial exchanges – could therefore limit the abuse of market power and improve efficiency.

Owing to the limitations of self-regulation, official regulation is therefore needed to underpin stability and growth in a modern economy. Regulatory success in achieving the sought-after goals depends, *inter alia*, in taking proper and balanced account of the self-interest of various parties. Here lies the challenge of the public authorities in designing appropriate regulations, and in creating incentives for good governance – the enforcement of which depends on relentless public vigilance.

With the Sarbanes-Oxley Act of 30 July 2002 in the USA, corporate governance principles – notably with respect to ascertaining the truthfulness of accounts – have become more enforceable, with potential penal sentences for violations made by top management.[39] The Act shores-up the honesty and transparency of corporate financial statements by requiring corporations to make, *inter alia*, real-time disclosure of material changes in their financial conditions or operations. Such disclosures are further strengthened by SEC oversight of the Accounting Board, which represents accountants and auditors.

Unlike other advanced economies – such as those of Western Europe and Japan – regulators in the USA have important enforcement powers. Thus the US SEC can carry out its own investigations, and can file civil suits or administrative actions. Compared to its peers, its enforcement of laws and regulations is deemed to be more effective. Such enforcement is vital for the legitimacy and growth of financial markets.[40]

Markets on their own do not produce efficient mechanisms of self-governance. Regulatory frameworks are needed to protect stakeholders and financial systems. Chapter 3 examines key regulatory issues.

3
Prudential Regulatory Norms

Regulatory frameworks – often introduced or changed in the wake of the outbreak of scandals or crises – have generally sought to align private incentives with public interest. A well functioning financial sector therefore needs the underpinning of well designed and effectively implemented regulations, along with sound public policies. This chapter seeks to identify the vulnerabilities pertaining to the financial sector. It focuses on those peculiar to banks that have required governmental regulation. Capital adequacy and safety of payments systems – which have received privileged attention in international co-operation – are reviewed, along with other complementary prudential approaches relating to financial intermediation.

3.1 Vulnerabilities

The vulnerability of banks is highest among financial intermediaries. It derives largely from a few interrelated characteristics, including the following, most important, ones:[1]

1. **Financial leverage and duration mismatch**. Deposit-taking banks are in the business of using third-party funding principally to finance credit-worthy clients. Third-party funding – often in the neighbourhood of 90 per cent of such a bank's balance sheet – is largely contracted in the form of short-term or demand deposits. The latter are bank liabilities which have to be honoured on sight or within a very short period of time, and at face value. Bank management has had a propensity to favour reliance on third-party funding whose nominal financial cost is *prima facie* generally below that of owners' capital – at least from the tax angle (in most juris-

dictions, when calculating corporate taxable income, interest paid is deductible but not dividends paid).

Banks tend to hold a small fraction of their callable deposits in liquid assets or cash (since these assets produce moderate income or no income at all) and employ the balance in illiquid assets. This phenomenon of funding illiquid loans of various maturities with liquid claims is often referred to as a 'liabilities/assets' mismatch in duration. This makes banks vulnerable to the loss of depositor trust, which could lead to the sudden large withdrawal of funds.

2. **Interdependence and contagion.** Banks are closely interconnected. They have inter-bank lending (without collateral), syndicated loans, joint clearing and settlement mechanisms, counter-party operations (for example, in foreign exchange transactions, or in over-the-counter (OTC) derivatives), agency relations, joint ventures, securities trading and other relations. The losses of a defaulting bank could spread through the payment and settlement system, and are thus bound to have an instantaneous impact on other banks in the system, leading eventually to their default.

The risk of contagion is direct when a bank is unable to collect the sum owed to it by a counter-party or a debtor whose exposure is not collateralized with safe securities – notably government securities. Indirect contagion arises when market participants expect other banks in the system to encounter the same problem. The impact of the failure of one bank on other banks can be one of (i) solvency, that is when the value of a bank's assets is below that of its liabilities to third parties, leading to the failure of one or more of the impacted creditor bank(s); or (ii) liquidity, to the extent the impacted bank(s) lack the means of payment to meet sight claims, although the value of their assets is above that of their liabilities to third parties.

3. **Opacity and window-dressing.** A bank's task of collecting data and reporting is costly. Moreover, banks do not generally have information systems that collect comprehensive financial data on risk exposures on a real-time (or near real-time) basis. Central banks and regulatory agencies would like frequent reporting of risk exposures, and recognize that this could be burdensome to banks. By accepting quarterly reporting at pre-set dates on their largest positions of risk, one central bank's source admitted that banks could resort to window-dressing to moderate their declared exposures to risk on the reporting dates – which would render the reported figures unrepresentative of the intervening periods. It was

also acknowledged that 'although the failure of a large bank from one day to another is an unlikely event, it does happen'.[2]

The lack of instantaneous complete transparency about their bank's risk profile is likely to make depositors panic, should adverse rumours spread. Depositors' runs on banks are prompted by a 'flight to security'. They are generally concerned about (i) the maturity mismatch of banks' liabilities versus banks' assets; (ii) the lack of reliable information on the risks that banks care to disclose to regulators or to the public; and (iii) the fact that banks have limited liquidity payable to depositors on a 'first come, first served' basis.

Depositors are prone to rushing to withdraw their funds, not only from unsound or unsafe institution(s), but also from other solvent institutions – notably smaller banks – lest other depositors do so first. In an environment of uncertainty and opacity, jittery depositors may suspect that their banks could be contaminated by the bank in default – given such close interbank relations. They may decide to 'play it safe' by demanding that their claims be paid instantaneously.

A bank run is not limited to traditional depositors. Increasingly, banks have a significant portion of their financing through the inter-bank market and short-term negotiable instruments. Information spreads more quickly among market participants than among retail depositors, and these participants can react rapidly – thus provoking grave liquidity problems in the bank(s) concerned.[3] Such runs would drive targeted banks to the brink of liquidating assets prematurely at sacrificed prices, in the absence of a willing lender of last resort. This latter function of ultimate provider of liquidity is normally assumed by the central bank, which has a monopoly on issuing legal tender (see also section 5.8 of Chapter 5). Such fire-sales of assets is bound to hurt the targeted banks' solvency, earnings and capital and consequently sap their capacity to honour fully all their deposits and their other liabilities.

Certain authors have identified two major potential interpretations for banking panics: (i) a sudden unexpected withdrawal by bank depositors which cannot be met readily by banks' cash reserves without the intervention of the central bank – called 'random withdrawal' theory; and (ii) depositors' perception that the banking risks have increased following news of deterioration in macroeconomic conditions without hard facts on their banks' assets values – referred to as 'asymmetric information' theory.[4]

3.2 Justification of financial regulation

The above-mentioned vulnerabilities of banks, and the importance of a well-functioning financial system to economic stability and growth have generally led the public authorities in market economies to pay particular attention to the regulation of the financial sector. Three principal areas of public policy's concern cover consumer protection, disclosure, and systemic risk – as explained below.[5]

First, regulation aims generally at *protecting individual consumers' legitimate rights* against fraud, unfair or deceptive practices, and other offences. Consumer protection is also needed in order to prevent any possible abuse of market power by one or more dominant firms. Corporations have generally sought large size (often through mergers or acquisitions) and market power, for multiple reasons. In the justification of the strategy of size, management often refers to motives of staying power, greater efficiency and higher returns. In particular, the following arguments are invoked: (i) an improved capacity at absorbing shocks, (ii) economies of scale (since the initial cost of setting up a financial activity and launching a product or service is usually relatively large, while the marginal cost of offering an additional unit is relatively low); and (iii) economies of scope (through the synergy created by cross-selling multiple products to satisfy various complementary needs of customers, and using infor-mation already accumulated about them). In market economies, approval of mergers or acquisitions is authorized on the assumption that the above-mentioned advantages benefit consumers, and that concentration in the business sector does not generate abuse of market power.

Second, the financial sector is characterized by *information asymme-try* – the latter indicating that the parties to a transaction do not have the same information. Borrowers have better information than lenders about their capacity to pay back a loan and depositors have incomplete or obsolete information on their depository banks. Regulators can require the latter to observe rules of prudence and disclose needed information to enable depositors and other users of financial services to make sound decisions based on transparent, reliable and understandable information. Small depositors and other bank consumers often lack the willingness, time, skill or resources to track and analyse the risks assumed by banks and other financial intermediaries. Accordingly, they favour delegating the function of customer protection to specialized governmental agencies that are legally empowered to obtain the needed information through regular or *ad hoc* unannounced inspections of financial institutions. Appropriate penalties would then apply to transgressors. The utility of transparency is not limited to depositors and creditors, however. It also concerns other stakeholders in financial institutions. This applies particularly to shareholders, who will bear first the eventual losses of their bank. Disclosed information needs to be truthful and comprehensible – an objective that presents a continuous challenge in an industry whose products and services are increasingly sophisticated or complex.

Third, appropriate regulation and effective supervision (see Chapter 4 for supervision) strive to eliminate or moderate *systemic risk* (discussed in section 1.2 of Chapter 1). This risk concerns the potential impact of the failure of a single financial intermediary (or a single country) to honour its financial obligations on other financial intermediaries (or other countries). The rapid transmission of risk can be explained by the fact that financial firms (or countries) are closely interconnected. Solvent but illiquid banks could encounter sudden massive non-rational draw-down from their panicking depositors – in favour of perceived safer banks (domestic or foreign), Treasury bills, foreign currency assets, precious metals, real assets and so on. These depositors, along with investors, are subject to collective 'herding behaviour' – which is often fuelled by group hysteria. This phenomenon could – in the absence of adequate liquidity to distressed banks – lead to 'fire sales' of financial or other assets, and the limitation or stoppage of credit lines. This would set going a cycle of price declines, and eventually of insolvencies among companies and banks. To address the above risks, various safety nets have been designed (see Chapter 5 onwards). Most are prompted by the objective of preventing or quelling bank runs, which could propagate rapidly from weak to stronger institutions.

3.3   The mission of public authorities

Public policy is concerned with protecting and enhancing 'public good'. Certain governmental policies relating to the financial sector of a market economy are deemed to be most conducive to welfare and growth. They include, notably, financial stability; efficient mobilization and allocation of financial resources; sound monetary policy; compliance with prudential standards; protection of consumers; appropriate fiscal charges and incentives; good governance; and the observance of social and ethical codes (see Figure 2.1 on page 12).

The stability and solidity of the financial sector is of particular concern to the public authorities in a modern economy in view of the fact that it is at the centre of: (i) the payment and settlement system; (ii) the mobilization of financial resources; (iii) the distribution of credit; and (iv) the creation of means of payment. Financial regulation has focused closely on banks within the financial sector, since banks, (i) supply a significant portion of an economy's stock of money (namely, cheque accounts) through the process of financing individuals, companies and other entities, and (ii) constitute the backbone of the payment and settlement system.

The payment and settlement system is part of the fundamental infrastructure of a modern economy, in so far as every economic transaction necessitates a payment. Besides legal tender – that is, bank notes and coins created by the monetary authorities – bank deposits belonging to individuals and institutions constitute a major means through which payments are effected. Since bank deposits represent a leading liquid asset held by individuals and institutions, banks consequently offer payment services linked to these deposits (and to overdraft facilities), and have thus assumed a central role in the payment system. The central bank has a patent role in influencing the banking sector in the lending process (for example, through the instruments of monetary policy). It has also a crucial role in building sound and efficient payment/settlement systems.

In view of the fact that banks jointly form the payment system through which most transactions in a modern economy pass, bank failures thus have a stronger adverse effect on the real economy, in comparison with the failure of other firms in a large number of business sectors. Indeed, the closure of one bank could affect the solvency and liquidity of hitherto healthy banks. Such failure destroys an economy's means of payments, in so far as the non-insured deposits could be totally or partly lost. It also freezes the insured deposits, to the extent that they are not likely to be reimbursed immediately. In the latter case, deposit insurance officials in several countries conduct legal investigations and assessment of assets and liabilities, prior to the compensation of insured deposits. Delays in reimbursing these deposits, along with the destruction of non-insured deposits, are bound to have an adverse effect on national saving, consumption and investment (see section 5.5.6 in Chapter 5).

One should add that banks are not the sole source of potential disruption in the financial system. Other non-regulated or lightly-regulated financial institutions – notably hedge funds – could be a potential source of vulnerability for the financial sector (see also section 3.7 on pages 57–9).

In view of the potentially important negative externalities of a bank failure – notably by reference to systemic risk – the public authorities cannot leave the setting and observance of prudential criteria to the sole discretion of bank managers. The latter in a given bank could be tempted by a strategy of excessive risk-taking in order to generate higher profits and higher bonuses for themselves. But this strategy could backfire and produce losses that could lead to the failure of the bank in question – with the potential of spilling over to other institutions in the domestic financial sector, and beyond (see section 3.1 on pages 28–30). The protection of public interest requires regulatory–supervisory frameworks aimed at preventing as far as possible the laxness that is a breeding ground for future financial crises. Expressed differently, financial regulation is concerned primarily with promoting efficient, safe and stable financial systems.

An efficient financial sector is essential to the growth and stability of modern market economies – at national, regional and international levels. Public interventions in the financial sector need to be specifically guided by the objectives of (a) setting prerequisite conditions for the safe and efficient operation of the banking–financial system; and (b) forestalling payments crises. Such crises (see Chapter 1) cause considerable damage – such as recession, disruption of production, destruction of business relations, social conflicts, loss of property or life, and pauperization. This is illustrated readily by the many crises, that have occurred in recent decades and in various parts of the world.

Failure to observe internationally recommended codes and best standards relevant to the sound regulation or supervision of financial intermediaries and markets is a potent source of systemic risk. This has been recognized by various international organizations or forums. Standards have been set by the Basel Committee on Banking Supervision (BCBS)[6] and its sister bodies – the Committee on the Global Financial System, and the Committee on Payment and Settlement Systems which operate within the BIS. They are focused on recommending safe, sound and efficient practices for banks, financial markets and payments systems. Their prudential objectives are shared by other global rule-setting bodies, such as the International Organization of Securities Commissions (IOSCO), and the International Association of Insurance Supervisors (IAIS). The IMF and the Financial Stability Forum (FSF) – in addition to national regulatory authorities[7] – have also specified sets of key macro and micro prudential standards. Rigorous implementation of sound international standards can make domestic financial systems less prone to crises.[8]

The BCBS is the foremost standard-setting institution in the banking sector. It does not have any supranational supervisory authority: its task is to recommend best practice standards and codes. Its clout derives from the importance of member central banks and regulators, and from the fact that its recommendations are reached collegially – thereby assuring the ultimate enforcement of these standards by important countries with large financial markets. The IMF (acting alone for the industrial developed countries), joined by the World Bank (for the developing countries), use the BCBS's standards as benchmarks in their Financial Sector Assessment Programme (FSAP). The latter is a voluntary comprehensive health check-up for a country's financial sector.[9]

The FSF was created in 1999 by the Group of Seven (G-7) with the objective of promoting international financial stability through co-operation among supervisory agencies. It assesses vulnerabilities and recommends remedial actions.[10] With the disappearance of barriers among various financial markets, the FSF seeks a comprehensive assessment and monitoring of transnational financial risks on a continuous basis. It attempts to build a global web of rules and relationships among regulatory, supervisory and multilateral financial organizations aimed at detecting potential problems and studying the optimal regulatory–supervisory methods for avoiding financial crises, or for managing them whenever they break out.

Developing countries have questioned the legitimacy of standards or codes elaborated by a small group of officials (for example, the G-10) belonging to developed countries. They contest the supremacy that a few have in setting principles and rules for the world financial system. They deem it desirable and more effective for the universal application of standards to have a global approach in these matters, in which all economic regions of the world are represented.[11] The general manager of the BIS and chairman of the FSF recognized this issue in these terms: 'We have to pay attention to the question of legitimacy because the standards have to receive world-wide acceptance. That is why the Basel Committee and other committees as well have engaged in a much more thorough process of consultation and review'.[12]

In their search for promoting global financial stability, monetary authorities have given their primary attention to the safety of payment systems, to the soundness of financial intermediaries, and to effective supervision. Hereafter, key issues of payment and settlement risks, and of optimizing banks' capital are addressed. Supervision is examined in Chapter 4.

3.4   The origins of international prudential co-operation: international payment and settlement risks

Formal international co-operation in prudential matters started in 1974, triggered by the outbreak of settlement problems following the demise of Bankhaus D.I. Herstatt in Germany and Franklin National in the USA. Both suffered from very large losses in foreign exchange transactions and were subjected to fraud by, respectively, the chairman and the biggest shareholder of the above-mentioned banks.[13]

Settlement breakdowns within a single currency, as well as within the foreign exchange system, would hurt the real economy. Settlement risks have had two main origins:

(i)   *Credit* and *liquidity risks* which represent the failure of customers (individuals, businesses, governmental agencies, banks and other financial institutions) to meet their obligations in full and on time. Typically, a customer's account is credited before receiving payment in quid pro quo – that is, before the transfer of funds is executed. It is possible that in the interim period the transferor of funds has become insolvent, or has encountered a liquidity problem.

(ii) *Operational risk* in the form of an interruption in the normal flow of activities. This could result, for example, from failures in information technology (IT) covering computer systems or telecommunication services, strikes, or other internal or external contingencies. Such problems could lead to liquidity or credit risks for a bank and its customers. If the shortfall in liquidity is substantial, it is likely to spread to other participants in the same payment system, and these participants might be unable to meet their obligations. Financial intermediation would then be subjected to systemic risk.[14]

More specifically in the field of foreign exchange settlement risk, because of different time zones, New York-based banks, for example, bear the risk that the dollars they purchased with other currencies in Europe will not be delivered. Such a stoppage in payment could be caused by operational difficulties or the default of a foreign-based counter-party. This was the case of Bankhaus D.I. Herstatt which was closed on 26 June 1974 at 4:00 pm Frankfurt time by German regulators (for reasons of insolvency) before it could deliver the US$600 million it owed in relation to the Deutschmarks it had already received. US dollar transfers have to be cleared in New York, where settlement operations begin at 10:30 am New York time, which corresponds to 4:30 pm Frankfurt time. The ensuing panic among banks was then so great that they stopped their outgoing payments, provoking a quasi-paralysis of the foreign-exchange market.[15] The risk associated with the failure to honour interbank payment and settlement obligations has been dubbed the *Herstatt risk*.

The demise of Herstatt and of Franklin National triggered the first attempt by central bankers and regulators to institutionalize their co-operation in the field of prudential standards for banks. This came about through the creation at the end of 1974 of the BCBS, whose secretariat is provided by the Bank for International Settlements (BIS)[16] in Basel, Switzerland. Its members currently comprise senior representatives of monetary, regulatory or supervisory authorities of major financial centres.

The global foreign exchange market had in 2000–03 an estimated US$1.5 trillion in daily transactions, and a crisis in this market can create havoc in the international economy. The Herstatt risk – in so far as it is akin to credit risk representing the counter-party's capacity and willingness to honour its obligations – can be managed by private market participants. Notable among possible approaches are the following: (i) a bank can constitute a capital cushion to meet eventual losses arising from the failure of its counter-parties; (ii) a bank can require a collateral (a safe liquid asset or a readily fungible guarantee) in a foreign exchange deal pending full settlement of the agreed transaction(s); (iii) participants can ask for an instantaneous 'continuous linked settlement' (CLS) of currencies; and (iv) a party can resort to netting *vis-à-vis* its counter-party.

The most active financial firms trading in foreign currencies (some sixty) agreed in 2001 to create the CLS Bank (incorporated in New York) to centralize their trade in seven currencies (AUD, CAD, CHF, EUR, GBP, JPY and USD) on a 'delivery versus payment' (DvP) basis, which began operations on 9 September 2002. This multilateral bank does not pay any party unless the buyer and the seller in the foreign exchange deal have funds available with the CLS Bank. Compared with the previous practice of foreign exchange settlement, which took on average two working days, CLS eliminates settlement risk, and reduces the liquidity needed in settling foreign exchange trades. It is envisaged that participating financial firms will be able to make payments on each other's behalf. Such operations, however, reintroduce an element of Herstatt risk if a partner does not honour commitments. Central bankers are still concerned about the possibility of systemic failure occasioned by a problem within the CLS Bank itself.[17] Direct oversight of the CLS operations is primarily assured by the US Federal Reserve System, but it will nevertheless entail the close co-operation of European and other supervisory authorities.[18]

Several central banks have already resorted in their national or regional payment and settlement systems to a continuous real-time process. In this process, funds are transferred and settled on a trans-action-by-transaction basis (called real-time gross settlement – RTGS), as and when these transactions are made instead of waiting for some later designated time. In several countries, central banks offer commercial banks intra-day credit for large-value real-time gross settlement – subject to full collateralization. The latter protects the central bank from losses,[19] and avoids liquidity gridlock problems.

Continuous on-line settlement has reduced the size and duration of banks' exposure to each other, as well as the credit and liquidity risks inherent in a payment's system. DvP and RTGS are thus reckoned to have reduced significantly the risk of contagion, and therefore also systemic risk.[20] Besides using real-time settlement, the potential for direct contagion could be further reduced by resorting to certain counter-party credit risk mitigation techniques, notably:

- *Ceiling.* This consists of setting upper limits for counterparty exposures. The EU regulation sets up that limit at 25 per cent of the capital base, although exposures between financial institutions of less than one year are exempted from the rule.
- *Netting.* Banks have important exposures *vis-à-vis* each other. The operation consists of netting both positive and negative positions against the same counter-party. These positions are sizeable in derivatives, and netting has reduced the credit position of Swedish banks by 55 per cent to 60 per cent for their fifteen largest counter-parties.[21]
- *Collateral.* Credit positions will be guaranteed by collaterals. The counter-party would be required to provide readily fungible securities. These are usually governmental debt instruments. Banks may not, however, have the amount of securities required, and the operation could be costly.

Absolute safety of the payment system – in which banks play a crucial role – implies that no bank could default. Such a situation is bound to be incompatible with market efficiency, which requires the demise of non-performing or poorly-performing institutions. Appropriate trade-off between levels of safety and efficiency of the payments system can be achieved by allowing for the failure of inefficient or poorly-run institutions, while keeping the payment system running in a reasonably orderly fashion, free from upheavals.

Payment, exchanges and settlement systems encounter, like other financial intermediaries, safety risks. Hackers, unauthorized users, outages and other accidents could disrupt financial markets, and compromise their integrity. Securities and derivatives exchanges – often self-regulated – are subject to the oversight and periodic inspection (on-site and off-site) of the regulatory–supervisory authorities.[22]

3.5 International co-operation in capital standards

3.5.1 Functions of capital

Both bank executives and the regulatory authorities consider capital to be the keystone for their risk management and control frameworks. At the enterprise level, raising capital levels reduces, *pari passu*, the bank's need for debt financing, cushions it against unexpected losses, and safeguards its solvency *vis-à-vis* creditors and other customers. At the sectorial level, adequate capital requirements strengthen the banking system's capacity to withstand eventual crises. It is thus understandable that the function of regulation–supervision of the banking system has focused on equity as the central foundation of financial prudence.

A financial firm's first line of defence against potential losses in a competitive market is its capacity to generate earnings commensurate with its risks – followed by its equity buffer. Regulators have often focused exclusively on the relative size of a bank's equity to assess its staying power in periods of difficulty. Equity represents owners' capital and reserves (disclosed or undisclosed), and is characterized by (i) permanency; (ii) a residual status in the distribution of income or assets; and (iii) bearing first and fully the impact of eventual losses. From the standpoint of regulatory prudence and market efficiency, a bank needs to hold adequate capital to serve several interrelated objectives, chief among which are the following:

First, capital helps a financial institution to withstand shocks and absorb readily possible unexpected losses over a given period of time.

The losses can be estimated using an institution-specific 'worst case scenario'. Anticipated losses can be covered by risk charges or premiums that financial institutions levy on portfolios, or on individual products and services. These anticipated losses can also be transferred to insurers, or covered by specifically-constituted reserves. Thus, an appropriate capital cushion for unanticipated losses allows some time for prompt corrective action that management can mount *before* the institution is driven ineluctably into insolvency and bankruptcy. Equally, such capital cushion gives the authorities more time to assist in finding an optimal solution to a beleaguered bank.

Second, from a dynamic perspective, the level of a bank's capital needs to be risk sensitive – that is, to move, in principle, commensurately with changes in the bank's holistic risk profile. While the risk premium over the cost of funds can be estimated on the basis of a long-run average, annual variability exists. It is possible that, in a year of recession, the actual loss exceeds the average *importantly*. In such an eventuality, it is crucial that the level of capital is sufficient to absorb the excess loss in that year and to protect the solvency of the institution. Furthermore, risk-based capital helps to achieve competitive equality with respect to equity among banks. Yet this objective could well prove difficult to measure and implement in view of the great diversity of economies and risk environments in which banks operate (for example, with respect to the synchronization of their macroeconomic cycles: from the growth phase to that of downturn), and the great diversity of financial institutions (whose activities can stretch from the narrowly specialized to the widely diversified, or from a local market to multiple markets).

Third, capital provides security to depositors by increasing the owners' stake in the bank through higher capitalization levels. This would ensure that the owners of the bank have a lot to lose in both invested capital and franchise value (which is the present discounted value of future profits) – should management engage in excessive risk. Owners would then become keen to retain a prudent-risk-taking management. Such higher levels of capital would, furthermore, help to moderate the interest charges the bank has to pay on deposits and other third-party funds. Regulatory capital should be reasonable, since excessive capital could induce banks' management to resort to riskier strategies in seeking returns capable of covering the higher costs of such capital funding – unless, in a concomitant process, the bank is able to attract deposits at lower interest rates.[23]

Fourth, capital serves to finance – in an environment of uncertainty – the start-up or the development expenses of a bank's business.

Various lines of a bank's activities require a gestation period of several months (possibly 2 to 5 years) before starting to produce income. Since business laws of various countries do not require that shareholders be imperatively remunerated at regular intervals or be reimbursed at pre-set dates (which is not the case with depositors or with investors in a bank's debt liabilities), management can therefore rely on capital for investing in activities which take time to fructify. These investments are often used for physical infrastructure, IT, know-how and talent, new projects, or the acquisition of other firms.

Fifth, suppose that disclosure practices of the business community are inadequate (a situation of opacity) or that bank management or the supervisory authorities are ill-equipped with resources to identify promptly problems which could be encountered by individual institutions in time to administer corrective action to overcome these difficulties. The banks concerned would, under these circumstances, need a higher capital cushion.[24] The higher the level of uncertainty or opacity encountered by depositors and other lenders to a bank, the greater the need for equity cushioning. Systemic risks' potential impact could be mitigated by requiring additional equity capital, although it is difficult to ascertain scientifically the amount(s) needed.[25] Regulators' concern in setting-up adequate levels of capital for banks and other financial institutions has been equally prompted by protecting the taxpayer and government-supported enterprises (such as their vehicles of deposit insurance), which could be called on to compensate the depositors of insolvent banks (see Chapter 5).

Instead of burdening the whole banking sector with additional capital charges to address the systemic risk issue, regulators often focus on creating appropriate incentives for individual banks to avoid strategies and practices susceptible to such a risk. The preventive approach of minimizing – through incentive-based regulation – excessive risk-taking and the chances of failure of individual banks appears to be more productive. Risk-prevention incentives would address, for example, (i) matching the relative importance of liquid and safe assets to that of sight or short-term liabilities;[26] and (ii) screening, monitoring and controling the operations of customers, counter-parties, industries and countries (see 3.6 below).

To sum-up, the higher the risk taken by a bank, the higher the level of capital buffer needed to absorb eventual unexpected losses. To the extent that a reasonable estimate can be made of the risk of *expected* losses, these can be covered by an appropriate risk premium or margin paid for by the customer. Capital – though difficult to tailor to each bank's changing circumstances and risk profile with any precision – is usually based on the banking sector's best practices. It should safeguard the survival and growth of the enterprise over the longer term, by absorbing eventual future losses in periods of difficulty, while providing shareholders and other founders with competitive remuneration for risks assumed. 'Core' capital is often defined as comprising:

(i)   paid-up ordinary capital – whether voting or non-voting – and published reserves; and
(ii) 'unrealised reserves' and preferential shares.[27]

3.5.2   Early co-operation in capital standards

The first two objectives of capital adequacy mentioned above have been advocated explicitly by the BCBS since 1988, but their implementation in national legislations has yet to be applied uniformly or universally. Indeed, several developed member countries of the BCBS, though ostensibly praising the paradigm of a market economy, have given patronage or specific advantages (for example, in the form of reduced capital requirements, governmental guarantees, favourable funding or fiscal exemptions) to chosen financial institutions. This favouritism exists in several leading market economies: the USA (with reference to federal mortgage-lending agencies Fannie Mae and Freddie Mac), Japan (for example, for the Housing Loan Corporation) and Europe (with reference to several state-controlled or state-supported regional and national banks)[28] – see also section 5.10 in Chapter 5. Although financial institutions owned or sponsored by the government have increasingly to conform to the BCBS's rules, their governmental links enable them to raise capital more cheaply than can private institutions, because of implicit or explicit state guarantees recognized by providers of funds.

Prudential rules for the safe and sound conduct of financial institutions have expanded considerably in the wake of problems or crises encountered by an increasingly complex and dynamic financial sector. These rules cover the definition of authorized activities, standards of liquidity and of asset safety, exposure limits and diversification, risk-adjusted capital, periodic disclosure of a wide range of information, use of sound accounting standards, appropriate internal organization, and efficient control systems. The latter include, *inter alia*, accurate job descriptions and the separation of functions for control reasons – in order to reduce the scope or temptation for collusion and fraud (see section 3.6 below).

Prompted by the dual objective of ensuring prudent behaviour and the competitive convergence of regulatory standards among banks at the global level, the BCBS has over the years formulated a series of guidelines for national bank regulators. With the approval of G-10 central bank governors and regulators, the Committee first recommended in 1988, for application by the end of 1992, a framework for minimum regulatory capital. Thus banks operating transnationally were asked to cover four categories of bank loan exposures with minimum capital levels, rising in accordance with their estimated average riskiness as follows: 0 per cent (OECD governments)[29] with no default record over the past five years; 1.6 per cent (banks in OECD countries); 4.0 per cent (residential mortgages); and 8.0 per cent (all other loans) – with reference to the face value of the respective claims. Capital has been defined as having two tiers: tier 1, or core capital, comprising essentially common shares and retained earnings; and tier 2 capital, comprising mainly medium–long-term subordinated debt instruments. Coming into effect from 1997, the BCBS enlarged its minimum regulatory capital to cover market risks, notably with respect to a bank's trading portfolio.

Capital standards adopted in 1988 were a compromise outcome of intense negotiations among the BCBS's members, and they helped to raise capital levels in some countries. Nevertheless, they have proved to be too simplistic, and often arbitrary or inconsistent in meeting the objectives of safety and prudence. Moreover, their applications in various countries has not been uniform, in order to produce a 'level-playing field' among financial institutions and products – with reference to the criterion of exposure to risk. For example, the Committee's rules apply the full minimum regulatory capital coefficient, namely, 8 per cent of the face value of these loans, for bank credit to the best-rated corporations (that is, AAA), in a similar way to lower-rated companies. Moreover, international interbank lending for up to one year has a 20 per cent risk-weight irrespective of the borrowing bank's rating and its home country's rating (for example, OECD versus emerging economies). Such rules encourage banks to operate perversely by favouring (i) the reduction of assets whose risks and capital charges are overestimated by regulators; and (ii) the increase of assets whose risks and capital charges are underestimated by regulators. The disincentive for banks to hold prime-quality loans is thus another illustration of moral hazard (see Figure 5.3, page 112).

The above rules are considered to have been one of the contributing factors to the Asian financial crisis of 1997–8. Foreign banks –

concerned about reducing their regulatory capital requirements – have thus favoured loans to emerging economies' banks and finance companies with maturities of less than one year, although they knew that the borrowers needed mainly long-term project financing. There was then a tacit understanding between the lending and the borrowing parties to roll over the short-term bank loans, under normal conditions. Judged with hindsight, the unbalanced maturity schedules rendered the lenders vulnerable to an appetite for excessive risk-taking.

To illustrate, short-term bank lending to Thailand, Indonesia and South Korea proved to be an important source of volatility in international financial markets in the second half of the 1990s – as compared to institutional portfolio investors. In Thailand, for example, of the total capital inflows in 1995 (namely US$25.5 billion), three-quarters were short-term bank loans to fund long-term baht assets, and a quarter were bond instruments and direct investments. With the rise of non-performing loans in Thai banks, foreign banks reversed their lending strategy and called in their outstanding loans. A US$1.9 billion *inflow* into Thailand in the first quarter of 1997 changed into a US$6.2 billion *outflow* in the second quarter – a swing of US$8.1 billion in three months, and this excluded the cancellation of unreported lines of credit. Even after the devaluation of the baht in July 1997, institutional portfolio flows remained positive until the end of 1998. Thereafter, foreign investors began to withdraw money from Thailand, as the recession caused by the banking crisis began to bite.[30]

The use of a static 'one-size-fits-all' approach for regulatory capital fails to address differences in the nature of banks, their diverse businesses, and their ever-changing risk profiles. Despite its limitations, the 1988 Capital Accord contributed to the increase in the level of capital buffer in several countries whose banks were deemed to be undercapitalized.

The standardized uniform weights have not been confined to credit risk; they have also been used in the case of market risks. The latter are defined as the risk of loss in a portfolio of financial assets over a chosen time horizon, resulting from changes in: interest/yield rates on debt or equity instruments, currency rates, commodity prices and various indices. Indeed, the BCBS recommended in 1997 a regulatory capital charge for the potential loss on the 'trading book' of a bank, set at a fixed minimum multiplier of 'three' for Value-at-Risk (VaR) – based on each bank's historical statistical data.

More specifically, VaR models provide a statistical estimate of the expected maximum potential loss that might occur in a portfolio –

under normal market conditions – caused by changes in market prices or rates, calculated over a specified holding period, and at a specified probability level. For example, a firm may generate a VaR estimate for a ten-day working period at 99 per cent probability and arrive at a figure of US$1 million. This means that 99 per cent of the time, it would expect its losses resulting from adverse movements of prices or rates over a ten-day holding period to be less than US$1 million. The holding period is normally chosen in relation to the time needed to liquidate a portfolio. The confidence or probability level is set subjectively, and regulatory authorities have favoured 99 per cent (or 2.33 times of σ, which is the standard deviation measure of the yield's dispersion around the mean). VaR has had an intuitive appeal to various parties, although the theoretical soundness of its agglo-meration of a variety of risk factors has been questioned.[31] Research works produce improved VaR models continuously, to cover varied conditions – including those pertaining to periods of recession or expansion.[32]

The multiplier factor of 'three' VaR of capital charge is required in so far as statistics of normal periods do not account for difficult situations. Moreover, there is an 'add-on of one' to make the total minimum capital requirement 'four' VaR, should the bank's internal model in stress testing (accounting for the impact of extreme market move-ments) prove to be flawed. Such stress testing estimates the potential loss resulting from large changes in key factors (for example, a 20 per cent fall in the stock market), which could occur in periods of extreme difficulty.[33]

At the start of a decline in the market value of certain financial instruments held in its trading book, the propensity of the bank's management would be to liquidate these instruments. If it deems the decline to be transient, the bank could shore-up its trading book with additional capital – assuming that it can mobilize the requisite capital readily.

The sale of assets of a bank's trading book in falling markets would drive prices down further, and given the above-mentioned VaR rules, prompt more selling. By comparison, non-bank institutional investors (for example, mutual and pension funds) do not face the same pressure of disposal – to the extent that they can readily pass market risk and losses on to individual investors in their funds. These funds' investment managers are therefore not obliged to pull out from the said instruments, unless their individual investors force them to do so.

3.5.3   Towards enhanced risk sensitivity of capital

After a series of consultations with regulatory authorities, banks and other interested parties during 1999–2003, the BCBS has elaborated and refined a new Capital Accord (Basel II) to replace its 1988 Capital Accord. The proposed Accord is based on a three-pronged approach: (i) making capital requirements more sensitive to each bank's risk profile; (ii) enhancing supervisory review; and (iii) increasing disclosure and transparency to foster market discipline in maintaining prudent capital ratios by banks. Basel II's three pillars (see Figure 3.1) are deemed mutually reinforcing, and are guided by the following principles:

(i)   Capital standards should be applied on a consolidated basis to holding companies of banking groups, with the objective of capturing all enterprise-wide risks. Special-purpose entities or accounts – which have occasionally been used to 'house' liabilities and losses outside the balance sheet – should therefore be consolidated properly within the balance sheet.

(ii)   Minimum capital requirements should take into consideration (besides credit and market risks) operational risks (for example, the risk of loss from internal control deficiencies, accidents, fraud, IT problems, destruction of data and premises, or legal risks such as money laundering).

(iii) The standardized approach of Basel II differentiates risk exposures of a bank among seven categories. Each category contains items of identical risk weights, requiring the same minimum regulatory capital charges. Risks are ascertained by credit-rating agencies accredited by the regulatory authorities.

(iv)   In estimating their customers' creditworthiness and their probability of default, banks with access to adequate statistical data and sophisticated techniques can use their own internal risk-based (IRB) approach (either the 'foundation' or the 'advanced' alternative) – subject to supervisory validation to ensure the observance of the BCBS's established methodological and disclosure standards.

(v)   Within the framework of credit risk control, due attention is given to techniques of risk mitigation relating to the treatment of collaterals, guarantees, credit derivatives and netting, as well as securitization. These techniques free-up capital which can then be used in more profitable activities, or returned to shareholders.

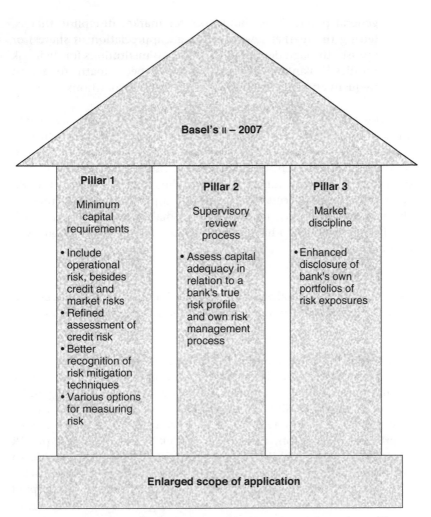

Figure 3.1   Towards an optimal 'regulatory capital' for banking: three pillars

(vi)   Supervisors have the authority to review upwards the minimum capital requirement of a specific bank above the standard 8 per cent on the risk exposures (12 per cent for risks below the rating of B–), if warranted by the higher risk profile of the said bank.

(vii) More information on the capital base, the risk exposures and the risk management process has to be disclosed to inform current and potential investors, counter-parties, customers and the general public. This should bolster market discipline that is, letting the market reward (through appreciation of shares) or punish (through depreciation of shares) institutions for their risk profiles.[34] Banking institutions have been loath to accept frequent and detailed disclosures of their risk positions.[35]

The IRB approach, in comparison to the 'standardized' approach, authorizes a bank to constitute lower capital requirements if warranted by the prudent strategy of the bank in question. Yet to set-up, operate and refine such a system, there is an important cost, both financial and in human resources. This makes, in effect, the IRB approach primarily accessible to large and sophisticated banks that are able to use advanced risk methodologies. Smaller banks, using the standardized approach, will have to hold comparatively larger amounts of capital.

3.5.4   Challenges

Basel II is due to be finalized before the end of 2003, and implemented by 2007. Its main features nevertheless pose several challenges, as listed below:

- **Internal-based risk models**. This applies to larger banks. Each concerned bank needs to develop the equivalent of 'mortality tables' for different categories of homogeneous loans. The validation of internal risk models (such as those of credit risk) by the supervisory agency requires it to have full access to the banks' private information, in order to check the truthfulness of IBR estimates of probabilities of default. Banks could be liable to underestimate risks – as shown by several past banking crises – and supervisors may not prove an equal match to the highly-paid and sophisticated talents recruited by large banks.[36] Moreover, in a dynamic environment, business activities change, and that makes it difficult to make valid comparisons of data collected over long periods. Moreover, methodological approaches vary within and across countries, and need to be harmonized accordingly. Best practice accounting and reporting methods need, furthermore, to be applied consistently and properly. Banks admit to the limitations of quantitative models based on assumptions that could turn out to be unrealistic, and recognize the crucial importance of qualitative judgement.[37] Since many of these models are very similar, there is increasingly a potential of systemic risk, based on herd-like behaviour.

- **Operational risks.** These comprise a wide array of factors (see Figure 1.1 on page 3) not yet clearly defined or agreed upon. Data and measurement methodology for these risks remain fuzzy. A formula-type 'one-size-fits-all' approach (for example, linking operational risks to gross revenues or to credit risk) would disadvantage the best-managed banks. Moreover, it would not provide an incentive for the worst-managed banks to improve their internal control systems – thus creating a moral hazard factor (see section 3.6 below). The control of operational risks is best suited to Pillar 2, rather than Pillar 1 in figure 3.1. Certain models used by banks to calculate their capital adjusted to risk exposures do not account for operational risks or bankers' excesses.[38]

- **External raters.** Apart from a very few independent rating agencies (such as Weiss Rating Inc.), most rating agencies are paid by rated entities for their services. These agencies, moreover, offer their clients the opportunity to preview the ratings – if they are unfavourable – before publication. It is possible that certain rating agencies (which are paid by their rated clients) could compromise their objectivity and be tempted to supply, in response to the pressure of these clients who demand better ratings in order to raise capital more cheaply than would have been warranted by strictly objective criteria. Rating agencies have therefore to watch out for their reputation – that is, their credibility *vis-à-vis* supervisors and investors. Profit-seeking rating agencies are also enticed to push through the sale of their quantitative risk models (for example, those used to assess regulatory capital) to banks.[39]

  Lacking full and immediate knowledge of the fast-changing risk conditions, rating agencies are often unable to anticipate failures of borrowers. Downgrading debt instruments have in several cases happened belatedly, after the issuing entities have declared their difficulties. For example, they gave Enron an investment-grade rating in 2001 just before it collapsed (see also Chapter 4, section 4.2). Rated corporations or governmental entities do not necessarily provide 'full and accurate disclosure of all relevant information' – according to a major rating agency.[40]

  Another concern with respect to rating agencies is that two long-established US-based institutions (Moody's, and Standard & Poor's) dominate the market of accredited raters. This high concentration often makes the rated institutions dependent for their international credit standing on the judgement of a couple of leading agencies that are not immune to shortcomings – as past events have demonstrated.

- **Standardized risk weights and compromises.** Proposed standard-ized weights of risk exposures – though representing improvements over those of 1988 – are still rough and static estimates insensitive to dynamic conditions. They are often the product of lengthy negotiations ending in compromises made at a given 'point in time' by representatives of national supervisory authorities of the world's main financial markets. Thus the capital charge on loans to small/medium-sized enterprises (SMEs) and on loans to retail customers have been lowered, below levels justified by statistically-based risk estimates. Increasing equity charges commensurate with the credit risk of long maturities was, furthermore, considered unac-ceptable to the German government and to the European Parliament, since this would also raise the borrowing costs of SMEs.[41] In these circumstances, banks are likely to continue to resort to 'regulatory arbitrage', namely by favouring activities whose regu-latory capital (when compared to the economic capital) underesti-mates their effective risk.
- **Market-assessed risks.** Disclosure of data – assuming that it is pertinent, accurate and timely – can help participants in financial markets to price financial instruments issued by a bank, with a better knowledge of their risk–return profiles. This applies notably to their subordinated notes and debentures (SNDs)–see section 5.5.2 of Chapter 5. Nevertheless, problems do exist with reference to the adequacy of market valuations – especially when certain bank items, such as loans, do not have an active and liquid market. One approach to address this situation is to resort to 'fair value' account-ing, which purports to be a proxy for market value. Fair value, however, is based on individual models and assumptions which 'would offer a considerable amount of discretionary scope for valua-tion which would seriously impair the reliability of the accounting items calculated in this manner'.[42]

  Fair value accounting is, furthermore, expected to lead to a greater volatility in the recorded value of assets, and this is bound to affect the capital requirements of banks, and the stability of the banking system. This, in turn, would prompt banks to shorten the maturity of their loans to reduce the scope of likely changes in the market value of loans. The European banking industry and its regulatory authorities are opposed to fair value accounting. The German central bank is even in favour of limiting transparency through the use of 'undisclosed contingency reserves', arguing that they 'provide scope for discreetly smoothing the result so as to avert a threat to the company's ability to continue as a going concern caused by excessive market reactions, such as a run by depositors [due] to deteriorating profitability, and in order to buy time for corrective countermeasures'.[43]

- **Procyclicality.** The more risk-sensitive the equity basis, the more reluctant will banks be to lend in a downturn characterized by rising business difficulties. Banks would then raise their exigencies from potential borrowers. In the rising phase of the business cycle, with the surrounding general prosperity, banks are likely to moderate their exigencies since borrowers would benefit from improved ratings.[44] A 'through the cycle' approach needs to be developed, with the bank building up capital protection in good years to underwrite potential losses in periods of recession. Though it is difficult to predict the timing of changes in the direction of cycles,[45] a 'through the cycle' approach authorized by regulators and the tax authorities could strengthen the resilience of the financial sector: regulation should allow the management of banks to resort to transparent precautionary provisioning, whereby capital buffers are accumulated in periods of expansion when profits are high and losses low, to cushion the negative impact on capital in downturns.[46]

- **Complexity.** Excessive complexity of capital regulation is a drawback for those expected to make good use of it. This judgement was clearly stated by the chief of one US oversight federal agency that charters, regulates and examines some 2100 national banks and 52 federal branches of foreign banks. Despite the fact that the USA is one of the world's most sophisticated financial markets, he stressed that 'bankers, examiners, legislators, and policy makers need to be able to comprehend the structure and content of the new [Basel] accord without having to plow through reams of mathematical *minutiae*.'[47]

- **Diversification.** The BCBS needs to address a bank's diversification of risks – not only by reference to its different credit portfolios, but also by reference to different lines of financial activities under Pillar 2 in Figure 3.1. Such enterprise-wide calculations for a financial institution can produce an overall risk profile that can be higher or lower depending on the correlations in defaults and/or credit losses within, as well as across, different concentrations of risks. A bank's scope for diversifying risk in many emerging markets is smaller when compared to advanced economies. Nevertheless, the gains of diversification are difficult to measure precisely. Moreover, there can be risks in diversifying too far and too fast – in so far as management fails to cope efficiently with the challenges or opportunities attendant on the development of new markets or lines of business.

Some analysts have found that focus (or specialization) is not necessarily less rewarding in terms of risk-adjusted return – in comparison to diversification.[48] Empirical studies show that the diversification of bank lending to different industries, different sectors and different geographical areas can lead to a decline in return. This is largely because the diversification process often moves into new and riskier activities, and is characterized by a deterioration in the bank's monitoring quality. The diseconomies of diversification derive, therefore, from reduced effectiveness in the span of control, lack of experience in the new activities, and increased rivalry (for example, through lower charges) caused by the entry of newcomers producing lower returns.[49]

- **Methodology.** A fundamental concern about the underlying approach of Basel's capital requirements is the tendency to *uniformity* in models, standards and data used. Such a situation could well create a herding effect, which could prove detrimental to the stability of the global financial system.

- **Adequacy.** The requirement of a minimum regulatory capital of 8 per cent for credit at risk is not verifiable objectively, and many financial institutions hold capital above the legal requirements. Bank managers opting for higher capital buffers can be prompted by the objective of obtaining favourable ratings – in order to tap financial markets at lower interest rates. The level of capital in fact held can also reflect the bank managers' subjective propensity for risk exposure.[50] In some countries – such as the United Kingdom – regulators set a bank-specific target ratio above the minimum capital requirement (known also as a 'trigger ratio'). The said target ratio is deemed necessary to prevent an accidental breach of the trigger ratio.[51]

The challenge of setting the appropriate level of risk-adjusted capital discussed in this chapter should not only be concerned about 'insufficient' capital. It should beware equally about 'idle' capital. In the latter case, bank management could use that capital less productively, or be tempted to move into higher-risk activities. Such a situation would yield equity owners lower returns than they could otherwise obtain in alternative investments of similar risk. Should *excess* equity capital, as defined above, exist in a firm, it behooves management to return it to shareholders – for example, by larger dividend distributions or through purchases of the said firm's stocks. This will enable shareholders to exercise their prerogatives to dispose of their entitlements as they see fit.

Considerable advances are being made in measuring economic capital requirements – for individual risk exposures, as well as for enterprise-wide risks that take into consideration diversification effects. Historical data on default risk or migration probabilities (that is, the likelihood that a borrower will be reclassified from one credit grade to another) are building up. New forecasting methods are improving the reliability of computing default risks.[52]

* * *

It is unrealistic to expect regulators to assess accurately optimal capital requirements for all potential risks that are likely to be encountered by a financial firm. Basel II seeks, nevertheless, to promote prudent behaviour among banks and a 'level-playing field' – world-wide – despite the complexity, diversity and continuous change in economic–financial situations. Challenges remain with respect to the identification, measurement and forecasting of risk factors – whose significance depends on various assumptions of market perspectives and time horizons. Moreover, adequacy of equity in a financial institution cannot be dissociated from that of liquidity. Indeed, insufficient liquidity could cause an otherwise properly capitalized and solvent bank to resort, in periods of excessive sudden net outflows of funds, to costly measures. These would include onerous external financing, the forced sale of non-liquid assets at sacrificed prices,[53] or the stoppage of lines of credit to solvent customers who, in turn, could be driven into default. All the foregoing situations would hurt the bank's capital base. These and other situations of distress in 'worst case scenarios' should incite bank management in adopting prudent risk control processes.

3.6 Risk mitigation

While the role of capital as a buffer for the absorption of possible losses is undeniable, it is generally recognized that capital alone is not sufficient to address such eventuality. There is indeed a wide spectrum of proven prudential principles and rules whose strict observance is most conducive to avoiding losses and fraud, thereby consequently protecting the capital buffer. They are related notably to restrictions on categories of acceptable activities, risk mitigation techniques, efficient and safe organizational structures, management procedures and controls, and others (see Figure 3.2).

The growth and resilience of financial institutions depend on judicious business strategies and sound risk management. Successful institutions are those whose management are able to choose strategies and business activities in which they command a competitive advantage. This calls for the identification of opportunities and their attendant risks. Management will then avoid or transfer risks that they cannot fully comprehend or manage profitably (see Figure 7.3, page 194).

Existing risk management techniques are being refined continuously, and new ones being developed, with a view to improving the transfer or mitigation of exposure to risk. These techniques comprise: limits set on connected or related lending and on the size of various types of risk exposure (relative to capital); use of readily marketable and safe collaterals (that is, with reasonably constant values) for credit exposure; insurances; hedging; derivatives (inclusive of credit derivatives); geographic and product line diversification; reducing existing excessive risk concentrations (for example, by resorting to asset sales, securitization, factoring, debt syndication and so on); effective screening and monitoring of customers; rigorous independent controls to ensure compliance with rules, procedures, regulations and directives; the efficient recruitment, training and supervision of employees; and an appropriate system of rewards and sanctions for management and staff. This is often referred to as the development of a risk 'culture'.

The institution of limits is a commonly used risk-mitigation technique. It promotes granularity and diversification by restricting a financial institution's exposure to a single borrower (individual, institution or country) or to a group of borrowers whose risks are highly correlated. Credit limits, traditionally, have been fixed in relation to book capital. More recently, economic capital has been used. The newer approach calls for raising premiums (i) as concentration risk increases; and/or (ii) as the grade of risk attributable to an obligor increases.[54]

Among risk management techniques, the use of collateral – as a guarantee for the honouring of a loan or obligation – has expanded considerably in recent years. Fungible collaterals, readily seizable and negotiable by lenders, lessen the need for these lenders to assess the credit worthiness of individual counter-parties. Such collaterals also assist lenders in overcoming the problem of asymmetric information (namely, the lack of transparency with respect to the intentions of the borrower, as communicated to the lender). Furthermore, collateralization mitigates credit rationing, broadens access to markets, enhances competition, fosters deep liquid markets, reduces information/transaction costs, moderates interest rates on loans, and promotes sound payment and settlement systems. When a collateral deteriorates in market value, it must be supplemented.

No risk-mitigating technique is, however, foolproof, and each technique has to be evaluated. For example, a credit default swap

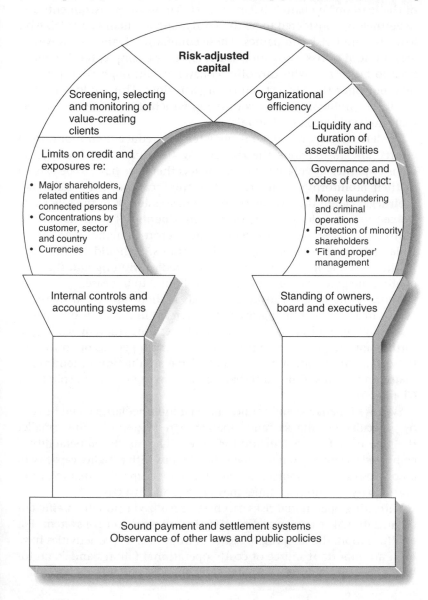

Figure 3.2   A bank's portal of regulatory prudence

allows a creditor to transfer credit risk on a customer to a counter-party in exchange for regular periodic payments, while retaining the funding of the loan on the bank's balance sheet. These swap instruments are, nevertheless, considered to be too costly, and are mainly available on loans to prime risk companies. These companies' loans are, however, least in need of risk mitigation.[55] For another example, funds tend to flow to borrowers who can offer collaterals, although their projects may not offer the highest return or cash flow. This could present a particular problem for new companies which do not yet own assets that can be pledged as collaterals.

Lenders relying on collaterals may tend to reduce their monitoring efforts, and to overlook the risk arising from excessive leverage by counter-parties in volatile markets. Banks therefore have to be careful in their monitoring – with respect to the location of the collateral, their legal claim, their capacity to take possession, and the sale value (forced versus orderly liquidation).[56] In a period of financial uncertainty, lenders or guarantors would then resort to higher margins on collaterals, thereby creating liquidity strains.[57] Should all financial institutions adopt the same strategy of credit rationing and flight to quality, the potential for systemic risk is bound to increase.

Another challenge of using collaterals is their impact on financial cycles. In a period of high growth, the increase in the value of collaterals could fuel additional borrowing and spending, thereby leading to further upward pressures on prices and values. In periods of downturn, the decline in collateral values could force a reduction in lending to maintain margins, thus exacerbating further the downward spiral (see Chapter 5).

Even well-managed and sound financial intermediaries could be hurt by speculative attacks and market stress events. The smaller the size of a financial institution, the higher is its vulnerability – compared to larger and more diversified groups with a higher capacity to absorb losses. Furthermore, it is argued that 'diversification that mitigates portfolio risk in "normal" times may fail to do so in a crisis'.[58]

Mitigating operational risks can best be realized through an efficient organizational structure and an effective internal control system. For an illustration, the lumping together of front/back office activities have been an important source of costly operational failures and fraud for banks (see also Chapter 4). As stated by one US regulator:

> A one-size-fit-all approach to operational risk – such as formulaic capital charge based on some percentage of gross revenues or a

percentage of the charge for credit risk – while simple to apply, would disadvantage the best managed banks and provide undeserved advantage to the worst managed. Worst of all, it would provide no incentive to improve internal control systems.[59]

National regulatory–supervisory agencies can exercise their judgement in the evaluation of a bank's risk profile, and take appropriate action. However, in the supervisory review process of Basel II, Pillar 2 (see Figure 3.1 on page 47) there is no guarantee that the said agencies will be guided by the same criteria and that they will enforce them uniformly. In view of the existent heterogeneity of banks, the above-mentioned US regulator privileges judgment. He said 'Judgement and the ability to make individualised decision – are crucial. We must not tie examiners' hands with inflexible rules'.[60] Burdensome and unfathomable complexities of Basel II capital rules led US regulators in a volte-face to renege unilaterally in 2003 on the comprehensive application to all US banks of the proposed new capital rules, and to confine their application to the large internationally active US banks (fewer than twelve), as stated by the US Comptroller of the Currency before the London-based Centre for the Study of Financial Innovation on 13 March 2003.

3.7   Regulatory gaps

Basel II, like its predecessor, targets only banks. As such, it fails to guarantee a level playing field with non-banking financial institutions, which have products that compete with those of banks. Moreover, a harmonization of regulatory rules applying to diverse operators within the financial sector is essential to the promotion of safety and soundness for the whole sector, and to the reduction of systemic risks.

Within the financial sector, institutions in the hedge-fund branch are generally under no obligation to disclose their investment strategies or risk exposures. The majority of these funds are *highly leveraged institutions* (HLIs). Their main owners are composed largely of a few sophisticated financial institutions or wealthy individuals. They are often organized as limited partnerships with no disclosure requirements – so far. The general partners (unlike the case with other types of funds) risk their own money and are responsible for the day-to-day management, while the limited partners provide their funds with no direct influence on management. HLIs' management have often followed speculative investment strategies: they have taken 'long' positions in certain securities anticipating their prices will rise and 'short' positions in others anticipating their prices will fall – with extensive use of market derivatives.[61]

Late in September 1998, the US Federal Reserve regulators intervened to avoid the collapse of a sizeable HLl, Long-Term Capital Management (LTCM) – after a loss of US$4.6 billion on more than US$1 trillion of derivatives in the wake of the Russian debt crisis. In particular, the Federal Reserve Bank of New York engineered a bail-out of LTCM by creditor-investor firms. Regulators

> were concerned that rapid liquidation of LTCM's very large trading positions and of its counter-parties' related positions in the unsettled market conditions of September 1998 might have caused credit and interest rate markets to experience extreme price movements and even temporarily cease functioning. This could have potentially harmed uninvolved firms and adversely affected the cost and availability of credit in the U.S. economy.[62]

Some HLI managers use offshore centres to avoid disclosing information on their investment strategies and risk exposures – which they consider to be 'proprietary'. By disclosing its strategy, a large HLI could find itself being taken advantage of by counter-parties or other players, especially when it needs to liquidate its positions. It is accordingly more realistic to enhance supervisory control over fund providers to HLIs, and notably the creditor banks. Without resorting to mandatory disclosure of HLI information on risks, regulatory prescriptions can require banks to announce to their supervisory authorities (on a regular basis) details about their major risk exposures – if any – *vis-à-vis* these and other institutions. This information will assist supervisors to assess not only the vulnerability of individual banks, but also the potential of systemic risk likely to be encountered by the banking sector.

To perform its monitoring/supervisory role efficiently, it pays regulators to centralize information on large loans. This is explicitly the position of financial regulation in several advanced financial markets. Switzerland, for example, requires each bank to communicate to the Swiss Federal Banking Commission (SFBC) the ten largest positions exposed to risk. This list does not include certain specific positions deemed riskless, for example OECD sovereigns.[63] Comprehensive and frequent reporting should prove more helpful to the regulators–supervisors' assessment of the changing risk profile of individual banks. While Swiss regulation requires, furthermore, individual banks not to lend at any given moment beyond a ceiling (set at 25 per cent of its equity) to a single customer or a counter-party, after 'netting',[64] stricter regulations would require lower limits and can thus serve to promote granularity and diversification. Since the near collapse of LTCM, supervisors of banks and financial markets have sought to enhance their regulatory requirements over banks with credit relations to HLIs, and have called on banks to adopt, *inter alia*, strong counter-party risk management.[65]

In the US legislative system, lobbying is legally authorized as a means of 'informing' lawmakers. The latter have not only been informed, however; they have also been influenced by financially and politically well-connected lobbyists representing powerful business interests. This was the case with Enron whose executives lobbied the US Congress intensively to block federal oversight of its activities. Enron sought and was granted, that the OTC derivatives would remain largely unregulated – despite recommendations to the contrary made by the Futures Trading Commission following a total loss of US$11.4 billion incurred by customers over derivatives during the decade ended March 1997. Enron's core business in the last years of its existence was 'derivatives trading'. In that business, Enron made in the year 2000 ostensibly more money than LTCM had over its entire history, and had attained in that one year a market capitalization of US$70 billion. This was wiped out in late 2001, along with its defaulting on billions of dollars of debts extended by major banks.[66]

* * *

The strengthening of the financial sector can be increased further by changes in tax laws. The provision that interest on debt is deductible when calculating taxable income for all businesses – including financial institutions – while dividends are not tax deductible, encourages management to resort to debt in lieu of equity. This tax feature, existent in most legislations, creates a bias in favour of debt, and discourages funding through equity. The high level of debt among financial and non-financial firms is a source of vulnerability for individual enterprises, as well as for the economy at large. The above-mentioned bias in favour of debt at the expense of equity needs to be resolved to reduce the vulnerability of banks and other enterprises.[67]

Regulatory principles and criteria, when properly designed, are a mainstay for a healthy and efficient financial sector. These, however, need to be implemented effectively through monitoring, controls, discipline and sanctions – to yield the targeted levels of performance. This subject is addressed in Chapter 4.

4
Effective Supervision and Enforcement

This chapter is concerned with the implementation and supervision of prudential regulations relating to banks (discussed in Chapter 3). Various domains of supervision are addressed. They cover, in particular, internal control and audit, external audit, public oversight and market discipline.

Supervision of financial institutions has become increasingly complex. Several reasons explain that development, among which three are prominent. First, financial institutions have tended towards the espousal of conglomerate strategies – combining within one firm multiple lines of business (banking, insurance and securities activities). Second, products and services offered have become more sophisticated with risk/benefit components often being difficult to assess and control. And, third, the transnational spread of financial firms' activities poses difficult problems – mainly with respect to: the timely collection and diffusion of reliable, pertinent and comparable data; the use of rigorous accounting or measurement methods; and the conduct of effective cross-border controls.[1]

The complex nexus of supervision of a financial institution comprises principally four main layers: the institution's own control system, internal audit, external audit, and governmental supervision (see Figure 4.1). All should be concerned with the rigorous observance of various laws, regulations, statutes, norms, standards, directives and codes. Their function is to provide the requisite information and appraisals for shareholders and investors, the board of directors, senior management, and oversight/supervisory agencies. The collected information comprises various domains, notably those of prudence in risk-taking, propriety in activities, correct accounting and transparency – to protect the legitimate interests of owners, investors, creditors, staff and other stakeholders (see Figure 2.1 on page 12 for an outline of these interests).

4.1 Internal control and audit

Within the company, there are a few mechanisms which ensure that regulations and rules are duly observed. They include, first, the internal control systems whose efficient working is based on a set of 'checks and balances', underpinned by an efficient organizational structure, division of work, reporting and communication. The latter enable management at various levels to detect without delay any irregularities, mishaps or fraud. The variety of increasingly complex risks encountered by a bank (see Figure 1.1 on page 3) could thus be monitored properly

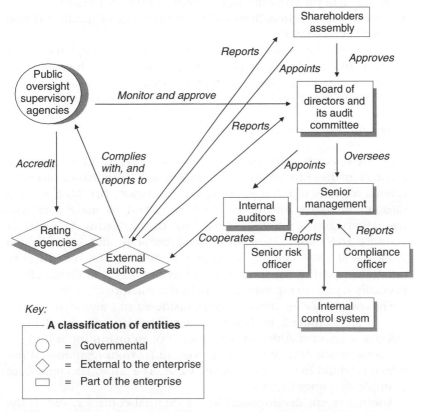

Figure 4.1   A formal supervisory structure for a bank: principal relations

and continuously. Internal control systems are checked by the internal auditors, whose functions include:

- the examination and evaluation of the adequacy and effectiveness of the internal control systems;
- review of the application and effectiveness of risk management procedures and risk assessment methodologies;
- review of the management and financial information systems, including the electronic information system and electronic banking services;
- review of the accuracy and reliability of the accounting records and financial reports;
- review of the means of safeguarding assets;
- review of the bank's system of assessing its capital in relation to its estimate of risk;
- appraisal of the economy and efficiency of the operations;
- testing of both transactions and the functioning of specific internal control procedures;
- review of the systems established to ensure compliance with legal and regulatory requirements, codes of conduct and the implementation of policies and procedures;
- testing of the reliability and timeliness of the regulatory reporting; and
- carrying-out of special investigations.[2]

As well as efficient internal control systems, most financial institutions have in recent times instituted a 'compliance officer' – often a member of the top management echelon. His job is to keep tabs on managers and other employees, and to make sure that regulations and directives – including those relating to codes of conduct and ethics – are understood properly and implemented correctly. Should managers or employees be in doubt, the officer in question can define the appropriate behaviour. The compliance officer normally reports to top management in the enterprise.

The compliance function is often considered an integral part of risk management. Indeed, by failing to comply (with laws, regulations, directives, codes of ethics, or best practices), an institution is likely to be liable to penalties. It can, moreover, suffer from reputational risk which is bound to hurt its franchise value. The latter risk applies, for example, to money laundering.[3]

Another recent development in the internal control system is the generalized creation of the 'senior risk officer' function. This consists of obtaining a holistic assessment of risks encountered at the level of the whole firm (including its subsidiaries/affiliates). This approach of integrating all risks faced by an enterprise can also be used with reference to a division, a subsidiary or an affiliate.

Investors, creditors, employees and other stakeholders could suffer from management's deficiencies in internal controls resulting, for example, from amnesia, smugness, or just lapse in vigilance. Indeed, this could be illustrated by reference to multiple incidents. For example, Michael Buckley, head of capital markets at the Allied Irish Bank (AIB), declared to the press in 1995 that his management's control structure would 'never' allow the emergence of a rogue trader similar to Nick Leeson, who brought down the then Barings by incurring losses in excess of the bank's capital of £540 million[4]. Unfortunately for AIB, however, Mr. Buckley (who became by 2001 its CEO) encountered in that year within his group a similar rogue trader. This was John Rusnak, who flouted the rules of prudence – notably those relating to the separation of 'front desk' transactions from 'back office' accounting and controls to carry out unauthorized operations and conceal losses incurred on those. Over five years, he was able to dissimulate losses totalling £485 million (US$691 million) by fraudulent foreign exchange trading at a US affiliate (Allfirst) of AIB. While one needs to be circumspect in admitting differences between the two episodes, it is worth noting that Nick Leeson commented in February 2002, 'I think the similarities are quite striking all the way through. It is frightening.'[5]

Effective internal controls require an approach of a clear division of responsibilities. Thus the 'front' office's activities – for generating and/or transacting business with clients – should be run by a personnel different from those responsible for the activities of the 'back' office, concerned with reporting, certifying or settling the said operations. The efficiency of internal control and audit systems within the firm has to be evaluated periodically by senior management, as well as by external independent auditors, and ultimately by supervisors from governmental oversight agencies. Their shared concern is to guard against flimsy risk controls that allow for irregularities, misconduct and fraud – guided by the objective of eliminating avoidable losses.

4.2 External audit

External auditors are appointed by the general assembly of shareholders and have the responsibility for certifying that no material misstatements are made in the firm's accounts. Should their audit of a firm reveal inappropriate accounting policies or practices, the external auditor should ask management to make the necessary corrections or adjustments. If no positive response is forthcoming, the auditor should then issue a qualified or adverse opinion on the financial statements in their reports to shareholders. The external auditor's judgement has to rely on the internal auditor's extensive work and the forthright co-operation of management.

Critical scrutiny, verging on professional scepticism regarding the accounts presented by management and their employees, has to be exercised vigilantly. As stated by BCBS:

> In forming an opinion on the financial statements, the external auditor carries out procedures designed to obtain reasonable assurance that the financial statements are prepared in all material respects in accordance with an identified financial reporting framework. An audit does not guarantee all material misstatements will be detected because of such factors as the judgement, the use of testing, the inherent limitations of internal control and the fact that much of the evidence available to the auditor is persuasive rather than conclusive in nature. The risk of not detecting a material misstatement resulting from fraud is higher than the risk of not detecting a material misstatement resulting from error, because fraud may involve sophisticated and carefully organised schemes designed to conceal it, such as forgery, deliberate failure to record transactions or intentional misrepresentation being made to the auditor. Such attempts at concealment may be even harder to detect when accompanied by collusion. Furthermore, the risk of the auditor not detecting a material misstatement resulting from management fraud is greater than for employee fraud, because boards of directors and management are often in a position that assumes their integrity and enables them to override the formally established control procedures. Therefore, the auditor plans and performs an audit with an attitude of professional scepticism, recognising that circumstances may exist that cause the financial statements to be materially misstated.[6]

To carry out its mission efficiently, the audit inspection function must be founded on certain general prerequisites. These include (i) the recruitment of honest, technically competent and discerning personnel, fully abreast of the latest developments in the financial sector; (ii) attractive incomes for auditors and inspectors comparable to those of the employees of the audited firms; (iii) secure jobs, and strong incentives to enforce regulations; (iv) access to information systems and vulnerability indicators capable of identifying without delay various risks; and (v) the legal power and the stamina to scrutinize freely the institutions under their supervision – without having to cave in to persons of influence within the firm, for venal reasons or for the sake of protecting or advancing their careers. By concealing delinquent actions and/or approving incomplete or inaccurate accounts, auditors mislead shareholders and other stake-holders who are concerned to ascertain the genuine substance of their company.

Auditing firms have not always certified objectively and rigorously their corporate clients' financial statements. Banks' and other firms' failures could be caused by multiple reasons. Inaccurate, incomplete or fraudulent accounting and auditing, along with opacity, could hurt the troubled firm's prospects. It would deny stakeholders the right to be alerted readily to warning signs, and prevent honest management from taking remedial action to change faulty strategies and redress the fortunes of the enterprise.

External auditor's challenges could be illustrated by reference to the difficulties of Arthur Andersen LLP in 2001–02 *vis-à-vis* Enron Corp. The latter – a derivatives trading company with US$70 billion of shareholder value in the year 2000 and the seventh highest in the USA – defaulted in November 2001. This was the largest corporate bankruptcy in history up to that year, but was surpassed in 2002 by Worldcom, Inc. It had hurt various stakeholders: shareholders, investors, creditors, customers and employees.

More specifically, Enron's external auditors agreed to the non-consolidation of special-purpose entities (SPEs) which had lodged large debts and other obligations. The US code of generally accepted accounting principles (GAAP) authorizes SPEs so long as 'outsiders' own a mere 3 per cent. By allowing companies to shift debt off their balance sheet and to deconsolidate loss-making start-ups, the US GAAP system is open to abuse.[7] That would not have been possible under international accounting standards (IAS) espoused by the European Union, where affiliates are generally consolidated should the parent company own more than 50 per cent of the capital – with the under-standing that the parent in control vouches for all the liabilities of its affiliate.

It is worth noting that large, US-based investment banks co-operated with Enron in setting up these SPEs. The latter have been legally recognized entities – although their structures were not transparent and were unknown to the average investor.[8] The Chairman of the US Senate Permanent Subcommittee on Investigations stated:

> Enron's deceptions were shocking, and equally shocking was the extent to which respected U.S. financial institutions like Chase, Citigroup, and Merrill Lynch helped Enron carry out its deceptions and mislead investors and analysts about the company's finances. These financial institutions weren't victims of Enron; they helped plan and carry out Enron's deceptions in exchange for large fees or favorable consideration in business deals.[9]

According to the CEO of Andersen:

> SPEs are financing vehicles that permit companies, like Enron, to, among other things, access capital or to increase leverage without adding debt to their balance sheet [sic] ... The accounting rules dictate, among other things, that unrelated parties must have residual equity equal to at least 3 per cent of the fair value of an SPE's assets in order for the SPE to qualify for non-consolidation ... There is no prohibition against company employees being involved as investors [sic].[10]

These SPEs were not independent from Enron: the so-called external partners/investors turned out to be employees who could be loaned capital by Enron. Furthermore, it was common to capitalize the SPEs by injecting Enron shares and guaranteeing that the level of equity is maintained at a specified minimum level: with the fall in the value of Enron's shares, the company had to inject more capital, and its credit rating was consequently downgraded.

Enron's external auditors, Andersen, accepted the year 2000 published accounts of the company as representing a *true and fair view* of its financial situation during that year. Yet Andersen's CEO admitted in December 2001 to : (a) errors of judgement made by his team with respect to the non-consolidation of SPEs which did not pass 'the 3 per cent test for residual equity' owned by third parties; (b) incorrect inflation of reported shareholders' equity; (c) concealed liabilities or losses through non-consolidated SPEs; and (d) the shredding of documents or deletion of electronic files relating to its audit work – the latter soon after learning about an impending congressional hearing on the Enron debacle.[11] The US Justice Department indicted Andersen in March 2002 on criminal obstruction charges in so far as it did knowingly, intentionally and corruptly persuade [its employees] to (a) withhold records, documents and other objects from official regulatory and criminal proceedings and investigations; and (b) alter, destroy, mutilate and conceal documents in relation to Enron.[12] The court finally declared Andersen guilty in mid-June 2002.

Investors, creditors and other participants in financial markets rely on external auditors to ascertain that revenues are not artificially inflated, losses are not concealed, and accounting subterfuges are not used. Auditing firms' objectivity and their aptitude to detect irregularities is undermined by significant consulting and other non-audit services (such as information technology systems, legal help, tax planning and recruitment services) they provide to their client firms. This situation of conflict of interest has compromised auditors' independence in a number of cases.[13] In a survey of twenty-one large companies that disclosed fees paid in 2001 to their auditing firms for consulting assignments (out of thirty companies in the Dow Jones Industrial Average), 73 per cent of the total fees (that is, US$725.7 million) was for services other than audit. J. P. Morgan Chase topped the list – with total fees paid to PricewaterhouseCoopers of US$104 million, of which US$18.4 million was for the audit.[14]

Bank regulators favour banning accounting firms from providing internal auditing and other consulting services to any financial institution they are auditing externally. They are also in favour of increasing current sanctions they can impose on auditors, and for requiring them to retain for a reasonable period the records and working papers used in their audit. They also acknowledge the shortcomings of accounting – for example, in the area of bank securitization.[15]

Episodes of Enron and the like illustrate vividly that the *accounting* crisis of the late 1990s-early 2000s reflects structural weaknesses in that profession and poses problems for the efficient working of markets. Notwithstanding that accounting is not an exact science, auditors have the primordial responsibility of attesting to the fairness and reliability of companies' accounts, with their assumptions clearly stated and consistent with economic reality. Such sound and honest financial reporting is vitally needed by the business community and by regulators to assess properly the reasonable value of assets and liabilities, and to assess the performance and prospects of audited firms.[16]

A strong legal-judicial system is essential to ensuring the success of supervision in enforcing contracts and protecting investors' or lenders' legitimate rights. Deviant, fraudulent or inappropriate actions should be timely and appropriately sanctioned, and bank owners or managers should bear the consequences of their actions. This could start with warnings, and extend to reprimands, civil money fines, naming and shaming, and severance of the employment of guilty officers, eventually culminating in judicial proceedings with criminal charges and higher levels of penalties. The latter could result in the rescinding of the bank's permit in the case of grave failures, and the appointment of a conservator or a receiver to take charge.

4.3 Official oversight and inspection

In protecting the public interest, public sector's supervisors must act as agents of two principals: (i) the taxpayer, who should be shielded against the eventuality of being called upon to share in the cost of bank failures; and (ii) the customer (whether debtor, investor or creditor), who needs safeguards against possible illicit exploitation by unscrupulous parties both within and outside the financial institution. For an effective supervisory system, fraud or abuse – such as selling worthless financial products, churning portfolios, underestimating costs or liabilities, overestimating earnings, exacting unwarranted high commissions and other malpractices – have to be unmasked by external supervisors without delay.[17] This may prove difficult when members of management are intent on covering up such actions.

4.3.1 Dereliction or forbearance

Supervisors in emerging and industrial economies, however, have not always acted decisively in the public interest. Indeed, some have procrastinated in addressing problems of troubled financial institutions for which they are responsible, often to cover up past mistakes of oversight and/or in the hope that improvements in the condition of the supervised bank might be forthcoming. They are often comforted in their attitude of 'regulatory forbearance' by their understanding that insured depositors are protected, and that an insolvent bank can continue to operate for a long period.

Low pay, and lack of authority and independence are impediments to attracting and retaining qualified supervisors. The prospect of getting high-paying private-sector jobs creates incentives for concealment and corruption among supervisors.[18] In so doing, conniving supervisors seek to ingratiate themselves with the top management of the bank under examination. They hope that the bank's problems are resolved quickly, or they expect alternatively to abandon their supervisory responsibilities before such problems blow up and become public knowledge.

Regulators' forbearance that allows looser accounting standards or the relaxation of discipline by delinquent financial institutions – whether based in developing or developed economies – has occasionally led to protracted crises. One notable example is that of Japan – the largest economy in Asia – where regulators tolerated insolvent financial institutions that continued to generate high levels of non-performing loans during the 1990s and early 2000s in a stagnating economy (past bad loans were not recognized, and existing loans became bad because borrowers failed to attain the hoped for growth).

The origin and scale of Japan's bad debt problem can be traced to its 'bubble economy' created by aggressive lending – notably to the construction/real estate sector, whose prices quadrupled along with those of shares between 1985 and 1991, only to tumble dramatically thereafter. Regulators in Japan should have declared several financial institutions bankrupt or seriously undercapitalized when judged against internationally accepted standards. The Japanese public authorities have nevertheless sought to shore-up troubled banks, securities firms and insurance companies[19] – to little avail, however. The authorities have been concerned about the adverse impact of forcing the write off of non-performing debts on the solvency of (i) numerous financial institutions; and (ii) ailing corporate debtors (mainly construction and retailing companies, in whose capital some banks have had significant participations). Non-performing debts of Japanese banks exceeded US$104 billion in mid-2001.[20]

Examples abound of financial crises which owe their origins to politicians who hindered supervisors in the exercise of their functions, and used state-controlled banks as a conduit for job patronage or for delivering financial favours to friends and voters. This was, for example, the case in Turkey in 2000–1.[21]

Furthermore, it might be questionable to resort to a relaxation of prudential rules to boost economic activity. This approach has nevertheless been the resort of some countries which had already suffered from financial crises – for example, in the case of Thailand, whose Finance Ministry early in 2002 eased provisioning guidelines for local banks, in an effort to encourage a growth in lending.[22]

Delays in disposing of an insolvent bank (that is, whose liabilities exceed the fair value of its assets), with losses still accruing, could well increase the cumulative losses ultimately sustained by such a bank. This, in turn, will aggravate the risk of losses spreading to other banks, and the potential bail-out cost encountered by the taxpayer, who would be called upon eventually to protect depositors by covering-up the losses of the failed banks. At the behest of the public authorities, supervisors could advisedly keep one or more insolvent banks afloat – especially when these institution are sizeable – and facilitate their recapitalization, should they be prompted by concerns about systemic risk (see also Chapter 5).

In the 1980s, the US supervisory authorities resorted to forbearance *vis-à-vis* banks by allowing them extra time to put their houses in order (to restructure loans in arrears) before declaring them insolvent. This was the case with several domestic lending institutions (namely the thrift industry), and major US international banks. A large number of the thrift institutions had large portfolios of bad loans – as judged by market values – and their outstanding capital could not absorb such losses. The support of the public authorities had cost the taxpayer an estimate of more than US$250 billion by the mid-1990s.[23] By comparison, forbearance *vis-à-vis* US major banks' lending to developing countries has allowed these banks to reconstitute their reserves and capital to absorb their losses without any outright support by public funds. A former chairman of the FDIC commented on the above episode:

> Sometimes forbearance ... is the right way to go, and sometimes it is not. In the S&L [Savings and Loan Associations] industry, all rules and standards were conveniently overlooked to avoid a financial collapse and the intense local political pressure that such a collapse would have generated. But in this case there was not a visible plan for recovery, so the result of this winking at standards was, as we know, a national financial disaster. On the other hand, in the case of Latin American loans, forbearance gave the lending banks time to make new arrangements with their debtors and meanwhile acquire enough capital so that losses on Latin American loans would not be fatal. Like medicine and the other healing arts, bank regulation is an art, not a science.[24]

Rich economies – compared to emerging economies – have evidently had a higher capacity to support their financial institutions – thereby enabling them to endure financial problems or crises. However, this situation could well induce laxity on the part of regulators. This can be illustrated by reference to the above-mentioned thrift institutions (or S&L) crisis during the 1980s and early 1990s in the USA, the protracted Japanese banking insolvencies during the 1990s and early 2000s, and

France's biggest-ever banking scandal of the state-owned Crédit Lyonnais in the 1990s (privatized in 2000).[25]

Compared to other developed economies, the Japanese banks' problem loans have proved to be particularly costly for the national economy. Problem loans increased from 5.38 per cent of total loans at the end of March 1998, to 6.58 per cent (that is, 32.5 trillion yen) at the end of March 2001. The injection of public funds for the rescue of twenty-seven banks in the fiscal year ended March 2001 totalled 8.5 trillion yen.[26] Three major problems have afflicted the Japanese banking system: (i) interest charges on loans have not generally reflected borrowers' risk for reasons of competition from government-sponsored financial institutions, external pressures on banks to provide cheap financing to small businesses, or traditional favourable financing charges to companies with long-standing relationships; (ii) the latter companies have often important cross-shareholding, and Japanese banks have large holdings of equities in various client firms that have suffered from a decade-long recession; and (iii) Japanese banks have relatively large holdings of subordinated notes and debentures (SNDs) of Japanese insurance companies that have encountered grave difficulties.[27] The apparent reluctance of Japanese banks to impose financial charges, commensurate with risks could be attributed to long-standing cronyism *vis-à-vis* many customers. Bad loans were thus renewed to companies in difficulty to avoid forcing them into bankruptcy – with the tacit agreement of the banking supervisory authorities.

The propping-up of insolvent corporate debtors by banks (which have acquired significant shareholdings in these corporations), has been a long-standing common practice in Japan. Some banks have allowed their debtors to avoid going into arrears by advancing new loans to meet repayment of the principal or accrued interest on old loans. Corporations have, furthermore, obtained refinancing from their banks at reduced margins. These margins have not taken proper account of the cost of capital, risk premia, operating expenses, and appropriate returns. The Bank of Japan sought to sever that double-dependency link between banks and their business clients by deciding on 11 October 2002 'to purchase some of the excessive shareholdings of corporate shares held by banks' – quite a novel approach for a central bank.[28] The Bank of Japan's purchase of corporate shares owned by banks (to be held for future resale, or for write-off until the end of September 2007) is, however, subject to the approval of the Japanese Government. The fumblings of the Japanese public authorities since 1992 have maintained a 12-year long economic stagnation, and a financial sector in crisis. Competitive forces have been

eviscerated by doling out subsidies to financial and non-financial institutions, and by allowing government-sponsored agencies to undercut
private sector financial institutions. Accepting the restructuring of the
business sector – involving the closure of loss-making companies, a rise in
unemployment, and the withdrawal of government subsidies – requires
political consensus. The cost to the Japanese taxpayer for solving the
financial sector problems was estimated late in 2002 to be roughly ¥ 120
trillion or 24 percent of Japan's GDP.[29]

4.3.2   Requisite expertise

Some countries may not have the human and material resources to
establish a soundly regulated and efficiently supervised and run
banking sector within a reasonable time horizon. For these countries, a
deliberate policy to welcome foreign financial institutions that are
well-managed and properly supervised on a consolidated basis by their
country of origin can prove to be a safe approach, to remedy the lack
of domestic infrastructure in regulation and supervision. The policy of
hosting the foregoing financial institutions could furthermore foster
macroeconomic discipline on the part of the host government
concerned – if that government is to maintain these foreign institutions'
involvement in their domestic economy. Such a policy has been
espoused by a few emerging economies, which have allowed foreign
banks from developed market economies to take over a major share of
their domestic banking sector, often in the wake of the failure of local
institutions.

Foreign financial institutions participating competitively in emerging
countries are likely to be more efficient – compared to their domestic
counterparts – thanks to economies of size and scope, lower operating
costs, and effective risk management controls. Equally, they can offer the
domestic host economy a wider range of products and services, and
special expertise. They may also serve as a conduit that facilitates the flow
of foreign investments. The trade-off for the host country is between an
improved regulatory environment, and vulnerability of the domestic
institutions to incoming competitors.

Domestic financial institutions need not be crushed by their foreign,
and often larger, competitors, if they make good use of their
knowledge of local markets and customers – comprising notably
individuals and households, and small to medium-sized enterprises –
where they have a comparative advantage.[30] If domestic banking
markets in developing economies are to be liberalized, it could

prove judicious that entry be made gradual, so as not to dislocate unwarrantably domestic financial markets and wipe out the franchise value of existing viable banks. Reputable foreign entrants can then create positive competitive pressures that stimulate – albeit over the longer term – efficiency, quality and innovation among domestic participants. The latter could well be induced to emulate the better standards of reporting and disclosure, of prudence and of management that foreign entrants adhere to – as required by their home country.

Talents are crucial to the mission of regulatory–supervisory agencies in developed and developing economies. Yet the said agencies often lag behind in expertise *vis-à-vis* commercial financial institutions, whose personnel and management are innovating continuously both products and services. New financial products contain risks that are not, however, easily identifiable or assessable by governmental examiners or supervisors–even in developed countries. As noted in one study:

> Continuing advances in technology have posed a different set of challenges for domestic and international regulation alike. The proliferation of financial instruments, coupled with innovative investing and trading strategies, keeps financial institutions several steps ahead of regulators who inevitably lag in gaining the requisite expertise required to assess the new risks.[31]

4.3.3   Supervisory approaches

On-site examinations

The personnel of supervisory agencies are often less informed, or belatedly informed, about the risks encountered by a bank in comparison to the bank's managers or employees. They need therefore to have timely on-site interviews with executives and staff, and to inspect ledgers and various other documents to ascertain risk exposures and how much the institutions under their purview respect the regulations. Such inspections can be rendered more effective when supervisory agencies are staffed with qualified and independent personnel. Moreover, the use of frequent surprise inspections can render the bank's management more vigilant. Nevertheless, this may prove too costly to realize.

In an environment of increasingly diverse and more complex risks, examiners have to evaluate the capacity of the bank's risk management systems to identify, measure and control risks accurately. This involves, *inter alia*, checking on the appropriateness of the criteria for screening loan applications, monitoring debtors and counter-parties, internal credit rating systems and write-off policies.

The US and other supervisory authorities use weighted criteria in their composite rating of banks (see Figure 4.2), referred to by the acronym CAMELS: Capital, Asset quality, Management, Earnings, Liquidity and Sensitivity to market risk. These ratings are done on-site at least once every eighteen months by US bank supervisory agencies, and ratings assigned to individual banks remain confidential.

Safe and sound	
1	Financial institutions with a composite *one* rating are sound in every respect and generally have individual component ratings of one or two.
2	Financial institutions with a composite *two* rating are fundamentally sound. In general, a two-rated institution will have no individual component ratings weaker than three.
Unsatisfactory	
3	Financial institutions with a composite *three* rating exhibit some degree of supervisory concen in one or more of the component areas.
4	Financial institutions with a composite *four* rating generally exhibit unsafe and unsound practices or conditions. They have serious financial or managerial deficiencies that result in unsatisfactory performance.
5	Financial institutions with a composite *five* rating generally exhibit extremely unsafe and unsound practices or conditions. Institutions in this group pose a significant risk to the deposit insurance fund and their failure is highly probable.

Note: CAMELS is an acronym for six components of bank safety and soundness: capital protection (C), asset quality (A), management competence (M), earnings strength (E), liquidity risk exposure (L), and market risk sensitivity (S). Examiners assign a grade of one (best) through five (worst) to each component. They also use these six scores to award a composite weighted rating, also expressed on a one-to-five scale.

Source: Federal Reserve Commercial Bank Examination Manual.

Figure 4.2   CAMELS ratings of bank solidity

Exposure to risk in banks can change rapidly. Supervisors, as well as shareholders and other stakeholders, are particularly concerned to learn as soon as possible about any changes, and notably any deterioration in the banks' financial conditions. The supervisors' aim would be to strive to alert management without delay to reverse the downturn. A momentarily troubled bank requires a comprehensive on-site examination to cover, *inter alia*, profitability, asset quality, liquidity, capital adequacy and risk control systems. In such circumstances, examiners perform their on-site inspection on a continuous basis until the bank's recovery. This type of inspection is bound to be costly in terms of the necessary skilled staff assigned to the job, and would put pressure on the management and the day-to-day activities of the bank.

Certain countries – though boasting banking secrecy laws – have come to accept on-site inspections by foreign supervisors, in addition to requiring more disclosures to markets by financial institutions operating within their jurisdictions. Switzerland, for example, has recently accepted the principle of 'regulatory attendance', with a view to implementing the inspection of international financial groups on a consolidated enterprise-wide basis. This principle allows a foreign supervisory agency in a country to undertake on-site inspections of foreign entities belonging to its home-based financial groups. Thus subsidiaries or affiliates of US banks operating in Switzerland can readily be inspected by authorized US supervisory agencies – subject to protecting the anonymity of customers. The latter's identity can only be disclosed (for example, for reasons of money laundering) in conformity with Swiss legal procedures.[32]

Several countries apply the above-mentioned 'umbrella' supervision. This is the case in the USA and thirteen other countries whose supervision is enterprise-wide, covering domestic and non-domestic entities belonging to financial groups headquartered in these countries. Through consolidated supervision, home authorities can capture the world-wide exposure of individual financial groups.[33]

Off-site monitoring

Off-site monitoring of a bank, in comparison with on-site examinations, analyses the situation of a bank on the basis of communicated information, without making a visit to the institution. In the USA, individual banks file on a quarterly basis with their regulatory–supervisory agencies selected information on their condition and income. This helps the agencies to evaluate the banks' risk profile, and assists the FDIC (see Chapter 5) to calculate deposit insurance assessments. From 2002, banks which have lending programmes aimed at sub-prime borrowers have to specifically declare that information. If such a loan portfolio exceeds 25 per cent of Tier 1 capital,[34] bank examiners would deem the institution concerned to be in a critical situation.[35]

In the identification of emerging safety and soundness problems, supervisors can use either (a) *surveillance screens*, which comprise a set of financial indicators for the bank and its peer group; or (b) *econometric models* designed to predict – on the basis of statistical tests – the future probability of a deterioration in the health of the bank.

The financial indicators used in the surveillance screen portray conditions at a given point in time. They normally lag in indicating current and prospective situations of strength or weakness, so they need to be complemented by the judgement of seasoned examiners in relation to the bank's observance of corporate governance principles and sound risk management. Econometric models provide an early warning with respect to the probability of failure within a fixed time horizon – for example, two years. To reach a credible evaluation, econometric models have also to consider qualitative factors (such as competence of management and risk controls) which could be reflected by certain proxy indicators quantitatively measurable, albeit roughly.[36]

The stability of the financial system could well be enhanced if best-practice rules tend towards becoming legally mandatory on banks – requiring supervisors to take 'prompt corrective actions' in specifically defined circumstances. Such a structured approach would be based on publicly pre-announced and well publicized objective norms which supervisors are legally mandated to enforce. Well enunciated norms – in comparison with the uncertainty and elusiveness associated with dis-cretion – give a needed sense of security to supervisors. They will thus act decisively in accordance with clear guidelines, and in co-ordination with the central bank and the deposit insurance agency. Bankers and their supporting politicians would not then threaten these supervisors with disciplinary action for alleged improper conduct.

Regulatory–supervisory norms could well include the mandatory requirement to sell the troubled bank to a healthy bank, or eventually to close a capital-depleted bank, at a specified time when capital is still positive. The foregoing assumes that (i) accounting and reporting of capital is ascertained objectively and communicated readily; and (ii) book capital is an adequate indicator of a financial institution's health. In reality, the true net worth of a bank depends on the market value of its assets, less third parties' liabilities. However, most of the assets of a typical bank are largely composed of illiquid loans with no market value. This situation can properly be addressed by a reasonable classification of loans with respect to their quality, and by making appropriate provisions for non-performing loans (see also section 3.5.4 in Chapter 3).[37]

In general, a very rapid increase in a bank's assets (notably loans) has been associated with a concomitant increase in risk. Moreover, a rapid growth in operations or declared profits of certain business lines (especially those involving 'fat' bonuses to operators) reflect higher risk-taking, and could possibly involve fraud. Equally, a higher concentration of exposures (for example, in commercial real estate, agriculture, telecommunication, IT and so on) renders a bank more vulnerable to increased losses should any of these sectors encounter difficulties. Vulnerabilities could also result from a bank's increased dependence on volatile funding sources – such as short-term deposits.[38]

Supervisors seek increasingly to apply tools or models which measure with greater accuracy the health of a bank, and whose predictive capacities are more reliable. Beyond macro data which provide a broad picture of the general health of the economy and the banking sector, supervisors now have models that monitor the risk profile of each bank, to identify serious situations that require urgent attention. Models applicable to banks with deposit-taking/lending activities have greater predictive power in comparison to models developed more recently for complex financial groups or those with new lines of business[39] (see also Chapter 7).

Prompt dissemination of relevant and reliable data should help market participants to sort out the efficient and healthy financial institutions from the troubled or mismanaged ones, and offer supervisors additional inputs for their assessments. Market risk premiums on debt instruments in competitive markets will become increasingly credible as early warning signals. Bank supervisors stand to gain incremental information from market data during the periods between inspections on the viability of banks, as distilled from risk premiums and equity prices.[40] Real-time market information would thus contribute considerably towards complementing the role of supervisors in mitigating risks in the banking sector (see section 4.5 on pages 83–6).

4.4 Integrated supervision: *quis custodiet ipsos custodes?*[41]

The blurring of traditional demarcations between financial products and services, and the development of conglomerates, have led to revisions in regulatory–supervisory structures. In a few countries, various financial functions (deposit-taking banks, pension funds, insurance, securities and derivative trading, asset management and investment funds) come under one single regulatory supervisory agency (for example, the Financial Services Authority – FSA – in the United Kingdom). First introduced in Norway in 1986 (through the Banking, Insurance and Securities Commission), this integrated financial supervision was adopted by Denmark in 1988; Sweden in 1991; the United Kingdom, Australia and Japan in 1998; Iceland in 1999; and Germany in 2001. Austria, Bahrain, Hungary, the Republic of Ireland, Malta and South Korea followed suit, and other countries such as Switzerland are, at the time of writing, preparing similar legislation.

Beyond national jurisdiction, the process of cross-linkage among regulatory and supervisory approaches and standards is proceeding gradually in the financial sector world-wide. In regional groupings – notably within the European Union (EU), this process has been considerably aided by the successful introduction of its single currency, the euro. This applies in particular to the regulation of banking and other financial intermediaries, deposit insurance and other safety nets, and the organization of financial markets. Much still has to be done in order to integrate the supervision of European financial markets, by producing, *inter alia*, an equivalent of the United States' SEC with its powers to impose sanctions and fines. There is equally a need for uniform European standards on company prospectuses, listing and filing requirements, clearing and settlement, market abuse, sanctions for the violation of rules, and a single passport to pension funds. EU regulations have yet to overcome certain member countries' protectionist policies, and to be guided by common objectives of simplifying and streamlining procedures, eliminating duplicated information, reducing the burden of excessive reporting, and promoting consistency.[42]

Integrated financial supervision is prompted by five main factors. First, it recognizes that traditional formal separations among financial intermediaries' products and services are becoming increasingly blurred, especially in view of the growth of financial conglomerates (covering banking, insurance, securities and asset management) and the increasing substitutability of several financial products and services. Integrated supervision will capture enterprise-wide, and industry-wide risks more easily. Fragmentation of regulatory–supervisory agencies in the financial sector could lead to information gaps and control loopholes (for example, in inter-affiliate transactions), and possibly to incoherent or discordant rules. Second, integrated supervision can be accompanied by economies of scale and scope. Lower costs will stand to benefit financial intermediaries and their stakeholders, who ultimately bear the cost of supervision. Third, financial institutions will be spared the overlap of multiple supervisory tasks if they report to a single supervisory agency. This should simplify relations with their supervisory interlocutors – especially if they have several lines of business. Fourth, integrated supervision can contribute to competitive neutrality – in so far as the principle of 'same risk, same rules' must apply. Fifth, separate agencies could produce *regulatory turf wars* within a single jurisdiction, while a single strong agency could recruit and retain more easily the necessary qualified personnel. At the international level, uncoordinated separate surveillance could be a source of friction with respect to the application of national laws and regulations.[43]

The four major arguments often adduced in favour of separate regulatory–supervisory entities are: first, it is more effective to have specialized and focused agencies; second, an integrated supervisory agency could lead to excessive concentration of power, may well prove too unwieldy to manage, and could be possibly subjected to political influence; third, competing agencies could lead to more efficient sets of rules for regulatees versus the possible 'ossification' of a regulatory monopoly; and fourth, there is a risk that a single all-comprehensive agency could falter without a counter-balancing force, and the potential impact of its faltering would raise systemic risk.[44] The institutional design of financial supervision is, in the end, a compromise of political economy, and is subject to the evolution of habits and customs.

Banks in the USA are free to choose the regulatory regime under which they would operate: state- versus federal-chartered, regulated and supervised banks. Many people see in the dual banking system 'a competition in laxity' – as put by a former Federal Reserve Board chairman, Arthur Burns. Others see in the dual system a reflection of US 'national value of competition, federalism and freedom of choice', and a source of innovation – to quote the US Comptroller of the Currency, John D. Hawke.[45] The USA has five federal regulatory–supervisory authorities for banks: the Board of Governors of the Federal Reserve System, FDIC, OCC, the Office of Thrift Supervision (OTS), and the National Credit Union Administration – in addition to the Banking Department in each of the fifty states – with some responsibilities overlapping among the different supervisory agencies. Moreover, wide discrepancies exist with respect to supervisory charges, since 'national banks pay on average two and a quarter times more in supervisory fees than do state banks'.[46] Other specialized state and federal supervisory agencies cater for insurance companies, pension funds and financial markets (with a few major submarkets having the benefit of self-regulatory bodies). The fragmentation of the regulatory–supervisory system for the banking sector in particular, and for the financial sector in general, is a potential source of multiple problems already mentioned above. Among these are notably the following: the costly duplication of work, gaps in oversight, dysfunctional 'turf wars', and a delayed response to solving problems.[47]

There are some who question the role of a central bank in carrying out bank supervision. They argue that such a role would lead to the perception that the central bank's traditional monetary function of lender of last resort would become unduly expansionary – to accommodate the supervisory concern of protecting weaker banks. The monetary–supervisory tandem within a single institution could therefore, become a potential source of moral hazard. Others see in this dual function a source of greater stability for the financial sector, in so far as the knowledge the central bank directly and readily obtains from supervision should enable it better to calibrate its monetary policy.[48] The preference for one approach over the other cannot be decided a priori. In a dynamic economic environment, a continuous re-appraisal is needed to ensure that the two functions – that is, the monetary and the supervisory – perform optimally.

The trend in the vast US financial sector is towards greater inter-agency co-operation, which is favoured by Congress. Indeed,

> while Congress has not encroached upon the chartering authority of the states, the balance of responsibility for the supervision and regulation of state-chartered banks has steadily shifted toward their federal regulators. For more than 30 years, almost every time Congress has imposed new federal bank supervisory and regulatory responsibilities, it has parcelled that authority and responsibility among the three federal banking agencies. That approach was originally shaped by concerns that some states lacked the resources to carry out Congress's mandates. As a consequence, the Federal Reserve and the FDIC today perform for state banks virtually every supervisory function that the OCC performs for national banks. The result has been to deprive the states of much of the opportunity to take full responsibility for the supervision of their own state-chartered banks.[49]

The US federal oversight agencies for banks are grouped within the Federal Financial Institutions Examination Council, with the objective of prescribing uniform principles and standards. The Council, further-more, co-operates with the Conference of State Bank Supervisors to improve the bank examination process. Such co-operation is bound to eliminate duplicative or outmoded policies and practices – thereby simplifying procedures and reducing the regulatory burden on financial institutions.

It is reckoned that miscommunication among US federal bank supervisors has hampered their co-operation, and their capacity to recognize promptly and correct quickly banking problems. It has precluded the supervisory agencies from taking timely measures to avoid the collapse of supervised banks, and to reduce the ensuing costs for the public authorities. This was notably the case with the Superior Bank (based near Chicago, Illinois) which was closed on 27 July 2001. The two supervisory agencies concerned were the OTS and FDIC.

The primary regulator, the OTS, 'denied FDIC's request to partici-pate in the 1999 examination', although both agencies are part of the US federal supervisory system. In this respect, the US Congress watch-dog, the General Accounting Office (GAO), found that problems of communication existed between the OTS and FDIC, and that 'federal regulators were clearly not effective in identifying and acting on the problems of Superior Bank early enough to prevent a material loss to the deposit insurance fund' [FDIC] – estimated upon the bank's closure on 27 July 2001 at between US$426–US$526 million loss for underwriting insured deposits.[50]

Not only national supervisors responsible for particular segments of the financial sector might fail to communicate and co-ordinate efficiently among themselves; they might also not act as rigorously as expected. This was conveyed clearly by the Inspector General of the US Department of the Treasury under whose aegis the OTS operates as a special supervisory agency for savings institutions. He attributed the failing of the OTS to its delayed supervisory response, ineffective enforcement action, examination weaknesses over valuation and accounting problems, undue reliance placed on external auditors, regulatory forbearance, and others. He said:

> In the early years, OTS' examination and supervision of Superior appeared inconsistent with the institution's increasing risk profile since 1993. It was not until 2000 that OTS expanded examination coverage of residual assets and started meaningful enforcement actions. But by then it was arguably too late given Superior's high level and concentration in residual assets. At times certain aspects of

OTS examinations lacked sufficient supervisory skepticism, neglecting the increasing risks posed by the mounting concentration in residual assets. OTS' enforcement response also proved to be too little and too late to curb the increasing risk exposure, and at times exhibited signs of forbearance. We believe that it was basically Superior's massive residual assets concentration and OTS' delayed detection of problem residual asset valuations that effectively negated the early supervisory intervention provision of Prompt Corrective Action.

We believe OTS' supervisory weaknesses were rooted in a set of tenuous assumptions regarding Superior. Despite OTS' own increasing supervisory concerns, OTS assumed (1) the owners would never allow the bank to fail, (2) Superior management was qualified to safely manage the complexities and high risks of asset securitizations, and (3) external auditors could be relied on to attest to Superior's residual asset valuations. All of these assumptions proved to be false.[51]

At the same hearings, the Inspector General of the FDIC recognized that if the lead supervisory agency (namely the OTS) had acceded to the FDIC's request to allow its examiners to be included in an on-site examination, the losses of the insurance fund would have been reduced. He stated:

Coordination between regulators could have been better. OTS denied the FDIC's initial request to participate in the regularly scheduled January 1999 safety and soundness examination, delaying any FDIC examiner on-site presence for approximately 1 year. The FDIC has special examination authority under section 10(b) of the Federal Deposit Insurance Act to make special examination of any insured depository institution. An earlier FDIC presence on-site at the bank may have helped to reduce losses that will ultimately be incurred by the Savings Association Insurance Fund. FDIC examiners were concerned over the residual interest valuations in December 1998. However, when the OTS refused an FDIC request for a special examination, FDIC did not pursue the matter with its Board. Working hand-in-hand in the 2000 examination, regulators were able to uncover numerous problems, including residual interest valuations.[52]

FDIC acknowledged that the OTS had approved flawed valuation and accounting statements (certified by external auditors Ernst & Young) allowing, *inter alia*, for the payment of unearned dividends and other financial benefits over several years (1992–2000).[53]

In the absence of a centralized institution, the appointment of a primary or 'lead' regulatory–supervisory agency within one country – or among co-operating countries – could help to overcome the above-mentioned lacunae of fragmentation. It will furthermore assist in reducing possible duplication or overlapping in supervision. Finally, it can help to move towards a more level playing field among banks and other financial services providers. Some countries, we have seen, prefer to maintain separate supervisory agencies for each identifiable category of financial functions – prompted by diverse reasons of division of labour, political-constitutional organization, convention, pragmatism, tradition, reputation and performance of the agencies concerned. Such separation of functions among different agencies need not preclude their co-operation.[54]

To sum-up, from the standpoint of regulated financial conglomerates with diverse activities operating in a given market, a single integrated supervisory agency spares them the costly burden of interfacing with a multiplicity of agencies with overlapping and possibly discordant rules. Moreover, consolidated supervision is crucial to assessing the overall risk profiles of financial conglomerates. Finally, integrated supervision could help in addressing systemic risk more promptly or effectively. The supervisory model chosen is not static. It is likely to evolve, influenced by both economic and socio-political conditions of the country(ies) concerned.

4.5 Transparency

Assuming rational behaviour, the timely availability of truthful, comprehensive, and readily understandable material information about financial markets should help all concerned: in particular, private and institutional investors, creditors, borrowers, managers of financial firms or intermediaries, and governmental entities. Informed judgements and decisions would then be made on sounder bases. This should help to bring under control difficulties and problems caused by opacity, and thereby reduce the occurrence of avoidable crises, and favour prudence – as sought by Basel II (see Figure 3.1 in Chapter 3).

4.5.1 Market disclosure

The relation between public disclosure of information or transparency on the one hand, and market discipline on the other hinges on the breadth and quality of information communicated to the public, and the capacity of stakeholders and other parties concerned to: comprehend and act on that information; and to reward or sanction the firm's management. Such a capacity will influence (that is, discipline) the behaviour of management – steering it towards higher sustained performance consistent with prudence. As put by a central banking study group, adequate timely information on a borrower's risk profile, and its current and prospective earnings, will enable funders and other parties to judge better the current and potential standing of that borrower:

> Market discipline means that a firm has private-sector stakeholders who are at risk of financial loss from the firm's decisions and who can take actions to 'discipline' the firm, that is, to influence its behaviour. Transparency in banking is a measure of the degree to which the stakeholders – equity holders, debt holders, and other counterparties – as well as securities analysts and rating agencies are able to assess an institution's current financial condition, prospects for future earnings, and risk. That assessment depends, in turn, on the extent and quality of disclosure, which refers to the public release of information on individual institutions about their financial condition and performance, the current value and collectibility of assets, and the value and cash flow requirements associated with liabilities, as well as information on risk exposures, risk management processes, control procedures, and business strategies.[55]

Central banks and regulatory agencies have the authority to collect, process, analyse and disseminate various types of information on financial intermediation and the real economy. Such information can influence the behaviour of participants in the financial system, and is thus very important to the safety and efficiency of the financial system. One should distinguish here between data and information. Data refer to facts and figures recorded and presented without any qualification or interpretation. Information – such as that provided by a research institution or a rating agency – interprets the significance of sifted data; it often carries with it implicit or explicit evaluations, as well as possible recommendations for action.[56] Information on assets' values and risks could be subject to individual or collective biases (see Chapter 7).

Accurate information calls for clear definitions and sound accounting standards to be applied internationally, thus enabling participants in global markets to make valid interpretations and comparisons.

Accounting rules are set by various national authorities and professional groups. Attempts at refining and harmonizing accounting rules and standards world-wide are made by the International Accounting Standards Board, the Global Investment Performance Standards Council, and others. The challenge of those setting accounting, performance and rating standards is to attain reasonable objectivity and accuracy. These standards are based on certain assumptions which should be presented distinctly. Some would argue for presenting accounts on the basis of different sets of assumptions.[57]

'Conventional wisdom' and consensus based on experience have often guided the decisions of standard-setting professional groups. This applies to proponents of transparency through fair-value accounting (based on 'marked to market') represented by the International Accounting Standards Board. Nevertheless, certain assets cannot be readily 'marked to market'; their valuations are subject to differing interpretations, particularly in the absence of meaningful and reliable market signals. This is notably the case with respect to the current valuation of non-marketable assets such as equity participations in privately held companies, bank loans held from origination to maturity, and over-the-counter (OTC) products, such as derivatives traded bilaterally.

Indeed, loan valuation methods could differ among the various parties concerned – the accounting profession, fiscal authorities and financial supervisors – in so far as they use different approaches for measuring loan deterioration and provisioning. This will affect bank balance sheets, and profit and loss statements. Accounting authorities stress the need for the *fair and objective* valuation of a loan (that is, the price the loan would normally obtain in an arm's-length sale in a competitive market) at the date it is reported. In the absence of such a market, the price has to be imputed.

By comparison, financial supervisors generally authorize that loans of solvent debtors held by banks until maturity be recorded at their face value. Nevertheless, these supervisors – prompted by prudence – have emphasized the need to build up sufficient provisions (notably through general provisions based on long-term average losses from defaults), as a buffer against future deterioration in credit quality. They argue that long-term, forward-looking provisioning would mitigate against the large falls in bank profits (and possibly in a bank's capital) that would occur in an economic downturn, and might reduce the pro-cyclicality of credit, financial volatility and financial instability.[58]

The generalization of fair value accounting to bank positions (such as assets held to maturity, in addition to intangible assets) poses computational difficulties. Such valuation – in the absence of a competitive market – is bound to contain a degree of subjectivity. It will also raise the volatility of a bank's capital requirements[59] if the valuation of the said bank positions were to be influenced by the vagaries of differing expectations or analyses (see also pages 50–1, Chapter 3).[60]

Some empirical evidence indicates that market transparency can contribute to the stemming of contagion. Stakeholders equipped with truthful, pertinent and timely information on actual risk exposure can then differentiate among banks, and sift the real from the false. This will reduce the likelihood of generalized bank runs, which occur in an environment of opacity.[61] As more comprehensive, reliable and timely information is made available to the public, and with the greater capacity of that same public to reach judicious decisions, market discipline will have a greater role to play in the evaluation of financial intermediaries, and their products or instruments.[62]

4.5.2   The case of credit registries

Transparency – that is, access to truthful, pertinent and timely information – is generally conducive to the development of markets, thereby benefiting a wider circle of economic agents on both the supply and demand sides of products and services. Thus access to credit could expand should potential borrowers make their payment histories readily available to potential lenders, including lenders with whom they have no prior business relations. By accepting a reduction in their privacy with respect to their track record of borrowing, eligible borrowers can obtain better terms, and available lenders are likely to increase their offer – compared to a situation of opacity. Furthermore, the benefits resulting from respecting contractual borrowing obligations (notably through lower interest charges and higher lending volumes) will prompt borrowers to act with rigour and responsibility.

A few countries have long authorized the creation of credit registries entrusted with the function of centralizing information on the risk exposures of borrowers. The functions of these agencies include in particular: (1) providing truthful and accurate credit information histories; (ii) the aggregation of exposures assumed by financial providers *vis-à-vis* individual customers (be they public entities, business enterprises or consumers); (iii) the communication of the aggregated information to lenders or underwriters who provide credit or guarantees to customers, as well as to the individual debtors concerned; (iv) offering credit scoring and fraud detection services; and

(v) supplying mailing lists and other marketing services for credit card and insurance companies, and others.

To protect their independence and neutrality, some jurisdictions (for example, in Europe) require the above-mentioned agencies to operate autonomously under the aegis of the regulatory–supervisory authorities. Other jurisdictions – notably in the USA – have authorized the development of private-sector credit registries both for consumers and for businesses (such as Dun & Bradstreet). Private firms are reckoned to be more exhaustive in their collection of needed information, and more efficient in their operations. Detailed information on sub-prime borrowers, for example, includes arrears beyond thirty days, court judgments, foreclosures, bankruptcies, debt service-to-income ratios in excess of 50 per cent, and so on.

Data on individuals can be obtained from a range of sources: credit card companies, mortgage finance, leasing companies, specialized car/student/consumer lenders, other finance companies and diversified financial institutions. Privately-owned debtor companies which do not publish financial accounts may also be included in the credit registries. The latter distribute complete, reliable and up-to-date histories on borrowers' track records to actual and potential lenders – on the payment of a fee.

Credit institutions in the USA have shared information voluntarily for nearly a century on the indebtedness and the payment histories of their customers via credit registries or credit bureaux. There were about 1000 credit registries in 2002, with four having national coverage and a combined size attaining about half of the industry's total turnover. Information communicated to credit registries was not always forthcoming; for example, lenders accounting for half of all consumer credit stopped communicating certain information on their clients in the late 1990s – such as credit limits and high debt balances. They were subsequently pressed by US financial regulators to communicate the requisite information.[63] To avoid economic abuse or possible criminal incidents, credit registries must observe security rules set and enforced by the public authorities.

Credit reporting systems are extending their services increasingly beyond national boundaries – in line with people's greater mobility. The ready availability of their services to lenders can assist borrowers in obtaining finance without delay from new lenders with whom they have had no previous relationship.[64] By accessing current and past information on a customer's risks, a lending firm is able to improve its evaluation of that customer and to manage the relationship judiciously.

Aggregated information on individual customers' risks available online to financial firms can help these firms to immediately avert excessive concentration of risk on one single customer or a group of like customers. It can also help management and regulators to take timely corrective action. Disclosed information on the indebtedness of various sectors can also be useful to a range of protagonists in the financial system, including policy-makers who would fine tune their actions in the light of that information.

US bank regulators (the Federal Reserve, the FDIC, and the Comptroller of the Currency) have shared information among themselves since 1977 regarding large, syndicated loans (those of US$20 million or more, held by at least three financial institutions). Adversely rated credits are summarized in three categories: substandard, doubtful loss, and special loans exhibiting potential weaknesses. These loans are, furthermore, classified by broad groupings of industries.[65] Similar information on non-syndicated loans contracted by financial intermediaries is not available.

4.5.3   Other inputs

Beyond information collected through the formal supervisory structure (see Figure 4.1 on page 61), other channels can provide supplementary elements – some of which could well aid corporate stakeholders and society at large in sparing them the costs of malpractices, errors, fraud and crises. Among these channels, one could refer to three major sources (see Figure 4.3):

- *The market* – comprising financial indicators, credit registries, think tanks, competitors and the media. Foreign exchange traders – according to various banking sources – are often the first to hear about potential counter-party problems. The latter are readily translated into the widening of spreads.
- *The public sector* – such as extensive critical investigations by the legislative and judiciary branches. The latter comprise the offices of attorney-generals, whose law-enforcement powers enable them to probe financial institutions. Prosecutors can identify fraudulent operations and accounting tricks. They can bring criminal charges against a bank's management, employees and customers.[66]
- *The enterprise* – notably whistleblowers from among the so-called gatekeepers (independent directors, shareholders, key investors or creditors, legal counsellors and employees), and from trading partners.

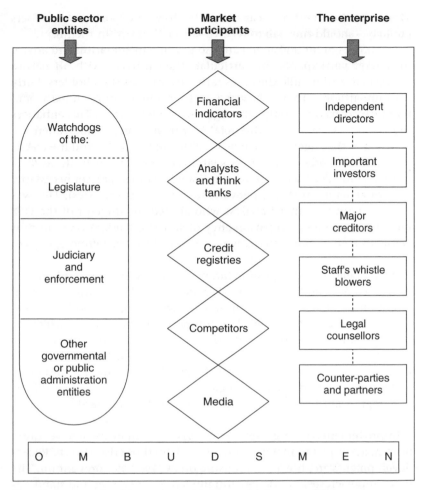

Public sector entities	Market participants	The enterprise

Watchdogs of the:

Legislature

Judiciary and enforcement

Other governmental or public administration entities

Financial indicators

Analysts and think tanks

Credit registries

Competitors

Media

Independent directors

Important investors

Major creditors

Staff's whistle blowers

Legal counsellors

Counter-parties and partners

O M B U D S M E N

Note: To be considered in tandem with Figure 4.1 (see page 61).

Figure 4.3 Additional inputs on banks and their stakeholders: the three perspectives

In particular, certain employees can be well placed to expose management's deceptions and fraud – by turning the spotlight on these malpractices. Various laws and regulations – for example, in Britain through the Financial Services Authority (FSA) – protect, in principle, 'whistle blowing.' In reality, however, whistle blowers are not rewarded for their actions and are often subjected to harassment within their firms when raising their concerns internally.

Moreover, they have no clear-cut protection for exposing wrongdoers publicly – should they fail to receive satisfaction within their firm.[67]

The offices of ombudsmen can also provide information and advice to market participants. In particular, they interact with all parties concerned, and handle the cases raised by various stakeholders, fairly and impartially. Their objective is to resolve, professionally and promptly, consumer complaints against financial firms. This enhances the public's trust in the financial sector at large. Ombudsmen are attached to state agencies such as the FDIC in the USA[68] and the FSA in the UK,[69] or to private-sector associations of financial institutions.[70]

Inputs provided by the above-mentioned channels are not necessarily used or acted upon by the relevant supervisory agency (ies). This was the case with a financial analyst who alerted the director of the OTS regarding the impending insolvency of Superior Bank, several months before its demise, but regrettably to no avail.[71] He, furthermore, argued:

> Many believe that deposit insurance creates a moral hazard, in that insured depositors care not a whit about a bank's or thrift's financial condition. But regulatory moral hazard trumps depositor moral hazard if regulators publish erroneous information on which to judge an institution's condition, as OTS did in the Superior situation, or if regulators inexplicably drag their feet in closing an insolvent institution, as the OTS did in the Superior situation. Although seldom discussed, regulatory moral hazard is the real issue Congress must now address, not depositor moral hazard.[72]

Improvements in regulatory–supervisory frameworks have often been made *ex post* to major problems, and are thus crisis-driven. Recent developments are, however, focusing on *ex ante* crisis prevention. The latter approach seeks to design and implement measures and standards capable of promoting a priori the efficiency, solidity and safety of national and international financial systems. Co-operation in that area has advantages for the longer-term growth of national economies, and for global financial and economic stability. The latter could be enhanced through: (1) disclosure of honest, pertinent and comparable information, and (2) the rigorous accountability of managers of financial institutions. Such an environment of judicious risk management and effective supervision/enforcement, although unlikely to eliminate the possibility of crises, is capable of building up defences, and of reducing the frequency of eventual crises or moderating their negative impact. Safeguards and safety nets to contain such crises are discussed in Chapter 5.

5
Financial Safety Nets

Public authorities' prudential regulations concerning financial intermediaries and their effective supervision (discussed in Chapters 3 and 4) are often considered to be the foremost safety nets. Their objectives are (a) at the micro level to ensure that individual financial institutions are well capitalized and well managed; and (b) at the macro level to safeguard the soundness, efficiency and stability of the financial system. Besides the regulatory–supervisory frameworks, specific post-failure and government-supported financial safety nets – discussed hereafter – are deemed to be valuable complements to enhancing savers' and investors' confidence, and reinforcing financial stability.

This chapter starts with a brief review of the coverage of safety nets (section 5.1). It then focuses on deposit insurance schemes and their desirable features – notably, those relating to: their efficient organization and management, premium assessment, use of market signals, and the challenge of large financial groups (sections 5.2 to 5.5). This is followed by an examination of investors' protection (section 5.6). The recapitalization of financial institutions (section 5.7), and liquidity provision to financial markets (section 5.8) are reviewed from the perspective of stabilizing the financial system. The insurance of non-commercial exposures is examined from the angle of mitigating non-controllable or non-actuarially assessable risks encountered by financial institutions and their clients (section 5.9). The chapter concludes with an interpretation of the impact of safety nets on market efficiency and discipline, and the 'entry–eviction' process (section 5.10).

5.1 Span of protection

Past events have shown[1] that the devastating impact of financial crises on society has prodded public authorities into overhauling or improving both their regulatory frameworks and their supervisory methods. Events have also led governments to seek remedies for the failure of financial systems or markets, and for controlling financial panics – by establishing and developing safety nets. These consist of rescue mechanisms for the benefit of the national economy, eligible financial intermediaries, and the general public. The objectives, scope and operational terms of safety nets have varied across jurisdictions and over time. Beyond regulation-supervision, major types of government-sponsored or government-supported financial safety nets are listed in Figure 5.1. They include:

- Deposit insurance schemes aimed at protecting depositors of insolvent institutions;
- Central banking institutions whose function is (i) to provide emergency liquidity to solvent financial intermediaries or depressed financial markets; and (ii) to ensure the efficient functioning of payment and settlement systems;
- Investor protection aimed at compensating investors who cannot recoup the financial assets held on their behalf by a defaulting securities dealer or investment enterprise. Compensation for customers is generally based on the face value of money accounts, and the market value of securities and other assets held in custody by these firms;
- Compensation of holders of insurance policies and of pension rights, upon the default of the institutions concerned;
- Compensation for certain losses arising from catastrophes;
- Protection against risks not usually insured by private companies, covering: loans, investments, and other rights or assets. The protection can apply to specified selected sectors and enterprises in foreign countries and the domestic economy;
- Recapitalization arrangements to overcome the insolvency of key financial institutions.

Guarantee, insurance or compensation schemes vary considerably with respect to the nature of financial claims or assets covered, the size of coverage per beneficiary, the funding of the insurance vehicles, the latter's type of management (private, governmental or joint), the obligation of financial firms to participate, the methods of calculating premiums or levies, and other characteristics.[2] To be credible, the 'saver, depositor, or investor' protection schemes need to be underpinned by appropriate regulatory–supervisory

	Principal direct beneficiaries	Vehicles
1	**Deposit insurance**	
	Consumers' deposits	Examples: • Federal Deposit Insurance Corporation (USA) • European Union: Directive 94/19/EC, 30 May 1994
2	**Ultimate liquidity**	
	Financial intermediaries: • Individual institutions • Financial markets • Payment systems	Central banks, as lenders of last resort
3	**Investors' portfolio protection**	
	Retail investors: • Personal portfolios with securities dealers and other financial institutions	Examples: • The US 'Securities Investor Protection Act 1970' • European Union: Directive 97/9/EC, 3 March 1997
4	**Life insurance policies and pensions**	
	Eligible parties	Examples: • UK Financial Services Compensation Scheme covers insurance policyholders, depositors, investors, and pensioners • Japan's Life Insurance Policyholders Protection Corporation • The Pension Benefit Guaranty Corporation (PBGD) protects the retirement incomes of about 44 million American workers in more than 35000 defined benefit pension plans.
5	**Natural and human-caused catastrophes**	
	Bail out of insurers and/or insured parties	Examples: • State guaranty funds of American state governments in the USA • UK government-backed, mutually owned 'Pool Re' • Government-owned Caisse Centrale de Réassurance in France
6	**Non-commercial risks insurance**	
	Enterprises' assets: financial and nonfinancial.	Examples: • Most industrial countries • Overseas Private Investment Corporation (USA) • Multilateral Investment Guarantee Agency (World Bank Group)
7	**External recapitalization**	
	Insolvent or undercapitalized financial institutions.	• National treasuries • State agencies • Obligated parties (for example stakeholders) • Others

cont. overleaf

Figure 5.1   Explicit major safety nets relevant to the financial sector

mechanisms, and the ultimate support of the monetary and fiscal authorities.

The British legislature decided as from December 2001, to group the compensation of consumers within the Financial Services Compensation Scheme (FSCS). The latter covers primarily private individuals and small businesses up to the following maximum levels: (i) £31 700 (100 per cent of £2000 and 90 per cent of the next £33 000) for a deposit claim in the case of the failure of deposit-taking companies; (ii) £48 000 (100 per cent of £30 000 and 90 per cent of the next £20 000) for a claim against an investment company that cannot return the investor's assets or money, or for the loss inflicted on an investor resulting from bad advice or poor investment management; and (iii) insurance claims for policies issued in the United Kingdom, when the authorized insurance company goes out of business (compulsory insurance is covered fully, and non-compulsory insurance – life and non-life – are covered fully on the first £2000 and 90 per cent for the remainder).

To fulfil its responsibilities, the FSCS has the power to:

- assess and pay compensation;
- impose levies;
- exercise rights of recovery; and
- compel the production of information to exercise its functions.

Though independent, the FSCS co-operates with other related official entities – namely the Financial Services Authority and the Financial Ombudsman. The rationale for a single financial compensation scheme is based on the advantages of rationalization, a single point of contact, and the ability to achieve greater coherence and improvements in systems and processes. The advantages of cost efficiencies become more pronounced in markets where consumers have the opportunity of diversifying their financial assets among substitutable or complementary financial assets or products.[3]

5.2 Deposit insurance rationale: moral hazard/protection trade-off

5.2.1 Genesis

Deposit insurance has witnessed many changes since the nineteenth century. In the past, bank defaults produced widespread tragedies among small savers, and this situation encouraged lawmakers to address the subject of protecting small depositors. With this paramount critical concern prevailing strongly, New York State was a pioneer with the Safety Fund Act of 1829. The purpose of that legislation was to create a mechanism for insuring bank obligations: banks had to pay a sum equal to half a per cent of their capital over six years to meet eventual liabilities of failed banks. The Act helped to restore public confidence in banks, and the fund – on its liquidation in 1866 – had a surplus, albeit small. However, several other deposit insurance schemes were not able to weather various panics.[4]

The New York legislature opened the way for other state legislatures in the USA and beyond. Safety funds in other jurisdictions, however, went out of business soon after their creation. Historians attribute the performance of the New York Safety Fund to a key regulatory–supervisory feature, which did not exist in other schemes, namely the appointment of three state commissioners to examine the status of banks and to report annually to the legislature.[5] Other deposit insurance systems 'produced very large bank failures, sufficiently large to bankrupt the insurance fund, and note holders and deposit holders sustained heavy losses.'[6] This was attributed primarily to fixed (that is, non-risk-sensitive) assessments, and very weak state supervision.[7]

Governmental deposit insurance exists at the time of writing in more than seventy countries. Though with differing structures, powers and coverage, most share the objective of protecting designated bank depositors – thus contributing to the raising of confidence in the banking system, especially in periods of volatility and uncertainty. They are also intended to protect soundly managed and healthy banks (and their stakeholders) from the contagion of defaulting banks and the potential danger of depositors' runs. Finally, deposit insurance schemes can thus serve to ensure the continued functioning of the payment and settlement systems – so essential to modern economies (see Chapter 3).

5.2.2 Opposition to deposit insurance

Some countries, such as New Zealand, have publicly informed all parties concerned – and notably depositors – that the government does not provide an explicit deposit scheme in any shape or form. All creditors are treated equally – whether domestic or foreign-based. The New Zealand authorities have chosen to promote the safety and stability of their financial system through regulation and disclosure, and not through any form of insurance of financial intermediaries' customers. The main objectives of their disclosure regime are to:

(a) increase the incentives for banks to monitor and manage their banking risks. Banks will have incentives to manage their affairs prudently, so as to avoid the need to disclose adverse events to the market;

(b) provide a more focused role for bank directors in overseeing, and taking ultimate responsibility for the management of banking risks; and

(c) provide depositors, financial planners, investments advisers and others with higher quality and more timely information on banks, so as to improve savers' and investors' ability to decide where to place their funds.[8]

Disclosures are detailed and extensive, made on a quarterly basis for all banks incorporated in New Zealand. Should a foreign-based bank with more than NZ$200 million in retail deposits not be subject to such disclosures in its home country, it will be required to incorporate locally.

A body of research analysed by a team at the World Bank and covering over a hundred countries

> suggest that, in practice, rather than lowering the likelihood of a crisis, the adoption of explicit deposit insurance *on average* is associated with less banking sector stability ... Deposit insurance has no significant effect in countries with strong institutions, but in weak institutional environments has the potential to destabilise. This result is reinforced by the finding that banks, exploiting the availability of insured deposits, take greater risks.[9]

The institutional environments referred to above consist mainly of prudential regulation and effective supervision/enforcement in a competitive market enjoying socio-economic stability.

5.3   Terms of deposit insurance

5.3.1   Adherence

The primary beneficiaries in deposit insurance schemes should be the small and unsophisticated depositors who do not have the interest, means, resources, time or skills to (i) obtain relevant and complete data on deposit-taking banks; (ii) understand and evaluate the risk-performance profiles of individual banks which could use complex financial products (for example, derivatives); and (iii) choose and monitor – with full knowledge of the facts – safe and soundly operated banks.

Supervisory authorities are often loath to disclose prematurely full information on individual banks in difficulty lest they trigger the precipitous demise of one or more fragile banks, with an adverse spillover effect on to the banks' customers and on to soundly-run financial institutions. This assumes that the said banks in difficulty are taking corrective measures to recover their soundness.

Several countries have required all their banks to adhere to national deposit insurance schemes. Voluntary participation allows individual institutions to 'opt out'. Typically, this will be the case with safe and solid institutions – a situation which would leave the deposit insurance scheme with the weaker institutions. To avoid such 'adverse selection', bank participation should become mandatory, and depositor premiums should be risk-based to take proper account of prudent policies and practices followed by safer banks, and to provide appropriate incentives for other banks to emulate prudent banks (see section 5.3.2 below).

Countries with compulsory comprehensive membership in statutory deposit insurance schemes – such as those of the European Union – have allowed certain segments of their banking sector to operate their own specific guarantees, subject to there being adequate supervisory safeguards. This applies to banks organized on a co-operative or mutualist basis that boast strong federations offering guarantee schemes (see Figure 5.2 for key characteristics of deposit protection in the German financial sector). The non-statutory protection schemes are subject to governmental supervision, and must respect official solvency and liquidity rules.[10]

To ensure an equitable policy and to avoid adverse selection, one could argue that it will be appropriate to make deposit insurance apply uniformly and comprehensively to all banks participating in a financial market. Austria, Germany and Italy have more than one deposit insurer with no level playing field. In Germany, for example, some banks offer deposit insurance for a maximum of €20 000, while major commercial banks offer practically unlimited coverage – in so far as each depositor can be protected for a sum which can reach up to 30 per cent of the capital of the depository bank. In defence of such diversity within a single market, one could state that the competition of systems could offer users a choice and allow them to test the additional net benefits provided by each system – over and above the statutory minimum. This would necessitate a comparative analysis of terms offered to depositors – including interest payments, withdrawal rights and other conditions.

The USA, despite its vast diversity, and the complexity of its economic structure, has moved towards the unification of its deposit insurance funds. This applies to the Bank Insurance Fund and the Savings Association Insurance Fund. Such unification produces a stronger and better-diversified merged fund – compared to each fund standing alone. It will, furthermore, preclude the possibility of premium disparity among banking institutions. And, finally, it will

Institutions	Institutional/statutory protection: depositor/investor	Voluntary deposit protection
Deposit-taking institutions *Under private law*		
Credit co-operatives and regional institutions	Institutional protection (operated by the Federal Association of German People's Banks and Raiffeisen Banks, regional co-operative associations)[a]	
Other deposit-taking institutions	Statutory cover up to 90% of a deposit[b] (maximum €20 000) and up to 90% of a claim arising from investment business[c] (maximum €20 000) (operated by the Entschädigungseinrichtung Deutscher Banken GmbH)[a]	Supplementary cover for deposits not covered by depositor/investor protection[d] per depositor up to 30% of the liable capital[e] of the institution concerned (operated by the Deposit Guarantee Fund of the Federal Association of German Banks)[a]
Under public law Savings banks, Land banks, public building and loan associations	Institutional protection (operated by the German Savings Bank and Giro Association, regional savings bank associations)[a]	
Other deposit-taking institutions	As in the case of other deposit-taking credit institutions under private law (operated by the Entschädigungseinrichtung des Bundesverbandkdes Öffentlicher Banken Deutschlands GmbH)[a]	Voluntary supplementary cover of a deposit[f] up to the full amount (operated by the Federal Association of Public Banks)[a]
Other institutions		
Credit institutions with: Principal broking Underwriting Credit institutions and financial services institutions with: Investment broking Contract broking Portfolio management Own-account trading Investment companies with asset management for others	Statutory cover up to 90% of a claim arising from investment business[c] (maximum €20 000) (operated by the compensation scheme of the securities trading firms Entschädigungseinrichtung der Wertpapierhandelsunternehm- en) at the Reconstruction Loan Corporation[a,g]	

Notes:

[a] Administration of a fund's assets for the settlement of claims, compulsory contributions by the co-operating/assigned institutions.

[b] Protected deposits, mainly account balances and registered debt securities denominated in euros or an European Economic Area (EEA) currency. Issued bearer bonds, in particular, are among the items that are not protected. The protected group of depositors/investors

cont. overleaf

Figure 5.2   Notes – *cont.*
consists mainly of individuals; financial institutions, public bodies, medium-sized and
large incorporated enterprises, in particular, are not protected.
c Protected claims arising from investment business are mainly claims to ownership or
possession of funds (denominated in euro or an EEA currency) or financial instruments.
Protected group of investors, see footnote b.
d Protected deposits are mainly sight, time and savings deposits as well as registered debt
securities, irrespective of the currency in which they are denominated (amounts owed to
customers). Issued bearer bonds, in particular, are not protected. The protected group of
depositors includes all non-banks (especially individuals), business enterprises and public
bodies.
e Sum of core capital and prudential supplementary capital, with the latter being included
only up to 25% of the core capital.
f See footnote d; certain public bodies (federal government, Länder, their special funds) do
not belong to the protected group of legal persons.
g Unless an institution is assigned to another scheme in specific cases.

Source: Deutsche Bundesbank, *Monthly Report*, Frankfurt, July 2000, p. 44.

Figure 5.2   Overview of deposit/investor protection in Germany

* * *

reduce the costs to insured financial conglomerates comprising diverse
banking institutions in tracking their separately insured deposits.[11]

5.3.2   Funding: *ex ante* versus *ex post* funding

As an institution serving the collective interest of all banks, the start-up
cost for launching the deposit insurance agency could be funded by the
banking sector. Should larger resources be required than banks are able to
mobilize, sizeable lines of credit could be made available by the central
bank or the Treasury – in order to give solid credibility to the deposit
insurance institution. The latter should preferably be operated as a self-
financing entity, by accumulating over the medium-to-long term reserves
from levies and premiums charged on banks and their depositors
sufficient to cover disbursements for the insured deposits of failed banks.

In the case of a systemic crisis where the whole banking sector is in
trouble, one cannot expect the deposit insurance institution to hold
sufficient resources to meet all insured deposits. In such a crisis
situation, governmental funding (that is, taxpayers' money) becomes
necessary for the rescue of banks and their depositors.

It is reckoned that regular, periodic *ex ante* payments of premiums
are safer and fairer than *ex post* payments. The *ex ante* method's safety
stems from (i) the fact that funds gradually accumulate to be readily
available for immediate disbursement to depositors of failed banks,
(ii) avoiding the problem of a time-consuming collection of funds
inherent in an *ex post* system; (iii) the general public's positive percep-

tion of confidence in the banking system's capacity to withstand crises; (iv) the greater ability of the deposit insurer to build-up reserves in normal or prosperous periods, prior to bank failures and the ensuing adversity that is likely to affect the financial system and the real economy; and (v) the potential capacity of the deposit insurer to borrow from the market against future regular premium income.

The *ex ante* method is fairer to the extent that premiums would have been levied on all banking institutions – the solid and healthy, as well as those that are subject to problems and potentially susceptible to fail. Some quarters may question whether governmental deposit insurers have the competence to obtain an attractive yield from their investment of reserves accumulated from premiums. Such competence could, however, be recruited and developed. One could also resort to joint private/public management of accumulated reserves by the deposit insurer – while cautioning against accumulating superfluous reserves, lest these are squandered.

5.3.3 Flat versus risk-sensitive premiums

In the same vein as the optimal calculation of minimum regulatory capital in a financial institution needs to be adjusted to risk (see section 3.5.3 in Chapter 3), it is equally desirable to have the payment of deposit premiums differentiated by reference to the risk profile of the deposit-taking institution. Such a linkage will in principle encourage bank management to operate in a safe and sound manner. At the limit, a deposit insurer could threaten to charge a banking institution punitively, in order to sanction its management's irresponsible behaviour until it heeds the summons to scale down the risks, as warranted. Care should be exercised in avoiding the destabilization of the said institution if the current management is willing and able to comply with the regulators' summons to improve the bank's conditions.

A flat premium applicable to all banks regardless of their risk profiles would be favoured in certain jurisdictions for reasons of the simplicity of such an approach. However, this regime is flawed, for two reasons:

(i) banks with high risk profiles receive in effect a hidden subsidy; and
(ii) well managed, prudent and adequately capitalized banks are surcharged.

A flat rate implies that weaker or less prudent banks can increase their risk without having to charge customers higher prices/margins/commissions on weaker quality products (for example, loans) and without having to pay higher interest on their funding (for example, deposits). Such a flat premium rate therefore distorts competition and raises moral hazard, in so far as banks do not have the incentive to contain their risky employment of funds. In a voluntary deposit insurance scheme with flat premium rates, the tendency for higher-risk banks is to join, while lower-risk banks opt out – a phenomenon known as *adverse selection*. To avoid this source of vulnerability for the insurance fund, membership of the deposit insurance scheme should be compulsory – we have seen – and premium assessment should be differentiated by reference to the risk profiles of individual banks.

Certain countries, such as Spain[12], have maintained a flat premium on insured deposits. Several arguments are invoked for such an approach. Notable among these are: (i) convenience, and acceptability of such a system by the banking institutions concerned; (ii) absence of full transparency on risks and inadequacy of current methods to allow for an objective measurement of risks and of changes therein; and (iii) risks are already deemed to be taken into consideration sufficiently through risk-adjusted regulatory capital required from banks. It needs to be emphasized that risk-adjusted capital is just one component in the management of the risk profile of a bank. Another component discussed in this section is risk-sensitive deposit premiums.

Both quantitative and qualitative factors of risk need to be accounted for in the calculation of deposit insurance premiums applying to individual banks' total activities. Objective quantitative criteria (such as capital, asset quality, liquidity ratios, large loans, sectoral concentrations, open positions, record of earnings/losses, and sensitivity to market/systemic risks) should be complemented by the key critical factor of quality of management. This is the CAMELS method (see Figure 4.2 on page 74) used by the US and other regulators and deposit insurers. The Canada Deposit Insurance Corporation (CDIC), for example, gives quantitative factors more weight (60 per cent of the total score) than qualitative factors (40 per cent of the total score) – see Table 5.1. The risk-adjusted differential premiums applying to insured deposits in 2002 cover four categories of bank, rising from two basis points (0.02 per cent) for the safest institutions to 16 basis points (0.16 per cent) for the weakest ones – see Table 5.2.

5.3.4   Cyclicality and limits on insurance funds

All insured financial institutions have to be charged premiums. As the chairman of FDIC acknowledged, institutions 'that are extremely well

Table 5.1 Overview of CDIC's differential premium system: criteria and scores

Criteria	Maximum scores
Capital Quantitative:	
Capital adequacy	20
Assets to capital multiple	nd
Tier 1 risk-based capital ratio	nd
Total risk-based capital ratio	nd
Other Quantitative:	
Return on risk-weighted assets	5
Mean adjusted net income volatility	5
Volatility adjusted net income	5
Efficiency ratio	5
Net impaired assets (including net unrealized losses on securities) to total capital	5
Aggregate counter-party asset concentration ratio	5
Real estate asset concentration	5
Aggregate industry sector asset concentration	5
Sub-total: Quantitative Score	60
Qualitative:	
Examiner's rating	25
Extent of adherence to CDIC standards	10
Other information	5
Sub-total: Qualitative Score	40
Total Score	**100**

nd = not disclosed.
Source: Canada Deposit Insurance Corporation, Ottawa, 9 January 2003, (www.cdic.ca).

Table 5.2 Overview of CDIC's differential premium system: premium categories and rates

Score	Premium category	Premium rates (basis points % of insured deposits)		
		1999/2000	2001	2002
≥80	1	4	4	2
≥65 and <80	2	8	8	4
≥50 and <65	3	16	16	8
<50	4	16	33	16

Source: Canada Deposit Insurance Corporation.

run offer some risk to the FDIC'. Yet, a 1996 US legislative Amendment to the FDIC Act authorized a zero premium payable on insured deposits by all banks, apart from those that were poorly capitalized or had significant problems, once the insurance fund had accumulated reserves equivalent to 1.25 per cent of insured deposits (known as a designated reserve ratio – DRR). This led to the exemption by mid-2001 of approximately 92 per cent of the US bank deposits from assessment, a situation which is at variance with the spirit and practice of commercial insurance. A US congress member expressed eloquently the basic principle of insurance thus 'I have a stellar driving record and my insurance company may have more than adequate cash reserves, but I still pay a premium for insurance coverage or I can't drive my car.'[13] Indeed, the insurance institution has to be provident and forward-looking to cover the eventuality of an unexpected future loss.

Risk-sensitive premiums have continuously to be readjusted and refined in the light of pertinent objective and qualitative factors, properly weighted. An FDIC study shows that an important portion of top-rated institutions (CAMELS 1 or 2) filed for bankruptcy after two years of the said top rating in the following percentages: they represented 34 per cent of the 1617 bank failures between 1980 an 1994, and 33 per cent of the 30 bank failures between 1995 and 2001.[14]

For periods of prosperity, risk-adjusted differential premiums are likely to be lower than in periods of downturn and recession. This cyclicality of premiums presents particular hardship to weak banks with little or no profits in periods of financial distress. To moderate this problem, pro-cyclical premiums should be smoothed or even made counter-cyclical. In the latter situation, the insurance fund would be building sufficient financial reserves on the 'sunny days' to be readily available for the 'rainy days'.

Charges for deposit insurance should therefore take into consideration the business cycle. Similar to commercial insurance, risk-based premiums need to be modulated and collected at sufficient levels and essentially in good times, to cover losses in bad times when banks and the economy are in recession. The challenge of any insurance scheme is to accumulate adequate resources – thereby avoiding having reserves that are too large or too small. Adjustment rules could be set up (i) to give banks credit towards future assessments (based on past contributions); and (ii) to make up for deficits with additional levies.

Several scholars and policy-makers have reservations on statutory pre-fixed ceilings on the accumulation of reserves in the deposit insurance fund. They question, therefore, the economic soundness of an approach that mandates cash payments out of the fund, or rebates or credits towards future assessments. Such a commitment on the part of the insurance fund could well undermine its capacity to face unforeseen major disasters.[15] One seasoned analyst pointed out:

> A capless [not subject to an upper limit] without rebates would obviously result in a larger and stronger fund, thereby instilling even greater depositor confidence. Former Treasury Assistant Secretary Greg Baer, in his February 16, 2000 House Banking Subcommittee hearing, expressed one of many reasons why rebates should NOT be paid: 'Thus we believe that allowing the insurance funds to continue building up reserves through interest income during good economic times is good policy.'
>
> Rebates would make a bad 'moral hazard' problem even worse. With 92% of the industry and all new institutions paying no insurance premiums, the marginal cost of adding an extra dollar of insured deposits is zero. The only thing worse than this would be to make the costs negative through authorizing rebates. As the above-cited former Treasury Assistant Secretary stated: '... rebates would exacerbate what is already a poor set of incentives around deposit insurance.'[16]

5.4 Systemically-important groups

5.4.1 The consolidation process

The dismantling of barriers within the financial sector (for example, through the 1999 Gramm–Leach–Bliley Act in the USA), the development of monetary zones (notably that of the Euroland), and the spectacular developments in information technology have helped the process of consolidation in the financial sector – mostly through mergers and acquisitions (M&A) – at both national and transnational levels. Financial consolidation can achieve some diversification gains for individual institutions, but can also be a source of potential risk for these institutions – in so far as: certain merged activities are not within the core competencies of management, operating risks and managerial complexities tend to increase, and savings or efficiency gains are not realized.

Financial consolidation has been of concern to the public authorities of major financial centres to the extent that systemic financial risk can be transmitted more readily – nationally, and transnationally –

through these large and often increasingly interdependent institutions. As put by one central banking source in Sweden, where 'four large banks cover at least 80 per cent of the system ... contagion could in general be expected to be a bigger problem in a concentrated system, since the large banks have fewer alternatives to deal with in the interbank markets'.[17]

Deposit insurance is generally aimed at protecting small depositors, and not banks' shareholders and/or management. The moral hazard factor increases with a concentrated market composed of large institutions. The latter could result from mergers and acquisitions, joint ventures among institutions sharing common services, or strategic alliances. To unsophisticated people, large groups often signify quality and solidity. Yet outsiders – such such as depositors and investors – have more difficulty in understanding a large financial firm's statements, if its accounts are too aggregated or if material information is skirted in brief footnotes.

The failure of a large group could originate from *internal contagion*, for example the collapse of one line of business or one affiliate (bank or non-bank). Unless segregated and contained adequately, such a collapse could eventually threaten the survival of the whole entity. Moreover, the process of consolidation, as we have seen, would lead to a concentration of counter-parties with increasingly large transactions shared among a small number of institutions. Their increased interdependence in various financial markets and their increased exposure to higher concentrations of risk would lead to a greater potential of *contagion across institutions*. Internal contagion and external contagion are reckoned to be important sources of systemic risk.

Large financial groups present important challenges to public policy. Among these challenges are those relating to (a) their dominant position in selected products or markets, and the potentially adverse impact they may have on fair competition, market efficiency, credit flows and consumer protection; and (b) governmental reluctance to close down such institutions whose safety and soundness are in doubt – lest their closure provokes a systemic risk. The latter challenge of 'too-big-to-fail' (TBTF) institutions has in fact often led public authorities to give implicit guarantees to all these institutions' creditors – including non-insured ones. Such guarantees exclude shareholders (who would lose their investments) and the board who, along with top management, would lose their positions.

Even in countries with no formal governmental deposit insurance, it is implausible that governments would not intervene to rescue sizeable banks – as recent crises have shown.[18] Such an implicit rescue policy is bound to increase the moral hazard problem and thus undermine market discipline in the management of mega-institutions. This is a clear case where the safety net (whether explicit or implicit) weakens management's incentives for risk mitigation, and vigilant controls. It also blunts market-pricing signals in the banking sector.

A management's perception that the survival of their institution is vital to safeguarding the integrity of the national or international financial system could therefore reduce their vigilance. Depositors would, furthermore, not worry about the risks taken by management to the extent they can count on the eventual support of the public authorities in time of difficulty. Regulators need, accordingly, to introduce strong incentives to counter bankers' lax behaviour based on the implicit support hypothesis. These could include especially dissuasive penalties. Moreover, national supervisors need to target these institutions with careful inspection and effective disciplining, in view of the disruptive impact their failure would have on the financial system and the economy of the country where they are headquartered, and/or other countries in which they have important operations. Several supervisory agencies have created special units whose task is specifically the continuous monitoring of such large financial groups.

5.4.2 Charging for the privileges of TBTF

Management often seeks enlargement of their enterprise for a variety of declared reasons. These include (i) expectations of cost savings through rationalization, economies of scale, and economies of scope (cross-sales between different business lines), leading to revenue enhancement through offering customers complementary products and services; (ii) the diversification of risk among submarkets, sectors, geographical areas, currencies and so on; (iii) critical mass which enables a large financial institution to seek large profitable deals (for example, in corporate banking and investment banking); (iv) market power yielding higher margins to the advantage of the large financial institution (for example, by reducing its cost of funding, and raising its charges on customers – the so-called monopsony/monopoly gains deriving from dominant positions); and (v) 'empire building' by top decision-makers motivated by 'ego' or prestige considerations from a higher market share and greater market power – and with larger potential financial benefits to themselves (see also pages 22–3 in Chapter 2).[19]

Large and complex financial firms typically serve a multitude of markets selling institutional and private customers a broad range of financial products and services, so-called 'one-stop shopping.'[20]

A number of studies have actually shown that large banks operate with negative economies of size. When the concentration is very high in a given market, and in the absence of potential competitors, small customers could, furthermore, encounter poorer services. At the macro level, the concern for systemic risk would increase in view of the adverse impact the failure of one big bank has on other banks.[21] This raises the issue of TBTF and the capacity of the deposit insurance to handle effectively a large bank failure, itself provoking in its wake other failures.

A market with few large parties participating in payment and settlement flows would warrant added vigilance on the part of regulators and supervisors – with the possibility of assigning to these institutions a complement of capital (in comparison to smaller banks) especially intended to cushion potential systemic risk. Alternatively, TBTF deposit insurance premiums could be raised: regulators and supervisors would thus add to the micro prudential rules (safety of an individual enterprise) a factor of macro prudential protection (safety of the system).

One researcher articulated the stance for a special deposit insurance assessment on US TBTF banks thus:

> The assessment, which might be in the 3–8 bp [basis point] range, would itself be risk based ... [and] would be on assets rather than deposits, because the potential risk exposure of the insurance fund arguably is with the entire company not just its insured deposits. (This is consistent with [the Chairman of the Federal Reserve Board] Alan Greenspan's view that, in the final analysis, there are no firewalls [*sic*].)[22]

These TBTF institutions defined as being the banks and thrift companies with over US$50 billion in assets numbered twenty institutions in 2001, representing about 50 per cent of their sector's total assets in the USA.

The proposition of a capital buffer for systemic risk, applicable to sizeable banks, is a subject of controversy. The said banks argue that such additional capital requirement – though difficult to ascertain – could well render these banks less competitive. Instead of additional capital requirements, it could prove more judicious in this case to have a system of prevention focusing on incentives that penalize undue risk-taking (see Chapter 3). Furthermore, to reduce the moral hazard factor (linked to depositors' and management's expectations that, once the insurance fund is depleted, the taxpayer will ultimately bail out a major bank), the government needs to establish a credible mechanism for allowing large problem banks to exit markets in an orderly fashion.

5.4.3 Resolution

The optimal solution with respect to insolvent but systemically-important institutions is to address effectively the challenging task of an 'orderly winding-up' of defaulting banks. Should a large and complex financial group become impaired, public authorities in one or more countries concerned could very well encounter difficulties in 'working out' or 'winding down' the said group in an orderly manner.

The total liabilities (on-balance sheet and off-balance sheet) of a large global financial institution could well exceed the resources of the deposit insurance fund or even the official monetary reserves of the country that has the ultimate supervisory responsibility. It is quite possible that such a country cannot muster adequate resources to 'bail out' or 'work out' one or more of its sizeable financial institutions. Public authorities would then be faced with the phenomenon of 'too-big-to-rescue' (TBTR). This situation could well prompt the top decision-makers of large institutions to exercise greater prudence and rigorous discipline – assuming they are concerned about their management's survival in a perennially viable institution.[23]

TBTF or TBTR would normally prompt enhanced vigilance on the part of the supervisory authorities. These authorities have in several countries recently increased the number of their inspectors, who follow continuously the operations of these banks, with some inspectors 'residing' permanently on the premises of the largest institutions – as is the case in the USA. It is likely that the large banks could prove 'too big to be disciplined' by bank supervisors – since they can lobby policy-makers for help in periods of adversity.[24]

Large financial institutions often have risk exposures in multiple products and sectors, and in extensive geographic areas. Characterized by innovative products, and increasing complexity and diversity, these institutions are accordingly not amenable to standardized rules for the quantification of risk. Each needs to build specifically designed risk models – for the assessment of its own risks and for the capital requirements related to those risks. In view of their potential impact on national or international systemic risks, large banks are examined closely by public supervisory agencies from various countries – with a lead supervisor from the country where the institution has its economic centre.[25] Such a supervisor would naturally assume a leading role in the eventuality of a large bank encountering problems leading to its demise and resolution.

Supervisory authorities rely often on independent external auditors (this is the case in Switzerland) to ascertain the soundness and safety of financial institutions, for evaluating their control systems and their risk models, and for verifying their compliance with various rules, standards and directives. These authorities need to be sure about the quality of work done by external auditors. Accordingly, they have resorted to the rating of auditing firms by judging the accuracy of inspection reports and the performance of audited banks.[26] An auditing firm's reputation and accreditation are at stake should they be implicated in the failure of an audited bank.

The larger the size of the troubled bank, the more challenging is the winding-up task, and the more costly for the economy is any delay in the closure of the bank and/or any improper disposal of its assets. Often a bridge bank is set up to acquire and manage all or a portion of the failed bank's assets and liabilities – until an appropriate final resolution is implemented. This method is used when more time is needed to permit the least costly resolution of the troubled bank.

An orderly process for failure resolution needs to have a number of features to protect public confidence in the financial system, and to minimize interference with market mechanisms. Notable features include (i) prompt payment of insured bona fide claims; (ii) application of techniques that are least costly to the economy in general, and to the deposit insurer in particular; (iii) a quick return of assets/business of the failed banks to the private sector; and (iv) legal actions in the case of negligence or other wrongdoing.

One should caution that a precipitate return of assets or business of the failed banks to the private sector is not always the best objective. Thus, the Canadian Deposit Insurance Corporation (CDIC) has in its stated policy the maximization of the recovery of assets on a 'net present value' basis. This may not always result in a quick return to the private sector.[27]

The institution of deposit insurance can be called upon to offer technical and financial assistance to a large, troubled bank susceptible to being revitalized by appropriate reorganization. Guided by the principle of 'slim and fit', the deposit insurer, along with other agencies, can thus help in the orderly downsizing of the 'too big to manage' institution. Downsizing through appropriate divestiture can improve the management's span of control and the efficiency of the 'de-constructed' institution, through focusing on core business areas in which it has a competitive edge – notably as a result of superior competencies.

In the absence of viable downsizing, an acquiring bank with the requisite financial and managerial strength would be a judicious approach for the resolution of a failed bank – assuming that the acquisition does not lead to a monopolistic situation. When no such healthy bank is willing to acquire the troubled institution, the deposit insurer would then have to recommend the liquidation of the remaining assets of the failed institution. In the USA, the FDIC can be named as the receiver. The proceeds of the liquidation will normally be disbursed to unpaid employees, uninsured depositors, senior creditors, subordinated creditors, and other claimants. Shareholders will be the last to benefit from the liquidation.[28]

* * *

The potential of systemic risk arising from the failure of a big bank – assuming no possibility for its acquisition by another financial group – can be contained substantially. This would call on the adoption by the regulatory and deposit insurance authorities of well-publicized measures to prevent panic and financial gridlock. These measures would, in particular, include: (i) resolving the bank whose net worth is nearly wiped out (and before it becomes negative), in accordance with clearly set criteria; (ii) paying immediately insured depositors; and (iii) advancing funds to uninsured depositors and creditors on a pro rata share of the estimated recovery value at resolution.[29]

5.5 Mitigating moral hazard

Deposit insurance – like all other safety nets – carries with it an important 'moral hazard' drawback. In particular, deposit insurance would: (a) reduce the vigilance of depositors and other creditors to monitor their bank; (b) induce depositors to entrust their funds to a bank at lower interest rates than would otherwise be warranted by the bank's risk profile in the absence of deposit insurance; (c) dilute the bankers' incentive for prudence, by enticing them to seek higher risks (in the expectation of higher returns and higher personal bonuses), knowing that third-party funds are unlikely to be withdrawn since these funds benefit from governmental guarantees; (d) enable a bank's management to expand its lending by financing customers at rates below those warranted by their risks in view of the lower interests paid by the bank on insured deposits; and (e) allow regulators and supervisors to accept laxity and forbearance with regard to the decisions they should take, notably on the timing and method of intervention in problem situations. The foregoing factors would lead to sub-optimal allocation of credit in the economy concerned, and would permit unsound business practices that could lead to potentially costly bank failures.[30]

Moral hazard, or the propensity of management and customers in a banking system covered by a deposit insurance scheme to neglect professional rigour, can be restrained. This can be done by a multi-dimensional approach: limiting deposit coverage, charging banks risk-adjusted premiums, appropriate regulation and effective supervision, credible sanctions for failure to observe rules of sound risk management, accurate pertinent disclosure of data on the real conditions of individual banks to allow markets to monitor their soundness, and other measures (see Figure 5.3).

A
Accounting/measurement

- Truthful
- Meaningful
- Usable
- Fair

B
Obligatory adherence of institutions

- Preclude adverse selection
- Avoid loopholes

C
Coverage limitation per beneficiary

- Ceiling of benefits
- Co-insurance
- Deductibles

D
Premiums/Levies

- Ex-ante
- Risk-adjusted

9 KEY LEVERS TO CONTAIN MORAL HAZARD

E
Effective supervision

- On-site examination
- Off-site monitoring
- Forward-looking

I
Equal treatment of institutions

- Small and local versus large complex, and transnational banks
- State-owned versus privately-owned banks

F
Market transparency of

- Debt/equity instruments
- Margins/interests
- Assets/liabilities
- Revenues/losses
- Risk concentrations, etc.

G
Disclosure characteristics

- Pertinence
- Timeliness
- Wide communication
- Easily understood
- Comparable rigorous standards.

H
Legal sanctions

- Appropriate penalties
- Termination of insurance
- Change of management
- Closure of institution

Figure 5.3   Key mitigating factors of moral hazard in deposit insurance

5.5.1   Explicit versus implicit protection

The absence of explicit deposit insurance creates depositor uncertainty. This could very well lead to greater nervousness and aggravate runs on banks at the first signs of vulnerability. It could accentuate the ultimate costs borne by the economy – as compared with explicit limited protection designed with appropriate incentives to encourage various interested parties to behave responsibly and rationally.

It is important to note that, in some countries without deposit insurance, the vigilance of depositors is extremely low because of their implicit belief in 100 per cent government protection. In such cases, the introduction of a credible limited deposit protection scheme might in fact improve the vigilance of depositors – particularly the larger ones who do not benefit from full coverage.

Certain developed countries do not have explicit governmental financial safety nets. For example, the Swiss regulatory authorities and the Swiss Bankers' Association (SBA) have examined the possibility of instituting a governmental deposit insurance scheme. The authorities have temporized, on three main grounds: (i) they want to encourage banks' management to operate with relentless rigour and avoid the moral hazard of a safety net; (ii) they deem sufficient the existing preventive measures of regulatory prudential rules (notably those relating to capital adequacy, liquidity, risk mitigation and diversification), if enforced effectively through vigilant control–supervision–sanction systems; and (iii) they have been concerned about the administrative and financial costs of setting up and operating efficiently a governmental deposit insurance institution. The Swiss authorities have so far been content with a voluntary interbank private scheme that guarantees depositors under specific conditions for a small sum up to 30 000 Swiss francs (see also section 5.5.6 on page 121).

Should a bank encounter insurmountable difficulties, the Swiss Federal Banking Commission (SFBC) can rescind the bank's licence to operate – it is hoped, at an early stage of the problem in order to protect depositors. The SFBC prefers, however, to co-operate with the SBA with a view to arranging a smooth take-over of an ailing bank by a healthy institution – without any adverse impact on the Swiss financial market. The SFBC and SBA, for example, nudged in 1994 thirty two small and medium-sized regional banks to cooperate closely, in order to enhance their solvency and improve their competitiveness. The said regional banks have consequently been successful in developing jointly RBA Holding – leading to improved efficiency and higher profits.[31]

One can reasonably argue that the Swiss authorities provide an implicit guarantee to each of the two (prior to 1999, there were three) major banking groups that control together about half of the domestic banking sector. TBTF's argument applies strongly in this case. One prominent event in this respect was the liquidity crisis faced in 1977 by one of the three major Swiss banks, the Crédit Suisse Group (previously known as Schweizerische Kreditanstalt – SKA). In mid-April 1977, the bank admitted responsibility for SFr2.2 billion of customer money invested in a bankrupt industrial affiliate, Texon. SKA's executive board primary concern was liquidity. The Swiss Central Bank, along with the two other major banks, offered a standby credit of SFr3 billion. This measure received the approval of the Swiss federal government, although it generated adverse publicity for SKA and had led to a further deterioration in its traded shares.[32]

Market signals could be built into the safety nets to ensure that participants in the financial system have strong incentives to behave prudently and efficiently. Such signals are premised on the existence of transparency. This calls for the collection, compilation, organization and timely dissemination of reliable, detailed and up-to-date information covering, *inter alia*, risk exposures and non-performing assets. In a transparent and competitive market place, the rational behaviour and prompt response of market participants on the supply and demand sides for funds should lead to appropriate market signals, and enhance market discipline. Various techniques have been recommended for the promotion of market discipline and prudence. Some are discussed below.

5.5.2   Uninsured negotiable liabilities

Insured depositors and creditors are not sensitive to risk to the extent they expect to be bailed out by governmental agencies. Regulation could require all banks – in particular, large institutions – to issue, besides their share capital, negotiable uninsured subordinated notes and debentures (SNDs) of given maturities for open public subscription with adequate disclosure of information. Investors are normally sensitive to the bank's 'prudence and performance' record. The higher the risk, the higher the yield spread over government bonds on the SNDs of the bank concerned – assuming the existence of developed, competitive and non-manipulated markets for subordinated debt. Well-informed – often institutional – investors in SNDs will exact higher spreads on uninsured debt instruments issued by riskier banks – if these investors do not expect public assistance should such banks encounter difficulties. Such higher risk premiums would eventually lead to the deterioration in these banks' share prices. These market indicators would thus prompt the said banks to moderate their risks, and reduce their borrowing costs.

Subject to easy access to authentic, accurate, relevant and timely information disclosed by banks, efficient and competitive markets could price the risk factor of individual banks properly – assuming that the collective judgement of numerous market participants is rationally based on value creation over set time horizons. Interest charges (including premiums on risks) on SNDs issued by a bank would, in these circumstances, increase, and credit availability would decrease in parallel with the increase in the risk profile of the borrowing bank. Uninsured holders of SNDs would then ask their bank to pay them adequate risk premiums, in comparison with insured depositors. They are, furthermore, likely to refrain from depositing with such banks and/or to withdraw their outstanding funds at the very first sign of doubt regarding these banks' solvency. The said banks will not be able to compensate easily for the loss of uninsured depositors by attempting to attract sufficient insured deposits.[33] The higher financing costs for such banks is a potent market discipline instrument which should induce them to limit their risk-taking.

More generally, a bank's disclosure of meaningful, reliable and consistent information on its risk exposures and the structure of its funding (including innovative, complex and hybrid capital instruments) will enable various market participants – financial institutions, investors, bank customers and public agencies – to better judge (i) the bank's capacity for generating profits and absorbing losses; and (ii) its management's competence in pricing risks. Objective price information on SNDs of the same maturity should therefore help all parties concerned in their ability to compare financial institutions and to make discerning rational decisions.

SNDs have their drawbacks, however. One is that not all institutions are in a position to issue such debt instruments. Moreover there may not be sufficient market liquidity (or even sophisticated investors) in many countries to make this technique successful. Questions also arise as to how the authorities and depositors would treat and react to high spreads or low ratings of SNDs. Finally, rational behaviour of market participants cannot be taken for granted (see section 5.6 below).

If investors believe that an implicit governmental guarantee extends to SNDs – for reasons of the too-big-to-fail argument for certain large institutions – the market rating of these SNDs will not reflect the intrinsic vulnerability of these institutions. If regulators want to dispose of this perception, they need to develop, publicize and apply clear mandatory rules for the closure of very large banks with no protection to uninsured deposits and non-deposit creditors. In accordance with the US Federal Deposit Insurance Corporation Improvement Act of 1991 (FDICIA), a bank whose book ratio of tangible equity capital to total assets is less than 2 per cent is automatically considered to be critically undercapitalized. Such a bank would, in principle, be put under the purview of a receiver, and treated as though it were insolvent and subject to resolution.[34]

Assuming ready access to market price data, changes in the interest a bank has to pay on its uninsured deposits – in comparison to peer banks – can also be used as an indicator of risk. Useful information on risk can additionally be derived from changes in the proportion of insured to uninsured liabilities in the funding of a bank. Uninsured liabilities in the US market can take the form of (i) certificates of deposit (CD) whose value per unit exceeds the federal deposit insurance limit of $100 000 per account, (ii) short-term securities, and (iii) senior bonds issued by a bank. All offer price signals which reflect the perceptions of market participants on risks assumed by individual financial institutions.

5.5.3   Limiting protection per depositor

The primary aim of deposit insurance – as we have seen – is to protect small (often unsophisticated) depositors who cannot properly or efficiently monitor their banks. The insurance scheme will have to aggregate all the deposit accounts per beneficiary in the market under its purview, to ascertain that the overall ceiling of coverage per depositor is respected. This will avoid the situation in which a large depositor, by spreading her/his deposits across several institutions, will attain a higher insurance coverage.

The individual depositor protection could be based on an average 'income per capita' benchmark in the country concerned. In periods of financial crisis, limited explicit legal protection of depositors was replaced with blanket guarantees to all creditors of banks (whether depositors or not) by governments battling with financial crises such as Japan, Korea, Mexico and other countries since the 1980s. The underlying objective of the authorities in these exceptional periods is to avoid the paralysis of the financial system, fearing dire consequences on the real economy.

It is generally accepted that such blanket guarantees can only be used over a limited transitory period, lest they distort market efficiency, subvert market discipline, and undermine sound risk control. Such was the case of the Japanese government which moved temporarily from a limited deposit protection to a comprehensive one to sustain its moribund banking system. Thus in 2001 it waived the 10 million yen ceiling guarantee per depositor set in 1996 and offered instead an unlimited blanket guarantee for all depositors and lenders to financial institutions until the end of March 2002, later extended for one more year.[35] The ceiling was due to be reinstated after April 2003.[36]

To favour prudence, the governmental deposit insurance should carry – besides a reasonably low coverage limit per depositor – a co-insurance factor. This will prompt each depositor to examine both *yield* and *safety*, since she/he bears the risk of self-insurance on a portion of her/his deposit. This co-insurance will render all depositors – in particular, the larger ones – less indolent and more demanding of transparency from their deposit-taking banks to track and assess the banks' safety and soundness. Depositors and other bank creditors will then have a greater incentive to monitor and discipline risky institutions. Should a bank deny its depositors and other creditors the requisite information, it would be shunned by existing and new customers, be obliged to pay a risk premium on its liabilities because of its opacity, and be more readily subject to bank runs at the first rumour or piece of adverse news. The eventuality of such bank runs would discipline bank management. To allow for the scrutiny of depositors or independent analysts, individual banks should therefore be subject to mandatory disclosure to the public of pertinent and reliable up-to-date information on their risks – readily and conveniently communicated to the public.

It is important to note that, even under co-insurance, individuals holding small balances in their accounts may not exercise monitoring because of a lack of financial incentive (the costs of doing so exceed the benefits). It is also important to be aware that the degree of co-insurance applied creates trade-offs between confidence/stability on one hand, and minimizing moral hazard on the other: the higher the co-insurance deductible – all other things remaining equal – the lower the protection and sense of confidence depositors will have, and the lower the 'moral hazard' factor.

5.5.4 Reinsurance

To evaluate the riskiness of their portfolios, governmental deposit insurance corporations should try to sell (that is, re-insure) a given amount of their total exposure (for example, the FDIC is authorized to do so up to 10 per cent) to market participants. Moreover, a deposit insurance fund can resort to credit derivatives to assess how the market prices its risk exposures.[37] Regulatory authorities could also require banks to insure a minimum portion of their total deposits directly with private insurers, or with mutual self-help schemes, on the basis of market-risk assessed premiums on deposits.

Selling a portion of the insured risk in a given portfolio of deposits implies that this portfolio produces realistic risk-sensitive premiums, and that the commercial reinsurer is able to derive from that operation reasonable profits over the medium–longer term.

It is reckoned that the rates charged by the FDIC in the USA to member institutions have generally been below market rates and contain, consequently, a subsidy factor. Avoiding governmental subsidies, or the safer banks subsidizing riskier ones, would require the deposit insurer to market-price risks. To reduce risk premiums on their deposit insurance, banks would then have to moderate their risk exposure or increase their risk-related capital standards.[38] Assuming that adequate monitoring of an institution's risk profile exists, risk-based premiums would incite banks to greater prudence, and would contribute to the enhancement of general banking stability.[39]

The FDIC has not yet succeeded in reinsuring any portion of its exposure, and private insurance groups have so far failed to show interest, presumably because they deem the premiums collected on insured deposits insufficient. Indeed, reinsurance was considered seriously by the FDIC in the early 1990s. The problem then was that the limited number of private reinsurers willing to participate wanted to reinsure only the FDIC's best risk exposures, notably those believed to benefit from too-big-to-fail protection.

5.5.5   Informing and training

Disclosure to the general public requires the availability of pertinent and reliable up-to-date data which uses rigorous accounting standards and is easily comprehensible. Truthful information on risks and earnings published by financial institutions will in principle assist participants to reach sounder decisions – as compared with a situation of opacity. It is also likely that markets will put a positive premium on a financial institution's frequent disclosure of appropriate data and will sanction opacity or irrelevance. One should guard against flooding the public with esoteric technical information, in so far as this approach does not serve market discipline.

To many informed observers, 'market prices set by bank creditors cannot simply be assumed to pass [the] Litmus test ... [of signalling] greater risk for higher-risk institutions'. This situation necessitates the maintenance of on-site supervisory reviews to evaluate the asset quality and risk management systems of financial institutions. Market data could be used as additional inputs in the judgemental process of supervisory agencies, and could help to allocate scarce and costly supervisory talents to identified 'problem' institutions and areas. The market signals would increase in value with a large number of market participants, reliable data, and objective analyses.[40]

The *efficient markets paradigm* is based on the assumptions: that all relevant information is disclosed accurately and communicated readily in a generally understandable way; that economic actors are rational; that they agree on the best way to measure risk and return; and that their actions are translated correctly and without delay into market signals. Information published by enterprises suffers from a variety of shortcomings. These include the use of various non-comparable accounting standards, lack of accuracy, non-simultaneous dissemination to all parties concerned, complexity of data given to consumers precluding easy and correct understanding, among other deficiencies. This situation will influence the ultimate actions of individuals, groups or institutions – whose interests, priorities and time horizons are often disparate. For various analysts and researchers, the efficiency of financial markets therefore remains a theoretical construction[41] (see also Chapter 7).

Deposit insurance institutions have recently taken the active responsibility of informing and training. Thus, the FDIC in the USA launched in 2001 the nationwide Money Smart training programme 'to help adults outside the financial mainstream improve their money skills and develop positive relationships with financial institutions'.[42] A campaign of general public awareness with respect to valid financial rules and sound techniques is needed to help individuals avoid predatory practices by financial intermediaries.

Communities lacking financial literacy could easily be deceived. For example, borrowers could become

> victims of abusive mortgage lending practices, which can include equity stripping, loans that carry inordinately high interest rates, excessive points or fees, required purchase of single-premium credit life insurance, mishandling of the borrower's payment to intentionally delay the posting of the payment, and prepayment penalties on loans that provide no economic benefit to the borrower.[43]

The FDIC, joined by other public and private institutions, started a relief project for victimized borrowers. With more complex financial products available to consumers, authentic knowledge could promote informed decisions by these consumers, and eventually reduce the cost of governmental protection through safety nets. Surveys are often conducted by compensation schemes to understand consumer attitudes towards the safety of their money and investments. Their results generally reveal that the public is not properly informed. This necessitates the raising of consumer awareness – for example, through the dissemination of well-designed consumer guides, financial education programmes, press releases, research works, conferences, telephone helplines, websites and so on.[44]

5.5.6   Constraints on depositors' rights

Although deposit schemes formally offer protection to eligible parties, the latter do often encounter practical problems in gaining full satisfaction for their legal rights. These problems result from implementation difficulties which generate potential losses for depositors (measured by reference to the full current values of their claims), or for the deposit insurance agency. Among these difficulties, one could mention in particular the loss of liquidity or value by insured depositors, for the following reasons:

(i)   Delays in the regulatory authorities' declaration of a bank's insolvency beyond the time that it is effectively economically insolvent.

(ii)   Delays between the time the said bank is legally declared insolvent while remaining in operation under existing owners and managers, and the time it is actually resolved.

(iii)   A protracted process for collecting and analysing data necessary to the identification of the insured and non-insured depositors, and to ascertaining their claims.

(iv)   Poor market conditions leading to the postponement of the sale of the insolvent bank or some of its assets to compensate various stakeholders.

(v)   The inefficiency of appointed receivers with respect to the distribution of the net sales proceeds of the insolvent bank to uninsured depositors and to the deposit insurance agency.[45]

These constraints and losses encountered by depositors have been aggravated by the eventuality of moratoriums on the activities of the official deposit insurance agency. A government can indeed default or renege on its deposit guarantees in the same way as it can fail to honour its sovereign debt. This happened with Argentina in 2001–02. Not only did the Argentinian government restrict deposit withdrawals from 2001, it also obliged banks to convert customers' dollar deposits into depreciating peso deposits. These governmental actions were deemed to be unconstitutional by the Argentinian Supreme Court of Justice – in so far as they violated property rights (judgments rendered on 31 December 2001 and on 5 March 2003), but the Argentinian Congress sought to counter the judgments by passing requisite legislation.[46] Argentina was seething with its worst-ever financial crisis in 2001–03. Depositors' fears of partial expropriation of deposits – for example, when deposits made in strong foreign convertible currencies are transformed by government diktat into domestic currency deposits subject to rapidly depreciating values – came true. Insured deposits (US$30 000 per account) by the state-entity 'Seguro de Depósitos Sociedad Anónima' could not be honoured in the currency in which they were deposited (namely US$). In accordance with a presidential decree issued in February 2002, depositors received peso denominated non-tradable and non-endorsable government securities.[47]

In private deposit insurance schemes, the uncertainty of depositors is much higher than in government-sponsored schemes. This is the case in Switzerland, where deposit insurance is a private agreement among member banks of SBA covering up to SFr30 000 per depositor. Payment to a depositor is in the form of an advance on her/his deposit account(s), and is made once the definitive verdict regarding default or liquidation is declared by courts – after all possible legal recourses have been exhausted. The maximum claim on member banks per event of default cannot exceed a cumulative total of the very modest total sum of SFr1 billion (about US$650 million in 2002) for total bank deposits of Swiss-based banks exceeding SFr 2000 billion in that year. Finally, the SBA can cancel with immediate effect – that is, without forewarning – the said agreement if it deems the liabilities to be too large following one or more bank failures. The SBA deposit guarantee agreement does not provide for the constitution of a reserve fund, and the eventual contribution of participating banks in the case of the bankruptcy of a member bank is collected *ex post*. That contribution applies to member banks whose gross revenues exceed SFr2 million, and is made on the basis of SFr250 per million of gross revenues (subject to a ceiling of SFr200 000 per contributing bank).[48]

The importance of moral hazard can therefore be reduced if protected stakeholders are uncertain with respect to the timing or the full payment of their legitimate claims. Seldom have financial guarantees – although they could be given by state agencies – been honoured immediately. Indeed, the beneficiaries of protection have had to accept (i) the financial costs of waiting – namely, losses in liquidity – which could stretch over several months; as well as (ii) losses resulting from underpayment, that is a reduction in the recuperation of the insured claims. Awareness of protected parties with respect to the eventuality of such losses and delays would raise their vigilance and improve market discipline. Consequently, insured and non-insured depositors would monitor the financial health of their banks more carefully, and would require, when warranted, higher interest rates in relation to greater perceived risk; otherwise, they would transfer their deposits to other banks deemed to be less risky.[49]

The weight of empirical evidence shows that explicit deposit insurance is, on average, an added source of vulnerability for the financial sector. Banks generally take greater risks by exploiting the availability of insured deposits – while protected depositors reduce their monitoring. Such vulnerability is higher in countries that do not have strong and effective institutions to carry out regulatory–supervisory functions, and do not have sound economic policies. Moreover, the institution of deposit insurance has been associated with lower financial-sector development.[50] As put by a World Bank study: 'Ironically, in many countries the very safety nets that were meant to limit the vulnerability of the financial system have been identified as the greatest source of fragility.'[51]

To summarize, experience has shown that there is no 'one-size fit for all' in deposit insurance, since countries have diverse socio-economic conditions. Nevertheless, the effectiveness of deposit insurance is based largely on eight pillars: (i) explicit legislation giving the scope and limits of this function; (ii) the compulsory participation by, and the equal treatment of, all deposit-taking institutions – small and large, private and state-owned – to avoid adverse selection, and to promote a level playing field; (iii) the immediate availability of sufficient resources to meet crisis situations and effect prompt reimbursement of insured depositors; (iv) effective regulatory – supervisory – enforcement functions to ensure that prudential rules are properly observed; (v) risk-adjusted differentiated premiums to moderate moral hazard, calculated on enterprise-wide consolidated activities of the bank (both on- and off-balance-sheet); (vi) a clearly understood limitation of deposit protection (for example, through ceiling and co-insurance features) to encourage depositors to exercise greater scrutiny of their depository banks; (vii) the adequate and timely disclosure of pertinent, reliable and easily understood information to allow depositors, investors, financial analysts and other market participants to reach sound assessments of the risk profiles of banks and make more rational decisions; and (viii) the eventual availability of the deposit insurer to co-operate in the task of efficient restructuring or liquidation of unsound banks.[52] The International Association of Deposit Insurers (IADI), founded at the BIS in Basel in 2002, should contribute towards enhancing among member countries the understanding of common interests and issues related to deposit insurance.

5.6   Investors' protection

Investors' portfolios held by brokers, dealers or other financial intermediaries belong legally to their customers. Should these financial firms become bankrupt, investors' outstanding wealth should normally be reinstated without delay. If this is not done (for example, for reasons of theft), governmental agencies or professional groups in a number of countries intervene to assist in the recovery of assets for their legitimate owners, or endeavour to compensate them. The *raison d'être* of this approach is to maintain investors' confidence in the financial markets.

Savers or investors often do not understand correctly the nature and extent of available financial protection. For example, in the USA, a country that boasts advanced rules of transparency, most investors (according to a survey conducted in 2001) erroneously believed that their stock losses generated by falling market prices would be covered by the federal safety net for deposits (the Federal Deposit Insurance Corporation – FDIC), federal regulators of financial markets (the Securities and Exchange Commission – SEC), or a non-profit trade association of securities firms (the Securities Investor Protection Corporation – SIPC).[53]

Unscrutinizing investors have often fallen for 'buy' recommendations by certain brokers or financial analysts – when some of the latter were selling or 'shorting' the shares of the same company(ies) in their personal account. One investment banker reportedly described the strategy of securities firms to lure investors to buy shares in badly performing technology firms in the late 1990s as a 'form of organised theft'.[54] The advice of independent analysts and brokerage houses with no underwriting relationship to companies' stocks under initial public offerings have provided their investors with superior results in comparison to securities houses with an underwriting relationship (see also section 2.2 of Chapter 2).[55]

With inadequate experience or skills, many potential investors are 'accident-prone'.[56] In this context, it is worth noting that bona fide financial journalists of leading media wielding much clout among readers have admitted candidly to erroneous diagnoses and/or prognoses.[57]

Depositors, creditors and investors who have no information, or distorted information, cannot therefore make sound decisions. Moreover, market participants may misread information and do not necessarily, or invariably, behave in accordance with rational economic standards. Their actions lead to excesses and herd-like behaviour. It is also argued that improperly presented data could, under certain circumstances, exacerbate contagion.[58]

The SIPC, mentioned above, is a safety net for US investors created by the Securities Investor Protection Act of 1970 (SIPA) under the oversight of the SEC. Most registered securities firms automatically become members of SIPC, although their affiliates are not obligated to do so. SIPC's function is to return customers' property (outstanding securities and cash) when a member firm fails, and if the firm is unable to do it. As put by the US General Accounting Office (GAO):

> Although SIPC's mission is to return the securities or cash that should have been in a customer's account when liquidation proceedings start, we found some evidence that investors are unaware that SIPC does not protect against decreases in the price of their securities. This type of misperception has led some investors to file claims for market losses in SIPA liquidation proceedings that were denied. The official explanatory statement that SIPC members can opt to use does not state that SIPC does not protect against losses from changes in the market value of securities.[59]

Unlike the FDIC, the SIPC is not an agency of the US government. It was chartered by Congress in 1970 as a membership corporation, the members of which must all be persons registered as brokers or dealers. Its Board is made up as follows: five members appointed by the US President subject to the approval of the Senate; one by the Secretary of the Treasury; and one by the Federal Reserve Board. A customer with an investment portfolio in a failed financial firm will receive all non-negotiable securities that are already registered in her/his name, or in the process of being registered. Concomitantly, the SIPC satisfies the remaining claims of each customer up to a maximum of US$500 000. This figure can include a cash claim of up to US$100 000. Beyond these limits, customers share pro rata in negotiable securities held by their bankrupt firm. Any remaining assets – net of liquidation expenses –

will serve to satisfy the remaining portions of customers' claims on a par with other creditors.

The above-mentioned ceilings on compensation limit moral hazard, by increasing the vigilance of investors. Losses resulting from fraud have ranged between US$10 billion to US $40 billion annually in the USA – while SIPC's reserves at the end of the year 2000 amounted to US $1.22 billion only. These reserves are constituted from assessments collected from SIPC members and interest on investments in US government securities. SIPC's delinquent members reached 287 out of about 35 000 broker–dealers who have been SIPC members during the previous thirty years of operation. In the year 2000, its members numbered 7033.[60] One should add that the Sarbanes–Oxley Act of 2002 gives additional compensation to harmed investors out of a fund that collects civil penalties levied by the SEC as a result of judicial or administrative actions.

To encourage investors to place their savings in stocks, some countries have exceptionally extended their financial safety nets – for example, by guaranteeing returns of mutual funds. This is the case in India, whose Unit Trust of India (UTI) has been rescued three times during the period 1998–2002. The latest bail-out cost the Indian government US$3 billion on 31 August 2002 (the previous two had a combined cost of US$1 billion). This was India's biggest-ever bail-out of a financial institution, and was meant to reassure 29 million investors and to preclude a distress sale of assets by UTI – the largest single investor in the Indian stock exchange. The Indian government agreed to pay 'unit holders' the difference between the fixed price it had guaranteed and the market value of underlying assets.[61]

If a government's macroeconomic mission is to protect the stability of the financial system, bailing out a financial institution cannot be justified in a market economy unless there is a threat of systemic risk. In the case of the UTI, no such risk was evident. Nevertheless, popular dissatisfaction and the desire to revive the then depressed Indian stock market weighed importantly in the bail-out.

5.7   Recapitalizing financial institutions

It is not the mission of a deposit insurer or any other governmental agency in a market economy to protect uninsured depositors or investors, and to bail out defaulting financial institutions and their shareholders. These institutions should bear the full market discipline which sanctions negligence and mismanagement. A mismanaged institution would have to exit the market.

Nevertheless, in a banking crisis characterized by persistent runs on banks, public funds are often needed to shore up the capital of banks, and reverse the tide of a bank deposit haemorrhage. In such a crisis situation, private capital is unlikely to be willing to take risks, and governmental action can be the sole credible means of restoring public confidence in the orderly functioning of the banking system. The latter's proper functioning is vital to the safety and stability of the payments system and financial intermediation, and thus to the sustainable growth of modern economies (see Chapter 3).

Governmental intervention in periods of distress needs to be underpinned by a broad political consensus, well thought out, and implemented promptly – to avoid the intensification and spreading of problems. Special entities need to be created to marshal resources, human and material, for public intervention. In particular, there is a need for a bank restructuring agency (BRA) to carry out governmental strategy. After a proper diagnosis, the BRA should carefully identify (i) essential and potentially viable banks; and (ii) dispensable banks that have to be closed down. The first group can be sustained through recapitalization or through the purchase of their currently impaired assets by a specially constituted asset management company (AMC). The latter's task will be to rehabilitate these assets – for example, through debt-equity conversions or through the lengthening of maturities. The design, organization and management of the BRA and AMC vehicles are a complex and time-consuming process. The characteristics of these institutions are bound to reflect the institutional, legal and manpower skills available to the distressed country. The success of these vehicles can be appreciated by reference to various criteria: the speed of stabilizing the economy, maximizing of returns on government investments, the tightening of risk management controls, timely disengagement of government from managerial responsibilities and capital ownership of rehabilitated banks, and the re-establishment of a sound competitive banking system. The latter would then be founded on effective corporate governance and market discipline based on transparency, accountability and limited deposit insurance protection.[62]

External recapitalization of financial institutions has been used as a safety net by various governments. Ostensibly, the reason is to protect the stability of the financial system and the economy. In reality, and over the long run, an often-used recapitalization policy can be a serious source of moral hazard: it would sap the solidity of the financial system – in so far as the inefficient, poorly run or insolvent institutions are maintained unjustifiably.

The recapitalization tool has been used, more or less widely, in both developed and developing economies. Leading examples of direct governmental recapitalization of financial institutions in developed market economies include, in recent years, the Crédit Lyonnais (France), Continental Illinois (USA), Johnson Mathey (United Kingdom), and several financial institutions in Japan, Norway, Sweden and Switzerland. Several emerging economies have also resorted to the recapitalization of their troubled financial institutions. Among emerging economies, Chile's experience in the wake of the 1982–3 banking crisis is noteworthy. The Chilean government succeeded in the recapitalization of distressed banks using various incentives – notably fiscal ones – and managed to resolve the crisis rapidly.[63]

Public authorities could summon the private sector to recapitalize ailing firms, whose survival is deemed to be in the public interest. In the absence of legal requirements (for example, calls for the unpaid portions of capital by existing shareholders), the authorities would resort to moral persuasion, 'jaw-boning' or 'arm-twisting'. This approach is often used *vis-à-vis* stakeholders such as creditors. A notable case is that of the LTCM in the USA (see section 3.7 in Chapter 3). The call by public authorities for the recapitalization of a firm can extend eventually to non-stakeholders.

Other jurisdictions are loath to come to the rescue of banks by recapitalizing them with taxpayers' funding. This is particularly the case in New Zealand, where a no-bail-out policy is openly stated – extending even to 'systemically important' institutions. The latter are defined as those with liabilities (net of amounts due to related parties) in excess of NZ$10 billion (equivalent to about 7.5 per cent of the banking system's liabilities in 2002).

5.8 Calibrating ultimate liquidity: from bubble to crunch

An adequate supply of liquidity to financial markets can also be considered as a safety net. This task is normally handled by central banks within their function of promoting systemic financial stability and efficiency. Though providing liquidity is part of their prerogatives as lenders of last resort (LLR), central banks undertake that function in the context of their price stability (anti-deflation or low inflation) long-term objective. They would generally intervene in an LLR capacity should there be a systemic liquidity risk. Moreover, liquidity support is normally provided on a fully secured basis.

Financial intermediaries hold capital to absorb unexpected losses. Similarly, they hold liquidity to meet unanticipated funding needs or cash outflows. The liquidity risk covers the firm's risk of being unable to fund its assets at appropriate maturities and reasonable interest rates, or of its being unable to liquidate a position without (i) undue delay; or (ii) a sacrifice in price. Should that risk threaten the survival of several solvent banks in the throes of a liquidity crunch, the central bank's liquidity support would avert a financial crisis.

The central bank's LLR function stems from its monopoly in issuing legal tender. Such a prerogative enables the central bank to influence national liquidity. It can supply additional liquidity to the national economy by funding (i) solvent banks that have solvent assets of designated categories (via the discount window, currency swaps, securities' repurchase operations, and other methods); (ii) financial markets (through open market operations); or (iii) the payments system (by offering intra-day lending) – see section 6.3.1 in Chapter 6.

To get central bank funding, banks offer eligible collaterals, namely high-quality, short-term negotiable assets readily fungible into legal tender with no delay and practically no loss in value. These assets are composed mainly of government securities, and of highly rated trade bills, certificates of deposit, commercial notes and similar instruments. Foreign convertible currencies could also be used as collaterals.

Commercial banks' accessibility to central bank liquidity raises fundamental queries. Could such recourse expand the banks' lending capacity (and thus monetary creation) at a time when the central bank's objective is to restrain monetary growth? Could monetary policy instruments (such as official interest rates, open market operations, limits on commercial bank lending and others) be used to moderate the business cycle in an economy? Should these instruments be used to forestall booms or busts in given sectors of the economy?

If the availability of liquidity to the financial sector is a safety net for financial intermediaries and their clients, its implementation presents several challenges. These pertain to the tools to be used, the correct range of adequate liquidity, the pricing of liquidity offered, the collaterals to be used, and the timing of interventions. Often, short-term interest rates have been relied on by central bankers to achieve their objectives of price stability (see Figure 5.4 for a set of relationships). In developed and efficient financial markets, a significant cut in interest rates can induce an increase in households' spending and in firms' investment.

Euphoric expectations of earnings in a given sector would encourage over-investment, and excessive borrowing, by individuals and firms. It would lead eventually to unwarranted increases in the prices of assets in that sector. Bubbles are bound to burst, as these expectations prove unrealistic. The adverse impact of bubbles on financial stability could well justify a macroeconomic stability policy of moderating excessive borrowing and investment. This could be ushered by increasing the cost of liquidity supplied by the central bank. The latter cannot, however, have the foreknowledge that increased activity in a given sector represents a *shift in fundamentals* (such as faster productivity growth) versus a bubble situation (such as an unsustainable growth in earnings).[64]

The chairman of the Federal Reserve Board had referred to 'irrational exuberance' in US financial markets as early as December 1996, and to the fact that 'evaluating shifts in balance sheets generally, and in asset prices particularly, must be an integral part of the development of monetary policy'.[65] That the Fed did not intervene in time to moderate

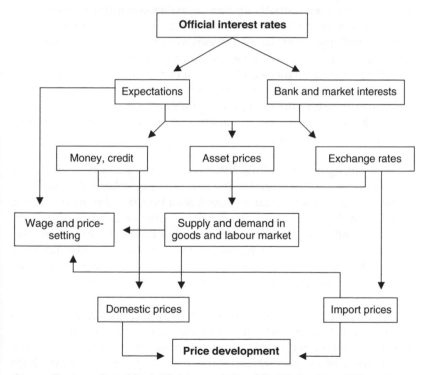

Source: European Central Bank, *The Monetary Policy of the ECB*, Frankfurt, 2001, p. 43.

Figure 5.4 Transmission mechanism from interest rates to prices: an illustration

the IT bubble of 1999–2000 is possibly attributable to the difficulties of diagnosis and prognosis.

The above-mentioned interventionist monetary policy is deemed to be helpful in containing financial bubbles. Yet it is reckoned that such an intervention could be a source of moral hazard, unless it is resorted to with restraint and in emergencies. Indeed, it can soothe private economic agents into a 'doze' thus reducing their vigilance and discernment at controlling risks and costs. Such a situation would weaken the financial system in the long run. Some analysts argue in favour of an 'intermediate' policy course that would avoid, on one hand, the unbridled overshooting of market forces generating excesses, and on the other, an interventionist policy that could degenerate into the administrative stifling of competitive forces.[66]

Central banks are guided primarily by the objective of price stability. If financial bubbles disrupt that stability, they could well be induced to integrate into their monetary policy measures conducive to preventing such bubbles, or at least to moderating their build-up and costly aftereffects. Similarly, potential disruptions in the payments system require the central bank's intervention as a protector of financial stability – notably to provide markets and financial intermediaries, as appropriate, with adequate liquidity to avoid or limit deflationary costs.

Central bankers cannot ignore a bubble that is likely to distort market forces, and hurt steady growth and financial stability. As put by one central banking source:

> By focusing on controlling inflation, central banks have made the concept of stability central to their action. Price stability does not only contribute to a more regular growth path for the real economy, it also helps to eliminate a major source of disturbance in financial markets by alleviating uncertainties and distortion created by large price fluctuations. While central banks are thus concerned about financial stability, this function should not be considered as a mere by-product or extension of their traditional monetary policy objective.[67]

Inflation has been defined conventionally as a sustained significant increase in the general price level of goods and services of an economy. It thus excludes asset prices. Whether the monetary authorities should introduce a more comprehensive concept of inflation to cover both goods and services, and asset prices – thereby accounting for the eventual situations of bubbles and their aftermath – remains a moot question. Using the comprehensive concept could help identify and control financial bubbles. The latter are a potential source of monetary and financial instability.[68]

Doubts exist, however, about identifying a bubble at an early stage, as well as about the effectiveness of central banking instruments (notably the interest rate) in controlling bubble formation. This situation has led to inaction on the part of central bankers. In particular, the chairman of the Federal Reserve Board stated:

> It seems reasonable to generalize from our recent experience that no low-risk, low-cost, incremental monetary tightening exists that can reliably deflate a bubble. But is there some policy that can at least limit the size of a bubble and, hence, its destructive fallout? From the evidence to date, the answer appears to be no. But we do need to know more about the behaviour of equity premiums and bubbles and their impact on economic activity.[69]

Certain quarters recognize that the leadership of the Federal Reserve Board had already by 1996 ascertained the existence of irrational exuberance. Yet no policy action was taken at that stage. They nevertheless argue that the monetary authorities should have – using their best judgement – attempted to 'prick the stock market bubble before it got too big' – even in the absence of a tested model.[70]

Some observers consider that the Fed has indeed a potent instrument in *margin requirement* (that is, the minimum amount that a client must deposit in the form of cash representing a given percentage of the purchase price of eligible securities bought on margin) to contain the stock market rise. This instrument can act as a warning signal to financial markets, and need not restrict credit to other activities. Others believe that the Fed cannot act alone in globalized financial markets. They deem that Euro-area high liquidity over 1998–9 led to massive investment in the American stock market, and that European central bankers' policies must share the responsibility of the US financial bubble.[71]

5.9 Non-commercial exposures

A vast array of risks is insured by commercial groups. These risks pertain to tangible and non-tangible assets – encompassing the physical, the financial and others. They include the insurance of credit, professional liability, computer fraud, physical damages, and material and non-material property rights. Some types of risks, however, are not normally insured by private commercial groups – because of the latter's difficulties in identifying, measuring, comprehending, assessing, controlling and/or predicting them. These risks belong notably to the category of non-commercial risks, which often include very large exposures.

Governmental insurance for non-commercial risks provides a safety net for the financial sector and other sectors of national economies. This insurance is offered in particular by governmental agencies to eligible persons or enterprises operating in (i) the domestic economies – for example, in the case of major natural or human-provoked catastrophes; or (ii) abroad – in countries deemed to be friendly and hospitable to foreign creditors and/or investors. Coverage for non-commercial risks comprises: political risk (war, revolution, civil commotion or terrorist attacks), expropriation of property, currency risks (inability of a buyer or debtor to pay owing to restrictions on foreign exchange transfers, depreciation or devaluation), default or refusal of debtor governments to honour their obligations, delivery risk (blockage of the normal delivery of goods or services), and very sizeable exposures (for example, large projects in such sectors as aerospace, energy, infrastructure or public utilities).

Notwithstanding the difficulties of identifying political risk, some research groups assign to it a significant weight in the credit rating of countries. For emerging economies, one rating agency gives political risk a fifth of the weight of country risk. The other four-fifths are distributed equally among: the solvability of the banking system, economic growth, internal macroeconomic stability, and the balance of payments situation. That agency has also established a high statistical correlation between political risk and the other economic components of country risk over the period 1997–2001.[72]

Because of the uncertainty of predicting the above-mentioned risks, private insurance groups have balked at entering this market – except on the basis of small, partial co-insurance or re-insurance (less than 10 per cent) for safer-risk countries, for periods not exceeding a three-year time horizon, and with the possibility of suspending their insurance after a period of agreed notice.

World-wide there are over fifty government-owned or supported institutions (national, regional and international) that handle non-commercial risks. In the USA, such insurance – often coupled with credit – is available to US investors with projects in more than 140 emerging markets and developing countries world-wide, through the government-owned Overseas Private Investment Corporation (OPIC), and the Export–Import Bank. Political risk coverage applies to bank loans, capital market transactions, cross-border leases, debt-to-equity investments, volatility of commodity prices, interest rate swaps, and others. Currency inconvertibility coverage protects against delays or blockages in the transfer of foreign exchange in relation to returns on capital, amortization of principal, interest payments, technical assistance fees, royalties and other remittances.

All export credit and foreign investment insurance institutions – although state-owned – are intended to be financially self-supporting over the medium-to-long-term horizon. Premiums are therefore assessed as sufficient to cover compensation for expected losses of the insured parties. These premiums are governed partly by agreements reached by the member governments of the OECD (signed in 1978, with a substantive amendment in July 1998) and the Berne Union (based in London, and comprising state and private export credit or investment insurers of over forty countries). These agreements set rules regarding the observance, *inter alia*, of anti-corruption measures, corporate governance, unsubsidized premiums (to avoid predatory competition in export markets), and respect of national and international laws.[73]

Significant portions of international exports and investments directed towards developing and emerging economies have taken advantage of these insurance programmes. Those eligible to purchase non-commercial insurance are enterprises whose operations are largely based in the countries offering the insurance coverage. They comprise mainly the developed OECD countries, in addition to a few emerging economies.

Inter-governmental regional development banks have their own regional insurance schemes, and the World Bank has the Multilateral Investment Guarantee Agency (MIGA). The latter is assuming a growing importance, and is furthering co-operation with national and regional governmental groups – as well as with private groups or syndicates (for example AIG, Lloyds, Zurich-American, Sovereign Risk Insurance Ltd, XL Capital Ltd, ACE and others).[74] Lloyds specifically offers protection against damage to corporate performance caused by war, riots, terrorism or civil unrest. Coverage includes loss of physical assets, loss of equity because of abandonment, repatriation costs for expatriate employees and their families, and personal accidents – each tailored to the particular needs of the insured corporation, and dovetailing with its other commercial insurance.[75]

The development of insurance for non-commercial risks is bound to have a moderating influence on systemic risks. In periods of great uncertainty, turmoil or violence, private insurance companies are likely

(i) to raise their premiums to prohibitive levels; or (ii) to withdraw their coverage. In these circumstances, governments become the insurers of last resort. This applies notably to insurance and reinsurance against terrorist attacks sustained by various developed or developing countries. Some countries provide support for insuring that risk in their jurisdictions, in the absence of adequate affordable coverage by the private sector. Such governmental support is already provided in Britain (through 'Pool Re'), in Spain (Consorcio de Compensación de Seguros), and in France (Caisse Centrale de Réassurance).[76]

At times of major disasters, national governments (as well as local and regional authorities) intervene generally to repair roads, government buildings, utilities and hospitals. They also provide for the necessary expenses and immediate needs of disaster victims (housing, unemployment compensation, physical and/or mental health treatment, dental care, funeral expenses and others).[77] On average, 60 per cent of the US infrastructure is insured for natural catastrophes, compared with less than 2 per cent for developing countries.[78] The latter countries, despite sound macroeconomic policies, are crisis-prone given their low income and limited resources available for compensation to victims of natural disasters (for example, hurricanes, typhoons, floods, earthquakes, drought).

5.10   Safety nets and contestable markets

The safety nets for deposits, investment portfolios, life insurance policies or pension rights are meant to protect the small customer and the financial system at large. They are not meant to protect poorly-run financial institutions. The failure of the latter often results from mismanagement. Institutions whose management indulges in excesses (for example, high compensation packages for executives and senior managers, expensive quarters, risky loans or investments) at the expense of shareholders and depositors should normally be replaced by a more responsible and competent leadership. If this avenue proves to be impractical, the sooner the financial firm is evicted from the market (by absorption, dismantlement or mere closure) the less are the losses sustained by shareholders, creditors and other parties concerned, including eventually by the taxpayer.

A *granular* market composed of numerous unrelated and independently-owned operators – in contrast to a *concentrated* market comprising a few operators – is deemed to be more conducive to competition with lesser scope for collusion, entente or cartel arrangements in price fixing and other anti-competitive conduct. A granular market is likely, furthermore, to limit the negative impact on the financial sector of a failure – since an operator's average size is bound to be smaller in that market, by comparison with a concentrated market other things remaining equal.

Should barriers to entry, exit or operation be non-existent (or relatively low), a concentrated market would not lead to restrictive practices. Such a market then becomes openly contestable in so far as the potential easy entry or exit of participants create an environment of competitive behaviour and lead to market discipline among the concerned economic actors. This presumes that the legal–regulatory framework actively combats anti-competitive practices.

Competitive markets are notably characterized by efficiency, and a diverse offer of products and services. Non-performing units or enterprises are bound ultimately to be driven to quit the market place. The judicious role of public authorities is to ensure that such departures are carried out in an orderly fashion – that is, with the least possible disruption to the financial sector and the real economy. The success of new entrants are attributable to their superior competitiveness, subject to the absence of protectionist barriers.

Figure 5.5 seeks to identify key factors of success [A], or failure [B] of intermediaries in a competitive financial market. Allowing a poorly managed bank to fail – with the evident costs sustained by various stakeholders (see Figure 2.1 on page 12 for stakeholders' interests) – should in principle act as a powerful alarm signal to other banks. Such a failure should prompt banks' management to exercise greater prudence, to promote efficiency and innovation, and to price profitably the risks they retain – if they are to survive and prosper in dynamic and uncertain markets. The failure of a bank could terminate with its take-over, break-up or closure.

It needs to be emphasized that the capacity to attract customers and to generate durably adequate income represent the first line of defence of a privately-owned firm *vis-à-vis* possible future adversities. Failures are essentially caused by managerial deficiencies and certain other external factors (notably those of a macroeconomic and political nature), whose relative importance could vary from one market to another, and over time. Excessive 'cut-throat' competition can also erode the franchise value of individual institutions, and eventually lead to an unstable banking environment. Such rivalry could make aggressive banks expand their business by reducing their margins and/or attracting riskier customers. The end result of this strategy

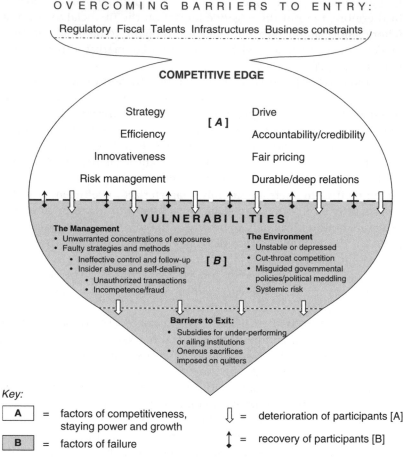

OVERCOMING BARRIERS TO ENTRY:

Regulatory Fiscal Talents Infrastructures Business constraints

COMPETITIVE EDGE

Strategy	**[A]**	Drive
Efficiency		Accountability/credibility
Innovativeness		Fair pricing
Risk management		Durable/deep relations

VULNERABILITIES

The Management
• Unwarranted concentrations of exposures
• Faulty strategies and methods
  • Ineffective control and follow-up **[B]**
  • Insider abuse and self-dealing
    • Unauthorized transactions
    • Incompetence/fraud

The Environment
• Unstable or depressed
• Cut-throat competition
• Misguided governmental
  policies/political meddling
• Systemic risk

Barriers to Exit:
  • Subsidies for under-performing
    or ailing institutions
  • Onerous sacrifices
    imposed on quitters

Key:

| A | = factors of competitiveness, staying power and growth | ⇩ | = deterioration of participants [A] |
| B | = factors of failure | ↕ | = recovery of participants [B] |

Figure 5.5 A 'contestable' market: entry–eviction process

could well be lower profits, and possibly losses that threaten the survival of these banks.

Authorities of a few developed and developing economies, although ostensibly adhering to the market-orientated model, have often adopted the stance that no bank or life insurer will be allowed to fail. The position of these governments has generally been motivated officially by an ill-conceived policy of upholding the reputation of their financial centres. This policy of 'barring exits' – often through financial subsidies or protection from new competitors – has proved over the longer term to be a source of moral hazard. Indeed, it has fostered negligence and mismanagement – to the very detriment in fact of the financial centre the authorities had tried to protect and develop.

Barriers to exit can also take the form of onerous sacrifices or penalties imposed on owners of financial institutions that decide to close their businesses – for example, by exacting large compensatory payments. Such barriers, regardless of their form and magnitude, cannot serve efficiently sustainable growth and build confidence in the national economy concerned.

In the case of a commercial bank's default and closure, management would – along with the employees – lose their jobs. Private shareholders would lose their capital, and so would uninsured creditors. In the case of public-sector owned or supported financial institutions, taxpayers' money is put at risk. In economies based on a free-market philosophy, the subsidization problem can be resolved by weaning these institutions away from the government through their effective privatization and independence.

The USA has, for example, Government Sponsored Enterprises (GSE), among which are privately-owned housing banks. There are three of these: the Federal National Mortgage Corporation (Fannie Mae), the Federal Home Loan Mortgage Corporation (Freddie Mac), and the Federal Home Loan Bank System (FHLB System). The first two are the largest and the more complex. They have enjoyed several privileges, among which are notably the following:

(i)   They issue debt instruments which have attributes similar to those of US Treasury instruments (such as eligibility for Federal Reserve lending or open market operations; exemption from registration with the SEC and the states; eligibility for unlimited investment by national banks, Federal savings associations, and Federal credit unions).

(ii) They have unique organizational structures and tax treatment; their charter is granted by Act of Congress; some of their board members are appointed by the President of the United States; their corporate earnings are exempt from state and local taxes; and a line of credit from the Treasury for US$2.25 billion is available to both Fannie Mae and Freddie Mac.

(iii) Their public mission is to provide stability to the secondary markets for residential mortgages, and to promote general access to mortgage credit, including to lower-income households.

(iv) Their risk mitigation consists of capping eligible mortgage financing up to US$300 700 per housing unit, and requiring the owner to provide 20 per cent equity or an acceptable credit enhancement such as insurance.

(v)   They benefit from regulatory forbearance in so far as they are not sanctioned whenever they are in insolvent situations. This was, for example, the case in 1981 for Fannie Mae, whose market value of its liabilities exceeded its assets by – US$11 billion. This event showed the inadequacy of the GSEs' capital requirements.[79]

(vi) Notwithstanding the complexity and size of their operations, these institutions have been allowed – so far – to apply capital standards significantly below those required from federally regulated banks. Their core capital adequacy requirements, as set by the Federal Housing Enterprises Financial Safety and Soundness Act of 1992, are 2.5 per cent of on-balance-sheet assets, and 0.45 per cent of outstanding mortgaged-backed securities and other off-balance-sheet obligations.[80]

The government sponsorship of enterprises raises concerns with respect to implicit insurance, and to 'level playing field' treatment. Indeed, creditors and investors view their special links to the public authorities as a competitive advantage over other financial institutions. This situation enables them to obtain lower funding costs compared to their competitors. The differential is equivalent to a subsidy, which has allowed them to expand their market share and their profits. Market participants thus deem Fannie Mae and Freddie Mac most likely to benefit from governmental rescue – similar to two, albeit smaller, US GSEs: the Farm Credit System rescued in 1987, and the special purpose Financing Corporation rescued in 1996. To prevent the default of these two institutions, the US government provided funding guarantees for US$4 billion and US$8.2 billion, respectively.[81]

The US Congressional watchdog, the General Accounting Office (GAO), in an extensive study of GSEs, has confirmed that 'the evidence presented in the report text supports the conclusion that GSEs' ties to the government have weakened the discipline that would normally be provided over completely private firms' debt securities'.[82] This interpretation was contested by the two top leaders of the Farm Credit System, who had benefited from governmental guarantees. They wrote, 'We strongly disagree with the conclusion reached that Federal backing promotes excessive risk taking. It is our opinion that there is evidence which can be cited to the contrary.'[83]

Government sponsorship has allowed the above-mentioned financial institutions to obtain explicit[84] or occult subsidies. The latter derive from the perception of lenders or investors that their debt instruments benefit from an implicit governmental guarantee. These lenders/investors are consequently willing to accept lower interest rates than those charged to the most creditworthy private firms. Part of the hidden subsidies has been transferred to homeowners, and the remaining part to employees through higher salaries and to shareholders through higher returns than those received by shareholders in competing financial institutions that have lost market shares. The foregoing is one example of a non-level playing field that distorts market mechanisms in the allocation of financial resources in the national economy. Measures to remedy that situation have been proposed.[85]

Level-playing-field competition can also be thwarted in several countries that allow mutually-owned or co-operative banks. These institutions had their origins in the meritorious philosophy: of mobilizing small savers' funds for the benefit of home-building and small enterprises, and of promoting solidarity. Nevertheless, these banks can in several jurisdictions buy listed institutions, while they have been protected by legislation from take-overs – in so far as they do not have owners with shares to sell. Moreover, their management is not under the obligation to produce for the participating mutualists returns comparable to institutions with private shareholders. They are thus able to poach business from listed banks in areas beyond their traditional activities – namely, servicing the small, lower-income customers. They have, furthermore, succeeded in obtaining funding from their unsophisticated depositors at lower interest rates – through their image of catering for the poor. Yet some of these institutions in Europe have moved into novel areas of investment or lending – for example, the Caixa de Ahorros y Pensiones de Barcelona by buying a 4 per cent stake in Deutsche Bank.[86]

Postal institutions have also entered the financial sector in several countries as providers of various financial products: savings, loans, insurance, foreign exchange and other financial products. As governmental entities, they have often benefited from extensive guarantees, tax exemption, and light regulatory requirements. It is understandable that the privately-owned financial institutions which lack such advantages dread their competition.

* * *

To sum up, safety nets, even if fitted with risk-mitigating safeguards, remain a potential source of moral hazard. Nevertheless, they are needed for emergencies to address systemic risk and crisis situations. Indeed, as put by a central bank, 'in a system crisis, the latent costs for the entire economy would be so great that the moral hazard aspects may need to be overlooked'.[87]

Safety nets were intended to contain losses arising from the spread of shocks within national economies and beyond. To make them effective and to mitigate moral hazard, safety nets need to be underpinned by strong prudential regulation, rigorous and vigilant supervision, sound accounting, adequate disclosure, appropriate sharing of risks among beneficiaries (for example, through risk-assessed premiums, limited coverage, and co-insurance), compulsory membership to avoid adverse selection, and a proper legal framework for the enforcement of sanctions in relation to irresponsible behaviour. These sanctions could culminate in the replacement of management and, eventually, in the closure of failed institutions, regardless of size.

The challenge of policy-makers and regulators is to design optimal safety nets – that is, that guard against a random shock developing into a full-blown crisis while avoiding moral hazard problems conducive to imprudent practices. Allowing for the orderly exit of an irremediably impaired bank before it starts posing a systemic risk is the most effective market disciplining technique.

6
In Search of Financial Stability

This chapter focuses on national and international financial crisis prevention and management. A stable global monetary and financial system is generally deemed to be a public good conducive to durable growth. Official multilateral institutions – such as the IMF, the World Bank Group, the Bank for International Settlements (BIS) and the Financial Stability Forum (FSF) – have important roles to play in promoting global financial and economic stability. Leading member governments of these institutions are those of the major financial markets in the world. Crises have prodded governments into co-operating with respect to (i) exchanging, pooling and disseminating reliable information pertinent to the efficient functioning of global financial markets; (ii) furthering co-ordination between national and international regulatory or monitoring bodies; (iii) designing and implementing common international best standards and practices; and (iv) co-ordinating their efforts in crisis prevention and resolution.

6.1 Crisis prevention/management and the IMF

Towards the end of the Second World War, forty-five governments participated in a United Nations Conference held in July 1944 at Bretton Woods, New Hampshire, in the USA. The leading allied countries considered various plans for establishing a new international monetary order. Their primary concern was to avoid economic policies such as those that contributed to the Great Depression of the 1930s. The IMF was launched in December 1945, when twenty-nine countries signed its Articles of Agreement or charter. At the beginning of the twenty-first century, the IMF has become the foremost monetary–financial inter-governmental organization, with universal membership (184 countries in 2003) and significant clout.

In accordance with the Bretton Woods Agreement, the IMF has several interrelated purposes. These are the promotion of financial stability, the expansion of international exchanges, the elimination of foreign exchange restrictions, and the offer of temporary financial support to correct members' balance-of-payments' deficits – subject to conditionality and monitoring requirements (see Figure 6.1). The IMF's Articles of Agreement constitute its code of conduct for member countries. Although it is not a lending institution (as is the World Bank Group), the IMF disposes of a limited pool of financial resources from which members can borrow in financial emergencies – subject to certain pre-agreed conditions.[1]

The Bretton Woods Agreements' objective of promoting and monitoring an open and stable international monetary system was to be achieved through the liberalization of member countries' current account transactions within a fixed parity system of member countries' currencies. The IMF left it to the sole discretion of its members to maintain restrictions or introduce new controls on their capital account

---

(i)   To promote international monetary co-operation through a permanent institution which provides the machinery for consultation and collaboration on international monetary problems.

(ii) To facilitate the expansion and balanced growth of international trade, and to contribute thereby to the promotion and maintenance of high levels of employment and real income and to the development of the productive resources of all members as primary objectives of economic policy.

(iii) To promote exchange stability, to maintain orderly exchange arrangements among members, and to avoid competitive exchange depreciation.

(iv) To assist in the establishment of a multilateral system of payments in respect of current transactions between members and in the elimination of foreign exchange restrictions which hamper the growth of world trade.

(v)   To give confidence to members by making the general resources of the Fund temporarily available to them under adequate safeguards, thus providing them with the opportunity of correcting maladjustments in their balance of payments without resorting to measures destructive of national or international prosperity.

(vi) In accordance with the above, to shorten the duration and lessen the degree of disequilibrium in the international balances of payments of members.

Source: IMF, *Articles of Agreement* (Article I).

Figure 6.1   Purposes of the International Monetary Fund (IMF)

transactions. It could even demand that a debtor country impose capital controls to safeguard its financial resources through clamping down on large capital outflows. The IMF-sponsored liberalization of cross-border transactions for the payment of goods and services was considered to be essential to the promotion of growth and employment. The IMF has nevertheless accepted that a member country maintains temporary restrictions on its international financial transactions, as the country works towards their elimination (Article XIV). Uncontrolled capital movements could threaten global financial stability in a system of fixed exchange rates. The Bretton Woods system of fixed parity sought specifically to avoid economic rivalry among IMF members by barring competitive currency devaluations and speculative capital flows – which were disastrously experienced between the two world wars.

The fixed parity system proved to be untenable in the early 1970s, in view of patent disparities among IMF members' economic policies, and in particular with respect to their anti-inflationary policies. Already by the 1960s, capital restrictions had begun to be circumvented, aided by financial innovations and technological advances (notably in information and communication technology). This encouraged several industrial countries gradually to abandon their capital controls.[2] The IMF's mandatory fixed parity was practically forsaken in March 1973. This step was formalized with the ratification of the Second Amendment of the Articles, which came into effect in 1978. Fixed parity has been replaced by various exchange regimes, covering, *inter alia,* free floating, controlled floating, and the pegging of a national currency to a single currency or a basket of currencies.

IMF functions originally centred on three core areas:

(i) *Annual country surveillance as mandated in Article IV*. This calls for an IMF staff team to meet government and central bank officials of each member country to review economic and financial developments and policies, and subsequently submit a report to the IMF Executive Board.

(ii) *Technical assistance and training*. The subjects covered are those within IMF's areas of expertise – such as central banking, fiscal policy management, exchange rate systems, and economic and financial statistics.

(iii) *Financial support to distressed member countries*. Virtually all forms of financial support are made conditional on the member adopting pre-agreed reforms to address the balance of payments problem that led to the request for the IMF support.

A country encountering a liquidity crisis (for example, resulting from sudden large capital outflows not related to changes in the country's fundamentals) may not be able to count on private-sector support. The IMF's mission is to help a member country to overcome such a crisis, before it becomes a *solvency* crisis – that is, leading to the reduction in, or destruction of, the country's productive assets and high forced unemployment. Admittedly, the distinction between liquidity and solvency crises can be made more easily in theory than in practice.[3]

Over the years, the span of activities of the IMF has widened, to include, *inter alia*, surveillance, setting standards and codes for strengthening national financial systems and global financial stability, and poverty reduction. Although its founding statutes clearly state in Article I that its general resources are available temporarily to member countries in difficulty, some twenty-five countries have been indebted to the Fund for more than thirty out of the fifty years since the Second World War. The consequence of this is that the Fund has been turned into a source of long-term financing.[4]

Judged with hindsight, governments whose countries encountered financial distress often belatedly sought external help, notably from the IMF. Assistance at the beginning of their troubles could have been more effective, and could have moderated some of the high economic and social costs of adjustment. IMF's support normally consists of loans, and is seldom offered as grants or concessional aid.[5] It would thus be misleading to equate such support invariably to a simple bail-out. These loans carry 'conditionality' requirements. Indeed, in quid pro quo for IMF funding, the beneficiary government of the borrowing country needs to commit to appropriate reforms.

A distressed country's required reforms extend over a wide area, stretching from legal regulatory frameworks to macroeconomic and financial policies – with a timetable of agreed targets – in order to eliminate the underlying sources of its external payments problem. The composition of the IMF's conditionality package has varied over time, with its scope broadening to cover a spectrum of reforms whose mix extends beyond the two traditional areas of:

- fiscal rigour, whereby governments undertake to work towards the elimination of unsustainable deficits in their budgets; and
- monetary restraint calling for a moderation in the growth of money supply – consistent with price stability.

More recently, the IMF conditionality mix has addressed other areas of structural problems, notably:

- the development of a competitive domestic market, and trade liberalization that often entails the privatization of state enterprises and the break-up of private monopolies (often politically connected), which distort efficiency, constrain growth and hurt welfare; and
- effective legal–regulatory–supervisory–enforcement frameworks, transparency, control of corruption, and other economic governance factors.[6]

To improve the reforms' chances of success, the financially troubled country needs to reach a national consensus among its main political parties, business community, trade unions, and other influential social and civic groups. Indeed, a society's long-term prosperity can be sustained through a realistic collective vision of wealth creation and of surmounting perils – founded on broadly-based domestic political support for the fair sharing of adjustment costs, and of the benefits of growth among the population. In a dynamic, competitive environment, markets will ultimately be the judge of the appropriateness of a country's policies and the resolve of its people.

At variance with the World Bank, the IMF has not tapped private financial markets: so far it has been content with government funding. In the allocation of its resources, the IMF Board can change its rules – especially when addressing unforeseen situations. Thus, total access to IMF resources obtained by member countries has varied considerably. For a few large emerging economies, this access far exceeded the statutory ceiling of 300 per cent of a member country's quota in IMF capital. The highest beneficiary was Turkey in 2001–2, which accessed over 2500 per cent of its quota (see Table 6.1). Moreover, these IMF's lending facilities have become more readily available, with over 60 per cent scheduled for disbursement during the first months of the approved programme. IMF lending arrangements have been used by governments and private financial institutions as a 'seal of approval' for other sources of financing. The latter include other multilateral developmental institutions (for example, the World Bank Group), official financing by major individual creditor nations, and commercial lending by financial institutions.[7]

Major funders – as expected – have wielded considerable influence over the IMF's decisions. This is particularly the case with the US government, which has the largest quota subscription in the general resources of the

Table 6.1   Major beneficiaries of IMF financial support (in percentage of quota)

Country/year	Total access
Mexico (1995)	688
Thailand (1997)	505
Indonesia (1997)	490
Korea (1997)	1938
Russia (1998)	449
Brazil (1998)	600
Argentina (January 2001)	500
Argentina (September 2001)	800
Turkey (2002) (includes undisbursed amounts from 2001)	2544

Source: IMF, Washington, DC (and note 3).

Fund – and a corresponding weighted voting power – among member countries (namely, 17.10 per cent in 2003).[8] Moreover, the US government is the largest contributor to the IMF through the General Arrangements to Borrow and the New Arrangements to Borrow (4250 million and 6712 million SDR,[9] respectively).[10] Its influence over the IMF has thus been prominent with respect to the decision to help debtor countries (large or small) in Latin America, Africa, Asia and Eastern Europe. The IMF Articles of Agreement require a qualified majority of 85 per cent to make certain decisions. Any state with more that 15 per cent of the votes – namely the USA – can, acting alone, exercise a veto power to amend the Articles of Agreement or to create SDRs.

In the conduct of its activities, two major issues continue to confront the IMF and its members. They are: moral hazard, and the choice of an optimal exchange regime. These interrelated issues are illustrated by reference to two episodes of crisis, discussed below.

6.1.1   Moral hazard – the tequila crisis

Assuming pegged exchange rates, lenders from a low interest market would finance assets in a foreign country with a higher interest to obtain an attractive margin – after due to consideration for risk. This can be, for example, between a low-interest creditor currency (say the US dollar) and a high interest debtor currency (the Mexican peso). Should conditions change significantly (for example, a jump in the US interest, a fall in Mexican interest, an increase in the country risk of Mexico, and/or the expectation of a deterioration in the peso/US$ exchange rate), the Mexican economy would then be subject to a precipitate massive outflow of capital. This should lead to the demise of the currency peg.

One well-documented illustration of IMF crisis management is the 1994–5 financial debacle of Mexico, known as the 'tequila crisis', and which led to dramatic capital outflows, and eventually the collapse of the pegged exchange rate of the peso (by some 50 per cent) on 21 December 1994. At the urging of the US government, the IMF quickly agreed to a stand-by arrangement for Mexico of up to US$17.8 billion, immediately after the US president announced financial assistance reaching US$20 billion. The total assistance package was raised to US$47.8 billion with Canada and the BIS offering additional financing – beefed-up with a supplementary funding commitment by the World Bank Group of US$2.8 billion.

Several officials of member countries complained that the IMF Executive Board was not consulted adequately on the above-mentioned Mexican rescue operation engineered by the Fund managing director, Michel Camdessus.[11] Moreover, the IMF's financing early in 1995 attained 688 per cent of Mexico's subscription quota, thereby 'transgressing' its statutory rule of the cumulative upper limit of IMF's financial support of some 300 per cent of the member's quota. The last-mentioned ceiling was originally agreed on to deal with the current-account problems of member countries. It has proved inadequate to address capital account crises.[12] The IMF's Articles of Agreement authorize the Board to make exceptions to statutory rules, and this happened at the time of the IMF's support to Mexico in 1995.

In the above-mentioned case, the US government was then concerned – it is pertinent to note – about the negative externalities of the Mexican financial crisis. These included, in particular:

- the threat of decline in US exports to Mexico with adverse effects on US employment;
- threats of default posed to US financial groups with large exposures to the Mexican economy;
- the risk that a collapse in the Mexican economy would create internal strife, and lead eventually to a burst of illegal emigration to the USA;
- the threat of contagion posed to other emerging economies;
- solidarity *vis-à-vis* a founding member of the North American Free Trade Agreement (NAFTA) comprising the United States, Canada and Mexico; and
- the concern that the Mexican approach towards an open-market economy and its political democratization (which has been espoused by other emerging economies) could be thwarted.[13]

Critics within the US Administration, the US Congress and other creditor countries of the G-10 had contested the validity of the above-mentioned argumentation for the rescue of Mexico. They further invoked the likely moral hazard created by this rescue, as well as that created by an earlier one in August 1982 when the Mexican government defaulted on its foreign debt. They argue that an anticipation of a ready availability of IMF's financial support in times of crisis renders lending institutions and investors – as well as borrowing countries – less sensitive to prudence in their actions and policies.

In both 1982 and 1995, the US authorities' support for a Mexican rescue – given the large size of the financial problem – was officially attributed to averting potentially grave damage to the US financial system and the US national economy. The official US reasoning has been that the Mexican economy is TBTF (see section 5.4 in Chapter 5). The then managing director of the IMF (Michel Camdessus) judged that the 1995 Mexican rescue package was justified – guided by the objective of avoiding potential systemic risk. That risk would have materialized if the Mexican government were to scrap its currency convertibility by instituting exchange controls over the Mexican peso – to avert a drastic domestic liquidity crunch. The imposition of exchange controls would then spread to other emerging economies in similar situation, prompted by their concern about the viability of the liberalization of their capital account.[14]

Some analysts consider that the IMF Mexican rescue of 1982 contained the seeds of the 1995 crisis. The rescue package for the Mexican debt problem of 1982 included, *inter alia*, the deployment of Brady dollar-denominated bonds (so-called in so far as they formed an integral part of the proposal by the US Treasury Secretary, Nicholas Brady, for debt reduction – introduced in 1989). These bonds are 'exit' instruments which gave creditor commercial banks of heavily indebted developing countries the opportunity of recuperating some of their claims on sovereign debt – subject to accepting reductions in principal and/or in financial charges, swapping debt for equity, or converting hard currency loans into local currency payments.

The Brady plan required notably that (i) the debtor countries carry economic reforms aimed at promoting growth and enhancing their debt-servicing capacity; (ii) the IMF/World Bank provide support in the form of new loans to debtor countries; and (iii) the creditor countries facilitate the write-off of their banks' foreign insolvable credits (for example, through tax incentives).[15] It was estimated that, under the Brady plan, shareholders of private lending institutions would forgive about a third of the US$191 billion of outstanding problem loans of the eighteen developing nations that subscribed to the said plan.[16]

The Brady bonds were not foolproof to default. Thus Ecuador was the first country to default on its Bradys, on 28 August 1998. Its Brady bonds, along with outstanding Eurobonds, were late in September 2000 exchanged for new Eurobonds with a debt reduction of about 40 per cent for Ecuador.[17]

Past IMF financial rescue operations could have encouraged emerging 'capital importing' countries to follow risky macroeconomic and financial policies. It could have encouraged foreign investors or creditor institutions to relax their tracking of risks.[18] A portion of the rescue funds served to reimburse 'free-rider' private creditors who comprised parties that were already enjoying relatively high interest rates when they chose to finance these countries.

Foreign creditors and investors – as well as debtors – could, on the basis of past rescue operations by the IMF and creditor nations, anticipate similar treatment in future crises. The IMF's promise (explicit, implicit or perceived) of financial support to selected financially distressed member countries, increasingly available with larger resources – and over longer periods for certain facilities – is deemed to be a potential source of moral hazard.

Some critics have claimed that IMF support 'is designed to absorb the losses of insolvent banks and their borrowers in developing economies, and to insulate international lenders from losses that they would otherwise suffer'.[19] No IMF rescue operation is, however, guaranteed or cost-free. Some private investors and lenders (domestic and foreign) have sustained, albeit to varying degrees, large losses during past financial crises – regardless of the IMF's and creditor nations' past rescue operations.

To reduce moral hazard and enhance market discipline, major protagonists – notably the policy-makers of borrowing nations – should have strong incentives for prudent behaviour in order to obtain private financing on attractive terms. Prudence could be fostered further by rendering IMF's support less certain and more discretionary, as well as being subject to more stringent rules. The private sector already participates in the costs of crises and in their resolution (for example through partial or total write-off of irrecoverable credits, additional funding, rollover of credit, rescheduling, easing of terms, conversion of debt into equity, and so on). In their lending to member countries, the IMF and the World Bank have always had some safeguards in terms of disbursement of funds linked to the implementation of agreed policy objectives, programmes and projects. Moreover, these two institutions benefit from a privileged status among creditors for the reimbursement of principal and interest.

The moral hazard creditor-side or debtor-side implications of IMF-led rescue programmes have been questioned. One study – sponsored by an association of the world's leading commercial financial institutions – conducted an empirical investigation into this subject. Its analysis has relied on emerging market bond spreads during the periods before and after the Mexican peso crisis of 1994–5. It refutes the claim that the IMF support to Mexico in 1995 has led subsequently to excessive risk-taking by private lenders, on the assumption that they would be expecting to be bailed out in future crises. It disputes the contention that this support exacerbated the financial crises of East Asia, Russia and Brazil in 1997–8.[20]

While it can be argued that the general formal commitment of the IMF to give confidence to members by making the general resources of the Fund available to them under adequate safeguards (see Figure 6.1) could lead to a moral hazard factor, the absence of such support could prove more costly for the distressed economy, and possibly for other countries. While an element of moral hazard can well exist in IMF lending, the evidence available does not reveal its specific significance in various past rescue packages.

Private creditors and investors have not been taken in by the illusion that the IMF would completely guarantee the debt service of its member countries. One can understand accordingly the large premiums levied for country risk on financial liabilities of emerging economies.[21] International creditors and investors have also borne losses in the various crises the IMF has helped to resolve, while the IMF has remained a privileged lender, assured of recouping its loans first.[22]

6.1.2   The breakdown of a currency board – Argentina

In the 1980s, Argentina encountered a dramatic period of socio-economic chaos: for example, in 1989, its GDP shrank by 6.9 per cent, and inflation rose to more than 3000 per cent per annum. The accession of Carlos Menem to presidential power and his commitment to espouse monetary reform, as formulated by his economy minister, Domingo Cavallo, led to a break in the cycle of hyperinflation. The reform consisted of the launch in April 1991 of a 'hard peg' of the Argentine peso at parity with the US dollar, backed by an automatic convertibility. This purported to have the advantage of limiting domestic money creation: the assumption was that the availability of dollars from exports or foreign capital inflows should govern monetary creation. Public deficits were deemed to be held in check – in so far as these deficits could not be monetized through the issue of money by the central bank. However, the central government and the provinces did incur substantial budget deficits in the 1990s that were financed not only by selling state enterprises to foreign investors, but also increasingly by borrowing from international financial markets.

A country's policy of a fixed parity – for example, *vis-à-vis* a reference currency such as the US dollar – could prove unsustainable, if clung to rigidly for too long in a changing context. The latter could well be a situation of protracted appreciation of the dollar (which could reflect economic conditions relevant to the USA rather than those in the said country), and/or the devaluation of the currencies of major competitors or trading partners.[23] This happened to Argentina, whose currency board from April 1991 until November 2001 based the peso on a 'dollar exchange' (one peso freely and mechanically convertible into one US dollar). With an appreciation of the dollar over the period 1995–2001, Argentina's exports suffered considerably. The situation worsened further with the large depreciation of the Brazilian currency late in 1998. The Argentine peso's automatic fixed parity conversion to the US dollar (or 'hard peg') at the above-mentioned rate thus proved unsustainable by the end of 2001.

Brazil has been Argentina's principal trading partner through the Mercosur customs union. The Brazilian currency, the real, maintained a 'crawling peg' band to the US dollar from 1995 to January 1999: this regime allowed successive controlled devaluations to accommodate several factors – notably Brazil's deviations from the US inflation rate, and other pressures against the real. Late in 1998, the real started depreciating, and in January 1999 the Brazilian authorities abandoned the peg for a free floating real: in March 1995, 0.9 real was exchanged for one US dollar, and the exchange rate fell late in January 1999 to 2 real per dollar.[24] The negative spillover on the Argentine economy turned out to be considerable, mainly through loss of competitiveness of its exports *vis-à-vis* Brazil and several other economies. Argentina suffered then from a lack of flexibility in several key factors: its exchange regime, its wages and its various other prices.[25]

The peso one-to-one fixed parity with the US dollar served for some ten years to eradicate Argentine's hyperinflation. It survived the tequila crisis, namely the Mexican peso devaluation of December 1994 (section 6.1.1 above). A fixed parity regime cannot, nevertheless, be maintained rigidly in defiance of changing macroeconomic and market conditions – both nationally and internationally. Domestic GNP in Argentina shrank considerably during 1998–2002, companies' average return on invested capital fell below the cost of capital, and unemployment rose to double-digit levels – producing domestic upheavals and violence. Considerable sacrifices were then inflicted domestically by austerity programmes, bank shutdowns or drastic restrictions on bank withdrawals and transactions, reduced pensions, and other measures – to no avail. In 2002, the floating peso depreciated considerably, and severe inflationary distortions (which wipe out the wealth of savers to the benefit to borrowers) resumed in an environment of political disarray, social instability and deep economic crisis.

Vulnerabilities summarized

As well as unfavourable external factors and shocks, important domestic difficulties were encountered by the Argentine economy over the period 1998–2001 before the situation blew up into a full crisis in December 2001. Domestic factors included in particular complacency in inappropriate policies, which led to rising unsustainable budgetary deficits at central and provincial governmental levels, financed by large increases in foreign indebtedness and/or the proceeds of the sale of state enterprises to foreign investors. A rigid labour market, bureaucracy and red tape, lack of an independent judiciary, and corruption had all hurt growth, and delayed reforms.

To avert the looming crisis, one can conclude, the Argentine government's deep spending cuts aimed at resorbing budgetary deficits in 2001, and the shoring-up of the peso/dollar parity came belatedly and proved insufficient. Furthermore, they hurt the productive sector and worsened the ambient recession. This had contributed to a further reduction in fiscal receipts, thus widening budgetary deficits. The authorities could not escape defaulting on the servicing of the US$150 billion sovereign debt in December 2001, the largest in history. The substantial depreciation of the peso in January 2002 hit various parties, mainly companies and their customers, the banking sector, and various creditors and investors – both national and foreign – who had funded the state and private sectors.[26]

Case studies on Argentina and other emerging or developing countries show that the lower-income segments of society are the hardest hit by financial crises. Moreover, when macroeconomic adjustment programmes are introduced by national governments – including spending cuts – the poor bear the brunt of such fiscal contractions (see also pages 155–6).[27]

Market access

In solving its balance of payments deficits, Argentina, along with other countries, is concerned about protectionism. Obstacles to international trade imposed by rich countries can be a critical challenge to heavily indebted economies which seek market access and export proceeds for their competitive products. Obstacles on exports can be overt or covert, and take different forms: high tariffs, import quotas (for example, on textiles or basic commodities), subsidies (notably for high-cost domestic products), arbitrary standards, or administrative red tape. Agriculture is one of the most protected sectors in the world's prosperous economies. Farmers' subsidies as a percentage of gross farm revenue were thus highest in Switzerland (69 per cent), Norway (67 per cent), Korea (64 per cent), Japan and Iceland (60 per cent), EU (35 per cent), and the USA (21 per cent) in 2001.[28]

Early in May 2002, US president, George W. Bush, signed a six-year law raising US crop and dairy subsidies to 67 per cent, adding US$6.4 billion a year to farm spending. Argentina's agricultural exports accounted for half of the US$26.5 billion-worth of goods it exported in 2001. It feared that the boost in US farm subsidies would have an adverse effect on its exports volumes and prices, hurting its economy that was already in recession.[29] The USA offered a bold trade liberalization proposal in September 2002, calling for a level playing field by reducing agricultural tariffs and other trade-distorting subsidies. The proposed formula invite the EU, the USA and Japan to reduce their trade-distorting tariffs and subsidies for agriculture over the period 2002–05 from US$67.2 to US$12.5 billion, US$19.1 to US$10.0 billion, and US$33.0 to US$4.0 billion, respectively.[30]

Inter-governmental groups, such as the Cairns Group (in which Argentina is a leading member),[31] and various representatives of developed and developing countries criticized agricultural subsidies. Australia's minister of trade, Mark Vaile, stated 'it is hypocritical to say we want developing countries to take part in the global market when they cannot get access'.[32] Unimpeded access for their products into the prosperous countries' markets could help their development, improve their capacity to honour their financial obligations, and encourage them to participate in global financial markets.

Already by early 2002, it was worth noting that the managing director of the IMF, Horst Köhler, pointed out that agricultural subsidies, in particular, are harmful to wealthy and developing nations alike. He stated:[33]

Thus, in my view, the true test of the credibility of wealthy nations' effort to combat poverty lies in their willingness to open up their own markets and phase out trade-distorting subsidies in areas where developing countries have comparative advantage.

It is unconscionable for the United States, Japan, and the European Union to spend hundreds of billions of dollars on maintaining marginal activities for the benefit of a few of their citizens, while devastating agricultural sectors that are central to peace and development in poor countries.

Evidently, trade is the best defence against debt problems, aid dependency, and IMF's rescues.

6.1.3   IMF's rescues – an evaluation

Any mechanism of insurance, protection or rescue is bound to contain a moral hazard factor. This applies to IMF financing of distressed member countries, as well as to damage insurance (for example, car accidents). The significance of that factor is not readily measurable. Nevertheless, IMF economists argue cogently that the Fund's co-operation is needed to avoid a further deepening of the financial crisis that hit member countries, and to facilitate the speedy recovery of distressed economies. Furthermore, the moral hazard factor could be moderated through (i) optimal IMF's conditionality requirements linking the Fund's financing for marooned member countries to fiscal and monetary discipline, coupled with realistic and sustainable foreign exchange rates; and (ii) greater involvement of foreign lenders/investors in the resolution of financial crises (see section 6.2.3 below).[34]

The apportioning of responsibilities in the prevention or resolution of financial crises among parties concerned is an intricate exercise. That the distressed country bears the primary responsibility for its problems is often true. Domestic policies and the failures of its political, economic and social leaders weigh heavily in the balance. Nevertheless, external factors – such as financial contagion, external price shocks, economic downturns, protectionist policies of wealthy nations, panic and herd behaviour – cannot be overlooked. Moreover, multilateral financial institutions, such as the IMF, could administer an inappropriate potion for the problem at hand. The former chief economist of the IMF, Michael Mussa, who had followed the Argentina drama over 1980–2001 conceded:

> In view of the Fund's deep and continuing involvement with Argentina's economic policies, its financial support for those policies, and the confidence in and praise for those policies that the

Fund so often expressed, it follows that the Fund must bear responsibility for the mistakes that it made in this important case, and must be prepared to recognise and learn from these mistakes.[35]

In admitting flaws in the design and size of its financial packages, the IMF has recently called on various academic and professional quarters to analyse and evaluate its policies and practices. In particular, the IMF's Independent Evaluation Office sought comments in 2002 on certain of the IMF's past policies that have been the subject of wide criticism, notably with respect to fiscal adjustment requirements. More specifically, concerns relate to their impact on (i) contracting output; (ii) efficiency, sustainability and equity; and (iii) the proper sequencing of reforms.

There has been well-publicized criticism from academics and social groups on the high social costs of the IMF fiscal adjustments required from countries benefiting from its programmes. These adjustments were deemed to be excessive – that is too large, too fast, and too skewed, with a negative impact affecting growth and the vulnerable segments of society. The poor have often been deemed to be the primary sufferers from the spending cuts that their governments choose to make – with primary education, health, and social assistance bearing the brunt. Moreover, some analysts consider that rapid trade liberalization has reduced tax revenues.[36]

Multilateral institutions, composed of human beings, cannot be immune from errors of judgement or from fumbling – no matter how well they represent various regions of the world, or how well-intentioned and sophisticated are their staff. These institutions have at their helm decision-makers who have to take into full consideration the views and interests of financially dominant governments that are strongly represented in their boards of directors. This is the case with the IMF, whose advice and financial packages have not always chimed optimally with social conditions in the distressed economies. It is gratifying to note that the IMF, according to its managing director, is looking towards '**improving the quality of our analysis and policy advice** and **enhancing its impact**'.[37]

Criticisms of the IMF have been varied and come from different quarters. They relate to the Fund's inadequate assessment of sources of vulnerability, and its inability to persuade the authorities to resort to timely crisis prevention. Moreover, critics question the Fund's crisis management rules and the expedient application of IMF conditionality. The latter nowadays covers five areas: (i) contractionary fiscal policies that produce substantial unemployment; (ii) rapid privatization that is of benefit to the privileged few; (iii) market-based pricing that often reflects dominant or monopoly positions, and hurts the poor in particular with respect to food and other essential items; (iv) capital account liberalization that enhances the vulnerability of weak economies to speculative short-term capital movements; and (v) freeing foreign trade with little concern for a level playing field with developed economies which protect their agriculture, and various other activities.[38]

The above-mentioned criticisms have been rebutted or qualified.[39] All parties recognize that the IMF's policies and practices need to be appraised continuously. This process should be followed by appropriate improvements to achieve their intended goals – taking full account of the changing national or international environment. Seldom do critics deem the IMF to be unnecessary, or call for its outright abolition.[40]

Strengthened by its experiences of past financial crises, the IMF is reforming its policies. This applies to capital account liberalization, and 'the IMF is now more vocal in pointing out the risks of rapid capital-account liberalisation'. It has conceded 'to the need to allow fiscal deficits to expand during crises to buffer the fall in output'. Reportedly, the IMF's 'conditionality is being streamlined to have fewer, less intrusive, conditions limited to areas critical to the goals of the programmes'.[41]

Should domestic political problems prevent the full acceptance of IMF conditionality, political leaders concerned should try their best to avoid being driven into a situation requiring IMF's help. This will encourage member countries to resort to greater self-reliance and to more rigorous policies to avoid the eventual need for an IMF rescue. This should also help in mitigating the moral hazard factor by reducing the propensity of countries to envisage dependence on costly or uncertain IMF remedies or rescues.[42]

6.2   Whither the IMF's focus?

The IMF's current multiple activities represent a considerable expansion in its original mandate. IMF's principals have over the last decades of the twentieth century favoured its greater assertiveness in global financial issues. Its widening functions currently stretch over a range of activities extending beyond the original temporary financial support facilities for balance of payments problems. They currently cover concessional lending programmes aimed at alleviating poverty in selected countries,[43] advising on policy reforms, standard-setting responsibilities, and various technical assistance tasks.

Some analysts argue that the widening of the IMF's activities brings in its wake a dispersion of its efforts, and an enlargement of its exposure to moral hazard. To contain the latter and enhance the benefits of specialization, it will be appropriate to refocus the activities of the IMF. This is the policy stance taken in 2002 by the largest contributor and leading protagonist in the IMF, namely the USA – as stated by one of its officials:

> The Bush Administration has encouraged the IMF to strengthen its capacity to detect potential trouble on the horizon, and to be willing to warn countries that are heading down a dangerous path to take appropriate action. Effective communication with markets is also key. And the IMF can be more effective and credible in undertaking these tasks if it focuses on issues that are central to its expertise – notably strengthening monetary, fiscal, exchange rate, financial sector, and debt management policies. In the last decade, the IMF became too involved in matters outside of these core areas.[44]

Several analyses and recommendations relating to the world's global financial architecture at the beginning of the twenty-first century deal with the IMF's desirable functions and the streamlining of these. A consensus among the largest contributors (notably the G-7) recommends: the avoidance of overlaps, an efficient division of labour, and effective co-ordination between the two sister organizations of the Bretton Woods Agreement of 1944, namely the IMF and the World Bank. The central function of the IMF that is generally underlined presently is that of crisis prevention and resolution. A few select aspects of that function are examined below.

6.2.1 Diagnosis of difficulties

In predicting the external financial vulnerability of a country, the IMF has based its diagnosis on a model comprising five key variables: the degree of 'real exchange rate' overvaluation of the domestic currency; the importance of the current account deficit relative to GDP; the growth rate of exports; the growth rate of monetary reserves; and the ratio of short-term external debt to monetary reserves.[45] As well as these factors, and in the light of recent crises, the IMF model's predictive capacity could be enhanced by integrating explicitly other related factors, such as: monetary expansion and inflation; volatility of international capital markets; domestic banking problems; effectiveness of financial supervision; and the extent of trade and financial interdependence of the examined country to other countries.[46]

Examples abound with respect to the difficulties of predicting crises or managing them. For one study of a central bank, 'in several countries hit by the Asian financial crisis in 1997, the crisis arrived almost out of the blue [sic] without macro-economic indicators giving any clear warning of its approach'. The public authorities encountering a financial crisis often have – according to that study – to improvise a solution 'without any guiding precedent', as happened in the Swedish banking crisis in the early 1990s.[47] Improved risk management tools, appropriate prudential regulation and effective supervision of the financial sector often become elaborated in the wake of crises.

Research work on crisis modelling in the light of recent experiences has yielded continuous improvements in the assessment of various types of risks. Early warning models are increasingly sophisticated. They include several pertinent and weighted vulnerability indicators whose predictive capacity has proved their superiority to single indicators – such as bond spreads (see section 1.2 in Chapter 1). Yet they do not send a consistent message with respect to the timing of the occurrence of difficulties or of crises.[48] Moreover, each crisis has unique elements which need to be addressed appropriately. Furthermore, seasoned researchers have admitted that 'it will be difficult to identify whether any measure – beyond strengthening the international financial architecture more generally – can reduce the risks of contagion specifically'.[49]

Given its vantage point as the foremost global financial organization with ready direct access to primary sources of information, thanks to its surveillance role, the IMF should in principle be more prescient with respect to country risks and global financial problems than are individual analysts, or rating agencies.[50] Its forecasting record has, however, been mixed. An independent evaluation in 1999 of the IMF stated: 'we found that the Fund – in both bilateral and multilateral surveillance – largely failed to identify the vulnerabilities of the countries that subsequently found themselves at the centre of the Asian financial crisis, except in the case of Thailand. In particular, it failed until rather late in the day to address a number of systemic issues. Moreover, to the extent that surveillance did identify these vulnerabilities, the tone of published Fund documents – notably [the

World Economic Outlook] – was excessively bland prior to the December 1997 update of WEO [and the *International Capital Markets Report*], after the crisis had erupted'.[51]

Those who examined the case of Indonesia over 1997–2001 understand the IMF's difficulties in anticipating the crisis and in prescribing appropriate remedies.[52] It was clearly 'recognised that none of the existing early warning models – including the regression-based models – anticipated the Indonesian crisis'.[53] The IMF attributes the failure to recognize the build-up to the Mexican crisis of 1994–5 and the Asian, Russian and Latin American crises of 1997–8 to member countries' lack of transparency on economic data, weaknesses of financial data, opaque governmental policies, and poor governance.[54] It further recognizes 'limitations of these models and vulnerability indicators as crisis predicators'.[55]

No matter how well endowed with expertise, one cannot rely on a single institution – such as the IMF – to be the sole whistleblower. Such a reliance is unwarranted, for two main reasons: (i) no institution is actually privileged to have a commanding wisdom and foresight to be able to offer a faultless prognosis; and (ii) a blunt warning given by one institution – assuming it has superior knowledge on the economic health of various countries – could trigger a crisis in the targeted country. Indeed, creditor institutions and investors would be prompted to cut their lines of credit immediately, and withdraw their investments from the flagged country. It would be more conducive to global financial stability to increase the number of independent monitoring and assessment centres. Moreover, individual lending institutions will be better served by relying on their own analyses and judgement, using relevant, reliable and timely information – instead of being led, herd-like, by a few credit assessors (for example, the IMF, the two main rating agencies, or a few major financial firms).

A granular market of independent analysts and raters would promote competition in rigour in that market, and would allow diverse assessments to have an optimal influence. It would preclude sudden and simultaneous movements of funders into or out of a country acting upon the signals of one of a few institutions. The multiplicity of assessments will therefore enable the market mechanisms to operate more efficiently and more smoothly in capital flows.[56]

Forecast models need to be built on the basis of a long and rich experience documented with extensive and reliable statistical data. Such data have been collected methodically for major advanced economies.

The evaluation of 52 000 forecasts made by 250 institutions for the GDP and inflation in these economies has revealed that less renowned forecasters have performed the best, and that the IMF and OECD ranked among the less successful – according to one central banking source.[57]

With the greater disclosure of pertinent information by financial intermediaries and governments, the IMF and other institutions, thanks to their vantage position, can improve their capacity to identify problems at an early stage. That information, if shared with the private sector on a timely basis, could very well contain problems before they develop into crisis situations.[58]

Early warning systems are often constrained by the unavailability of pertinent and reliable data – such as a country's net foreign exchange position, and financial institutions' position-taking in foreign exchange markets and off-balance-sheet items (derivatives, guarantees or undrawn contingent credit facilities). Several countries have found it politically impossible to require mandatory disclosures on the above items. Most financial firms resist the voluntary disclosure of proprietary information that they deem to be a source of profit. Moreover, these firms fear administrative and regulatory burdens. Several offshore centres, furthermore, do not collect statistics on their financial intermediaries. Other areas of opacity comprise 'black' or 'grey' markets whose activities are not covered by official statistics.

To address motley uncertainties, analysts, business executives and policy-makers are well advised to have recourse to simulation models and scenarios for possible future developments (based on different sets of assumptions covering interest rates, exchange rates, asset prices, growth rates, and behavioural patterns, among others). The scenarios would range from the very favourable to the highly pessimistic or worst case scenario. The analyst could then assign – in the light of her/his seasoned appreciation and after consulting with informed sources – weights of probability of occurrence for each scenario. Indeed, 'as it is very difficult to provide indications of developments in the future, these "what if" analyses may make a useful contribution to the analysis of financial stability'.[59] This approach of analysing a wide spectrum of possibilities could prove to be helpful to the parties concerned, taking into consideration novel factors that could occur in future crises. These scenarios could be consequently judiciously used to enhance the preparedness of these parties to various eventualities (see also section 7.2 of Chapter 7).

6.2.2 Ultimate liquidity provider?

One major advocacy is that certain IMF activities – such as those relating to development programmes, privatizations, reforms of financial institutions and poverty alleviations – should be an area of predilection for the World Bank Group. The latter already co-operates with the IMF and various other developmental agencies in the United Nations' system, as well with national and regional governmental or non-governmental organizations. The IMF would then be concerned primarily with providing liquidity during emergencies to promote the stability of the international financial system. It could also assume the function of catalyst in mobilizing other funders from both the governmental and the private sector. It is recognized increasingly that the IMF has a crucial role to play in controlling systemic risk, and preventing/managing financial crises – along with the ancillary functions of conditionality, monitoring and surveillance, and eventually issuing credible clean bills of health for member countries' economies.[60]

Indeed, according to its managing director, 'the IMF needs to work even harder to put crisis prevention at the heart of its activities ... [with] highest on our agenda ... work on early warning systems'.[61] Leading IMF creditor countries have also recently expressed a preference for an IMF relying less on direct lending and more on international surveillance capacity.[62] The European Central Bank expressed its views thus:

> The ESCB [European System of Central Banks] stresses the need for clear rules that would set out the respective responsibilities of the private and public sectors in the resolution of crises. In view of the limited resources of the IMF and because of moral hazard considerations, the role of the IMF should focus on the mobilisation of financial support and the formulation of appropriate policy advice. In this vein, the ESCB emphasises that public lending should be limited and that private sector involvement should be sought in all cases of international financial crises.[63]

Experience has demonstrated that it is unrealistic to envisage private LLR schemes to address liquidity crises. In the international economy, the IMF is edging towards a quasi-LLR function in relation to its (i) crisis management and (ii) crisis prevention. These activities currently cover:

(i) financial support to distressed member countries during and in the aftermath of a crisis: the IMF's help comes through various lending facilities, in addition to the Supplementary Reserve Facility (SRF) set up at the end of 1997. IMF disbursements are made in tranches – released as and when pre-agreed macroeconomic and regulatory reforms are realized; and

(ii) stand-by arrangements for countries with sound economies which do not currently need any IMF funding. Launched in April 1999 in the aftermath of the Asian–Russian crisis of 1998, Contingent Credit Lines (CCL) is a commitment to provide member countries with *ex ante* short-term financing (that is, up to one, or one and a half, years) to protect them against future contagion risks and speculative attacks – thereby precluding them from being driven to the costly approach of exchange controls.

The CCL facility is a precautionary line of defence that would be made readily available against potential balance of payment problems provoked from contagion. It is intended to send a message to the international financial community regarding the IMF's confidence in the credibility of a member's economic policies in achieving sustainable economic growth. Nevertheless, the criteria for approval for such a support are stringent, among which the pre-requisite that 'the member must be implementing policies that make it unlikely it will need to use the resources [*sic*] and it must not already be facing balance of payments difficulties as a result of contagion'.

CCL's support is intended for 'first-class' countries that comply fully with the IMF/World Bank *Report on the Observance of Standards and Codes* (ROSC). There are currently twelve internationally recognized standards and codes, spanning three areas: (i) macroeconomic policy and data transparency; (ii) financial regulation and supervision; and (iii) institutional and market infrastructure.[64]

The maximum size of the CCL is set at 500 per cent of the member's quota in the IMF. Similar to the SRF, it was originally subject to a surcharge of 300 basis points in the first year (plus 50 basis points a year for each six-month extension). The surcharge was later reduced to 150 basis points, and greater automation was offered in the release of the first one-third of the agreed support, in order to render this facility attractive to a soundly run economy.[65] The availability of rapid and extensive support would convince speculators that a bet against the said economy's currency could not be won. The CCL facility represents a novel redefinition of the IMF mission. Instead of being confined solely to crisis management, the IMF has thus become involved in the prevention of liquidity crises – somewhat akin to a central bank's LLR function aimed at avoiding a liquidity crisis in a national economy (see Chapter 5).

The CCL facility has not been used. It remains a moot question as to whether a government's recourse to it would signal that government's fear that something is wrong in the national economy, which could trigger a speculative attack. Moreover, there is no exit strategy that minimizes disruption for a country that loses its CCL status. And, finally, the one-year maturity of that facility, along with its costs, could reduce the interest of member countries in it, and in its disciplining prerequisites.

In a stable world economic environment, well-managed economies do not need to draw on the IMF's CCL facility if their foreign currency borrowing is finely tuned to their capacity to generate the necessary foreign exchange. Countries which have had relatively high foreign exchange reserves have been able to withstand external financial pressures. It has been demonstrated, furthermore, that a country's unimpaired foreign exchange reserves in excess of its external short-term debt reduce the depth of eventual crises during periods of international contagion. Such a level of reserves comforts foreign creditors about the capacity of the country concerned to honour its outstanding debt obligations.[66]

The IMF's quasi-LLR facilities can still carry a potential of moral hazard, however, if: first, decision-makers in an eligible country become less rigorous in their policies and practices on the understanding that they can count on an extra financial cushion in time of crisis; and second, creditors and investors become less exacting if they feel that the IMF is willing to fund the said country in a time of difficulty. The IMF's managing director cautioned that 'the IMF is not a global lender of last resort with the ability to create liquidity by issuing money'.[67]

In synergy with the IMF objectives, the Financial Stability Forum (FSF), was established by the ministers of finance and the central bank governors of the G-7 in 1999.[68] It functions as a co-ordinator for various institutions with the objective of reducing the risks of global financial instability. Its focus is on financial intermediaries, financial markets and payments infrastructure. Although the FSF does not have an operational mandate, it seeks a concerted approach of coherent support towards crisis prevention by international organizations and standard-setting entities (for example, the BIS, the IMF, the World

Bank and the OECD), alongside national regulatory agencies, finance ministries and central banks of the G-7 and those of other important financial centres.

6.2.3 Facilitation of debt restructuring

Financial discipline and full debt servicing serve the long-term best interests of both private and public borrowers. Borrowers that honour their obligations stand to gain from continued access to funds on reasonable terms. Should financial distress befall a borrower, however, judicious debt restructuring is the path to follow.

In national jurisdictions, when companies fail in their debt servicing, there are set procedures for resolving bankruptcies. In the case of the default of sovereign borrowers, there are no comparable clear procedures. The existence of such procedures can speed up the process of debt restructuring, lessen reliance on the IMF, bring greater predictability to international lending, and consequently lessen uncertainty and instability in the global financial system. They would also reduce the cost of adjustment to the parties concerned.

Since the early 1970s, a group of major creditor governments (from the OECD countries) have co-ordinated their policies in an *ad hoc* and flexible manner *vis-à-vis* defaulting countries within the 'Paris Club' – with the French Treasury providing the venue. The Club negotiates collectively – in close co-operation with the IMF – with countries that have defaulted on their foreign public debt, to reach appropriate means of relief. Governmental creditors generally require 'comparability of treatment' in the terms of restructuring the outstanding debt of a defaulting country – with respect to all members of the Paris Club, non-member governments, and private creditors. These terms cover, *inter alia*, a temporary standstill on debt servicing, lengthening of duration, reduction of interest, partial write-off of principal, and exchange of debt for assets or merchandise. Multilateral lenders – such as the IMF and the World Bank – are considered to be privileged lenders as pointed out earlier. Lenders of restructured debts (some of which have been securitized) would benefit from recuperating a significant portion of defaulted debts; and governments of debtor countries would also benefit by regaining the cooperation of the international business community (creditors, investors and exporters).[69]

The country in financial distress, by successfully negotiating resolution terms with its creditors, will therefore avoid protracted and costly litigation, the seizure of financial assets, blockage of trade finance, and other problems. The Paris Club expects the debtor country in difficulty to have obtained a prior agreement with the IMF on an appropriate structural adjustment programme, with a view to putting its house in order. This would encourage international investors and lenders to regain confidence in the country's prospects. Debt relief and financial support packages in favour of defaulting debtor countries have naturally been consistent with the national interests of creditor countries. Debt relief has also been directed towards prompting distressed debtors to reform their policies and to become credit-worthy.

Crisis prevention necessitates, across the board, political commitment and appropriate vehicles for the purpose of (i) analysing on a permanent basis financial indicators; and (ii) preparing contingency plans (at both national and multilateral level) for emergencies. A crisis can strike unexpectedly, and the authorities would not realistically be able to establish appropriate mechanisms without delay on the outbreak of a crisis, and to control or mitigate potential damages.[70] Preparedness – though very helpful in reducing the frequency and/or severity of economic disruptions, and consequently the magnitude of rescue operations – cannot rule out the occurrence of crises.

The management of a crisis remains, therefore, a perennial preoccupation of both public authorities and various actors in the private sector. Major financial groups (lenders and investors) operating in several markets increasingly seek collegial concertation – mostly through the Institute of International Finance (IIF) based in Washington, DC. Private financial groups have had *ad hoc* meetings (dubbed the 'London Club' since these meetings were held originally in London) to resolve on a case-by-case basis their loan problems *vis-à-vis* a country which had defaulted on its foreign debt – and in parallel to, or following on, the Paris Club negotiations. The guiding principle is to have comparability of terms among creditors.

With the development of sovereign borrowing through the issue of bonds in international financial markets, private creditors investing in these instruments number in the thousands, and belong to diverse groups and backgrounds. These securities are often traded, changing hands frequently among investors world-wide. The scope for reaching a general consensus on debt restructuring of a sovereign borrower – should the case arise – is more difficult to attain by diffuse groups of bondholders in comparison to a few major banks that have often resorted to syndicated loans. Several quarters have recognized the need to bring disparate bond lenders – currently subject to multiple jurisdictions and laws – to adopt generally pre-agreed procedures in the eventual default of a sovereign borrower.

Certain jurisdictions – for example, that of the State of New York – allow any small group of claimants to proceed to court in order to obtain satisfaction for their rights *vis-à-vis* a defaulting debtor. This could well delay or block debt restructuring, despite the fact that the majority of bondholders would be willing to reduce their claims on the defaulting sovereign borrower. Such delays could well hurt both the stricken country and the majority of creditors.

One proposal, dismissed in 2003, was to give the IMF a role in facilitating orderly standstills and debt restructuring of a country in financial distress. This could come through a change in IMF's Articles of Agreement.[71] One approach would be, for example, for a supermajority (for example, 60 per cent to 75 per cent) of creditors (banks, other financial institutions, investors in tradable debt instruments) to bind the minority in a debt restructuring agreement. All creditors would then be treated on an equitable basis. The IMF's function would be to help setting-up a forum to identify claims, oversee voting, adjudicate possible disputes and certify the debt restructuring agreement.

An alternative approach is to resort to 'collective-action clauses' (CACs) in sovereign or private international bond issues. These clauses provide for specific methods of resolution in the eventuality of default.[72] Although CACs could well be interpreted by some investors as indicating *ex ante* a potential creditworthiness risk that would warrant higher interest rates, borrowing governments of well-managed emerging economies can accept these clauses.[73]

Appropriate incentives for all parties are needed to participate in the resolution of a financial crisis – to avoid any dysfunction in the international financial system. If the private sector knows in advance that there are predictable limits and constraints on IMF lending, and that official finance (be it multilateral or bilateral) has priority over private finance, the scope for moral hazard could be reduced, and creditor–debtor willingness to co-operate could be more forthcoming. It pays all parties to have an efficient, equitable and expeditious debt resolution process, with the objective of making creditors and borrowers more vigilant, and market rates on capital flows more risk-sensitive.[74]

6.2.4 Capital account liberalization

The policy-making Interim Committee of the IMF (largely composed of developed countries' finance ministers and central bank governors) agreed in April 1997 that there would be global benefits to have the Fund assume an active role in promoting the orderly liberalization of capital movements. For the IMF, 'capital account convertibility means the removal of foreign exchange, and other controls, but not necessarily all tax-like instruments imposed on the underlying transactions, which need not be viewed as incompatible with the desirable goal of capital account liberalization'.[75] To prepare properly for global liberalization of all financial transactions (at both current account and capital account levels), the IMF needs an amendment of its Articles of Agreement (notably Article VI, section 3).

Entrusting the IMF with the mandate of working for the liberalization of capital transactions among its member countries with the same authority it has had for the liberalization of current transactions, remains a highly debated issue. The proponents argue that comprehensive unrestricted capital movements favour the productive allocation of resources and growth world-wide. Its critics are concerned about the potentially disruptive impact of unfettered 'hot' capital flows on national economies and international financial stability. Small economies are in principle more vulnerable to erratic capital flows than are the larger ones. Nevertheless, with sound macroeconomic policies, and an efficiently run and effectively supervised financial sector, the resilience of these economies can improve.

IMF surveillance serves to ensure that member countries attain the requisite conditions that permit an orderly liberalization of capital account transactions – not subject to reversal, except under specified rules.[76] Liberalization should therefore be preceded by macroeconomic reforms, along with sound regulation and effective supervision of the financial sector – to enforce prudential safeguards, authentic transparency, corporate governance and market efficiency standards.[77]

The liberalization of a country's capital account should therefore be gradual and founded on a robust domestic financial system (solvent, liquid, with well regulated and supervised financial institutions). Political leaders should give priority to the liberalization of their country's current account. With respect to the liberalization of the capital account, stable capital inflows – notably foreign direct investments (FDIs) – should be encouraged by providing an attractive business climate for the implantation of foreign companies that are likely to create net added value for the host economy. Unlike debt, FDIs do not need to be regularly serviced and cannot exit at short notice. Moreover, FDIs are more productive to the host country because of the know-how they bring, and their long-term commitment to create value in the investee economy.

It will be particularly risky to depend on short-term debt to finance longer-term projects – as some Asian firms did excessively in the 1990s (see section 3.5.2 of Chapter 3). One could equally consider the influx of 'hot money' investible in local stocks (for reasons of short-term capital gains) a potential source of vulnerability for the capital-importing countries – especially small, emerging economies. The latter would then become more readily subject to changes in international market sentiments, and to contagion. Financial market liberalization for developing economies has therefore both positive and negative effects on the domestic economy.[78] To enhance the benefits of opening their capital accounts, sound macroeconomic policies and a solid and prudent financial sector are, it has been established, essential prerequisites. When these are effectively in place, a gradual approach, giving top priority to FDIs, could pay off over the longer term in a volatile international market.[79]

* * *

In a globalizing world economy, it is unrealistic and possibly counter-productive to countenance the suppression of international frameworks of co-operation. The foregoing analysis has argued in favour of streamlined international organizations. In particular, it has found advantages in an IMF focused on working for greater efficiency in global financial markets, effective surveillance, and crisis prevention and resolution. In the event of a financial sector's breakdown of international magnitude, there is need for the rapid deployment of appropriate economic measures and safety nets (as illustrated in section 6.3 below) subject to avoiding pervasive and enduring governmental interventionism that could ultimately prove to be burdensome and counter-productive – undermining the efficiency and stability of the financial sector.

6.3   Financial co-ordination in emergencies

Major financial nations (the G-7 or G-10) happen to be dominant in nearly all multilateral financial institutions – such as the IMF and the World Bank. Their concerted actions are critical in addressing global financial crises, or in giving guidance to markets. These crises are not limited to emerging economies, and can very well hit any economy.

6.3.1 Dramatic losses of 2001

When major disasters strike – with the risk of the coumpounded impact of several dramatic events hitting simultaneously or consecutively – a rapid and efficient deployment of safety nets becomes imperative, to alleviate hardships and preclude the deepening or prolongation of a recession or a depression in one or more major economies. This was notably the case in 2001, which witnessed the bursting of the IT speculative financial bubble in the USA – the world's leading economy. This collapse rebounded on other stock exchanges across the world, with varying degrees of severity. The collapse of financial markets was further aggravated by the terrorist attacks on the World Trade Center in New York and the Pentagon in Washington, DC on 11 September 2001, which created liquidity problems. The New York Stock Exchange (NYSE) and the National Association of Securities Dealers' Automated Quotations (NASDAQ) did not open on the 11 September 2001, and remained closed for four days, unprecedented since the 1930s.

By the third week of September 2001, US broad price indexes had fallen a total of 12 per cent from their levels on 10 September.[80] On 24 September 2001, Dow Jones' Industrial Average was 27 per cent below its peak of 14 January 2000, and the high technology market – namely the NASDAQ – was 70 per cent down from its 'bubble' peak on 10 March 2000. Transmission of conditions in US financial markets to other major markets was rapid, though variable.

Destruction of telecommunications disrupted payment instructions and created liquidity dislocations, with some institutions unable to meet their daylight overdraft obligations. Connectivity problems hampered depository institutions from accessing their usual sources of funding, which led to delays in payment and settlements. Loss of life and destruction of infrastructure created serious disruptions in the financial markets – notably in the US Treasury bond and repo markets[81] – though several financial institutions put 'continuity of business' contingency plans into action.

It is acknowledged by the US regulatory authorities that there is a need for more robust business continuity plans to ensure rapid resumption of critical operations.[82] Moreover, international organizations have expressed their concern about 'operational risks engendered when financial institutions, markets or infrastructure are highly concentrated geographically. Moreover, when the firms involved are few in number, but account for a very high proportion of the global business, the risks of a massive systemic shutdown are clearly compounded.'[83]

The insurance claims for the September 2001 catastrophe reached almost US$40 billion for loss of life, property, workers' compensation and other liabilities (see Figure 6.2). Several international financial groups sustained heavy losses (see Figure 6.3). It was the worst disaster in the insurance industry's history – surpassing the previous claim of US$20 billion suffered in 1992 as a result of Hurricane Andrew.[84] Moreover, certain businesses also suffered heavily – notably the air travel and tourist industries in both the USA and world-wide.

New York City was particularly affected. Short term economic losses over September 2001 – June 2002 were estimated at between $33 billion and $36 billion. The said estimate includes $7.8 billion in lost prospective income of some 3000 deceased personnel; the loss of employment and earnings from affected sectors (e.g. finance, air transport, hotels, restaurants, and others) estimated at between $3.6 to $6.4 billion; and the cost of clearing, repairing or replacing physical capital stock put at $21.6 billion. The foregoing estimates do not address losses resulting from stress disorders, or alcohol and drug use whose impact on productivity is considerable – albeit quite difficult to ascertain.[85]

6.3.2   Prompt, effective response

To fend-off the prospects of a deep and protracted economic crisis, the US government and its agencies have promptly resorted to a multi-track approach, using various means to shore up the national economy. The stimuli are diverse and cover, *inter alia:* (i) *monetary,* through the central bank's reduction of its lending rates and the provision of liquidity; (ii) *fiscal,* through increases in emergency aid or subsidies, and reductions in taxes on individuals and businesses; and (iii) *regulatory,* through forbearance in accepting the expansion of credit lines without requiring lending institutions' to increase equity capital or guarantees commensurately.

Among various economic instruments at the disposal of governments in the management of aggregate demand or supply, monetary policy – which affects the cost and availability of short-term liquidity (see section 5.8 in Chapter 5) – has proved much easier to manipulate, compared with other instruments such as fiscal or trade measures. The latter take longer to be enacted and implemented – thus delaying their potential influence on the behaviour of economic agents. It is generally reckoned that monetary policy's contribution is most effective in maintaining inflation at a low level. By comparison, other governmental policies can be more effective in affecting the growth of output and

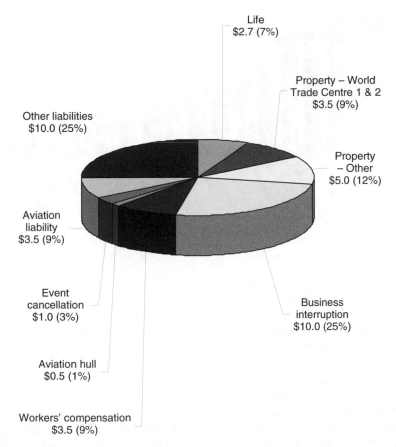

Life
$2.7 (7%)

Property – World
Trade Centre 1 & 2
$3.5 (9%)

Other liabilities
$10.0 (25%)

Property
– Other
$5.0 (12%)

Aviation
liability
$3.5 (9%)

Event
cancellation
$1.0 (3%)

Business
interruption
$10.0 (25%)

Aviation hull
$0.5 (1%)

Workers' compensation
$3.5 (9%)

Key: $ = US$ bn
Source: A.M. Best, International Insurance Institute, New York.

Figure 6.2   'September 11, 2001,' insured losses estimates (US$39.7 billion)

employment. They would include fiscal incentives to encourage work, saving and innovation; development of human capital through health and education; and vibrant competitive markets operating in sound and efficient regulatory frameworks.

Commercial banks in the United States and elsewhere were offered – in the wake of the 11 September 2001 attack – extra liquidity facilities for their payments within the clearing system. Figure 6.4 shows the various channels through which the Federal Reserve System provided additional liquidity in September 2001. One of its overriding

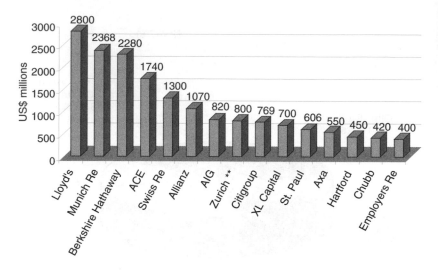

Notes:
  * Midpoint if company has announced range.
** Includes US$289 million for Converium (a global reinsurer associated to Zurich).
Source: A.M. Best, International Insurance Institute, New York.

Figure 6.3   Insured losses estimates*: top 15 groups (pre-tax; net of reinsurance), updated to 31 December 2001

concerns was to ensure the continued functioning of the financial and payments systems. Consequently, on 12 September 2001, the Federal Reserve (i) increased its holdings of securities through repos (see Glossary, p. xiv)[86] to US$61 billion (compared to an average of US$27 billion on the previous ten Wednesdays, and about US$12 billion almost a year earlier, on 13 September 2000); (ii) raised its lending to banks through the discount window by over 850 times, to US$45.5 billion (compared to the modest US$59 million average of the previous ten Wednesdays); (iii) authorized a 'float' (representing approved longer settlement periods for checks in the process of collection) of some 30 times to US$22.9 billion (compared to the US$720 million average of the previous ten Wednesdays);[87] and (iv) extended 'swap lines' of dollars for an equivalent amount of foreign currencies with foreign central banks – notably the European Central Bank (US$50 billion), the Bank of England (US$30 billion), and the Bank of Canada (raised from US$2 billion to US$10 billion) – to enable them to loan dollars to branches of European and Canadian banks operating in the USA.

	Repos	Discount window lending	Float	Deposits at Federal Reserve Banks
Average of Wednesdays from 4 July to 5 September 2001	22 298	59	720	19 009
12 September 2001	61 005	45 528	22 929	102 704
19 September 2001	39 600	2 587	2 345	13 169

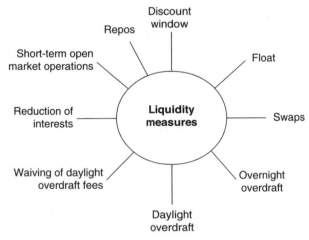

Note: Data were taken from the H.4.1 statistical releases from the Board of Governors. Only weekly averages and Wednesday figures are reported, in millions of US dollars. Deposits at Federal Reserve Banks comprise the sum of 'service related balances and adjustments' and 'reserve balances with FR Banks'.

Source: The Federal Reserve Bank of St. Louis, *Monetary Trends*, November 2001, p. 1.

Figure 6.4   Liquidity boost to US economy – September 2001 (US$ millions)

The liquidity position of banks consequently shot up more than five-fold, to US$103 billion on 12 September 2001, from a US$19 billion average on the previous ten Wednesdays. Furthermore, clearance and settlement periods for securities and other claims were allowed longer periods: daylight overdrafts peaked at US$150 billion on 14 September 2001 (60 per cent above usual levels), and overnight overdrafts increased to US$4 billion on 12 September 2001 (compared to a

US$9 million average for August 2001). For the ten days following the attacks, the Federal Reserve reduced or eliminated the penalties on these overdrafts, and liberalized its lending conditions.[88]

Hard on the heels of the 11 September 2001 attack, the G-7 ministers of finance and their central bank governors pledged to take 'all the necessary measures ... to insure the proper functioning of markets and the stability of the financial system'. Among the key immediate international measures taken was a 30-day 'swap line' of euros deposited with the Federal Reserve Bank of New York for US$50 billion received by the European Central Bank, aimed at meeting liquidity needs (see page 172).[89] This was followed by the ECB–Bank of Japan interventions in the exchange markets over 24–27 September to counter the depreciation of the dollar and the 'intense and undesirable upward pressure on the Japanese yen'.[90]

The Federal Reserve Board and its Open Market Committee, the lender of last resort in the USA, between January 2001 and November 2002 reduced twelve consecutive times the federal funds rate, to 1.25 per cent, and the discount rate to 0.75 per cent. The latest rates attained historic lows and edged below the current rate of inflation. The Fed's cheap credit policy, with its large potential of liquidity, might have – over the medium term – adverse inflationary potential. The policy actions of the Fed were emulated to some degree by the central banks of the other major market economies, and in particular those of the European Union and Japan. These simultaneous actions taken in the wake of the financial bubble's collapse and the 11 September tragedy were prompted by averting further dramatic falls of financial markets and economic activity. As stated in a Federal Reserve press release:[91]

> The Committee continues to believe that an accommodative stance of monetary policy coupled with still-robust underlying growth in productivity, is providing important ongoing support to economic activity. However, incoming economic data have tended to confirm that greater uncertainty, in part attributable to heightened geopolitical risks, is currently inhibiting spending, production, and employment. Inflation and inflation expectations remain well contained.
>
> In these circumstances, the Committee believes that today's additional monetary easing should prove helpful as the economy works its way through this current soft spot. With this action, the Committee believes that, against the background of its long-run goals of price stability and sustainable economic growth and of the

information currently available, the risks are balanced with respect to the prospects for both goals in the foreseeable future.

Monetary policy instruments, and notably changes in interest rates – compared to other economic instruments – can be implemented more quickly, flexibly and reversibly. Monetary policy's effectiveness, however, has its limits. It will depend on the 'interest-sensitivity' of demand for credit investment, and of consumer spending (see Figure 5.4 on page 129 for an illustration of the transmission mechanisms of interest rates). To achieve a given macroeconomic target, a coherent multi-track approach would prove more effective.

National consensus on the nature, composition and size of fiscal stimuli – such as aid to national enterprises and social groups – is always difficult to reach. The difficulties of consensus are further compounded at the international level. The common concerns among the G-7 in the synchronization of their measures is to attain greater efficiency and to avoid market distortions.[92] Stimuli packages could beget inflation, although this is deemed to be more acceptable if kept within 'reasonable' limits, than an enduring deep global slump.

Laissez-faire liberal governments or administrations metamorphose into *interventionist* ones in the wake of severe slumps. For example, after 11 September 2001, President George W. Bush's Administration deployed all existing safety nets, increased public spending, and cut some fiscal charges – with the objective of revitalizing the flagging national economy. The US government moved from a *laissez-faire* economic stance to fiscal activism, regulatory interventionism, and bailouts: subsidies or guarantees were offered to ailing companies that had sustained heavy losses (notably airlines and insurance groups), and aid to laid-off workers or to those who had suffered from the September 2001 attacks.

Regulatory authorities also relaxed their solvency rules for financial institutions in the first weeks after 11 September 2001. This was notably the case for insurance companies. The regulators' objective, as put by the British FSA, was 'to obviate the need for forced selling of equities at a nervous time'.[93]

Insurance companies, in the aftermath of the above-mentioned attacks, raised their insurance premiums on 'terrorism cover' for airlines considerably in 2001–02. Some have even hugely reduced or suspended their coverage. This behaviour forced governments to intervene and offer back-stop state guarantees. The largest US insurance group, American International Group, led a consortium in 2002 which offered passenger and third party 'war and terror risk' insurance amounting to US$360–US$540 per flight departure ($2 to $3 per air ticket for a fully loaded Boeing 757) as compared to US$7.50 per flight insurance provided under the aegis of the US Federal Aviation Administration and the Department of Transportation. The latter offered coverage of up to US$1.5 billion per aircraft and per event – compared to AIG's US$50 million in the primary aviation market, supplemented with up to US$1 billion to cover third-party risk. European companies have also had their governments involved in insuring certain types of terrorist risks.[94]

The effectiveness of easy monetary policy, corporate or personal tax reliefs, state guarantees or subsidies, and various other governmental spending – as stimuli over short or longer periods – is not predictable with any certainty. Transmission mechanisms and the interaction of various forces may not allow these stimuli to translate readily into increased investment, higher consumer spending and growth. There are bound to be time lags. Moreover, the pattern of differentiated support to various sectors of the economy or segments of society is often the subject of sectional interests, with each party claiming it is favouring efficiency and/or welfare.

Political wrangling and squabbles over the nature of economic stimuli are often the product of competing vested interests and partisanship. Politicians have had a tendency to hand out favours when deciding on the composition of their spending or tax cuts. Such behaviour will deprive governments of their moral authority as neutral arbiters of national equity – a lofty goal that is seldom realized.[95]

Regulatory authorities of financial intermediaries have relaxed their rules in periods of emergencies. This is the case with the FDIC, which declared the attack of 11 September 2001 to be a 'national disaster'. While assuring the public that federal deposit insurance is in full force, and money is safe in insured accounts, the FDIC and other regulators called on supervisors to exercise tolerance *vis-à-vis* banks that resort to loan restructuring, extended terms for repayment, or new lines of credit to respond to customers' needs in the aftermath of these tragic events.[96]

The IMF and the World Bank, encouraged by their rich member countries, came to the rescue of various nations heavily burdened by foreign debt – such as Pakistan and Turkey – that promptly joined the broad alliance fighting international terrorism, under the aegis of the USA. Economic stimuli at national or international levels would not bear fruit, unless confidence set into motion the economic engine. The longer-term impact on the world economy has been variously assessed. Costs are likely to come through notably increased spending on business security, higher insurance premiums, a shift of resources from civilian to military activities, and reduced international economic liberalism.[97]

In a dynamic environment, policy-makers and regulators would need to innovate to address unfamiliar events or unchartered paths. In view of unanticipated factors, different sets of instruments may have to be designed and used to attain, or get close to, desired objectives. Existing multilateral institutions are adapting to changing conditions – albeit too slowly for the liking of some principals or analysts. In Chapter 7 we shall take stock of the role of judgement in addressing financial uncertainties, and propose a sketch of a model for the dynamics of regulation.

7
Overview and Conclusion: Regulatory Progress

The perennial quest of human beings to foresee what the future holds is prompted by the goal to better their lot, and secure or manage their lives satisfactorily. This vital concern has spurred research by various parties – including scientists and practitioners – in all realms of life. Such research applies to the field of social studies, of which economics is an integral part. In the natural sciences, theories and laws on physical phenomena – with respect to their determinants and their manifestation – can be established with certainty or a relatively high degree of confidence and accuracy. By comparison, social phenomena are less amenable to precise definition, measurement or forecasting: the definitive understanding of underlying causes and interactions among various key variables in this area is still elusive. Consequently, predictions often contain a significant degree of uncertainty – especially in view of the likely occurrence of unanticipated factors. Nevertheless, large strides have been accomplished in recent years to improve methods and tools of analysing and forecasting economic phenomena. Empirical investigations have sought to identify key regularities of factors, actions, behavioural patterns or expected outcomes in social phenomena – such as financial crises. Objective analysis should help all concerned to better comprehend past and current events, and to influence future developments positively – be it at the level of the firm or at that of the national economy.

A correct and early diagnosis of an economic/financial problem should enable those responsible for its management to adopt timely and appropriate defences or therapy to avoid shocks, or to contain and moderate their ill effects. This chapter reflects on key challenges regarding the management and regulation of risks.

7.1 Micro-level alerts

Various quantitative models have attempted to identify and measure an enterprise's leading indicators of strength or weakness. These are intended to alert management and other stakeholders about serious problems that could lead eventually to the demise of the enterprise.

To forecast likely future developments in corporate performance, one could refer to early models which use simple linear equations. One such model sought initially to measure the solidity of individual manufacturing companies in the USA, and was later adapted for non-manufacturing companies. It uses five financial ratios readily available from corporate reports (working capital/total assets, retained earnings/total assets, earnings before interest and taxes/total assets, preferred and common equity/total liabilities, and sales/total assets). This model applied to US enterprises had in the 1970s and 1980s a predictive value in excess of 80 per cent, across a two-year time horizon.[1]

Models can be useful when applied to a branch of economic activity whose enterprises share common characteristics. Moreover, the models in question can only be valid if enterprises in the sector concerned apply consistently and with rigour well-defined identical accounting standards, and if reporting is fair, truthful and accurate.

The US Federal Reserve System and other central banks have developed econometric models that estimate a bank's probability of failure within a one- to two-year periods. For Fed-supervised banks, data used are from the latest quarterly reports of each bank. Moreover, CAMELS composite ratings of the US supervisory agencies have also been used as indicators of vulnerability for individual banks, with a predictive value valid for a two-year horizon.[2] The components, which include both quantitative and qualitative factors, comprise capital, asset quality, management competence, earnings, liquidity, and sensitivity to market risks (see Figure 4.2).

Increasingly diverse and more sophisticated models on the prospective performance of business are used to alert various parties, notably members of the financial community. For example, central bank analysts seek to measure the impact of the failure of non-financial enterprises – largely determined by their rapidly increasing levels of unsustainable indebtedness – on their respective lending institutions, the banking sector, and overall financial stability. These models thus link the vulnerability of the financial system to fluctuations in real activities.[3]

Model factors have to be analysed carefully. To illustrate this point: one econometric study reached a counter-intuitive conclusion with respect to leverage (that is, debt/equity). It found that low leverage (using as benchmark the banking sector's average) was statistically significant as an indicator of bank failure. This was the case in the British small banks' crisis of the early 1970s. The 'low leverage' factor represented, in this particular case, the lack of confidence of the banks' creditors – since the fragility of these banks was presumably common knowledge. In comparison, several other econometric studies have concluded that the 'low leverage' factor is an indicator of strength. One should caution, accordingly, that variables valid for a particular situation and a given period of time may well not apply to other situations or periods that do not have identical conditions. Beyond econometric equations, one needs to have a seasoned judgement regarding the interpretation of variables, parameters and computational results. Analysts should also take into account the propensity of management to window-dress their firm's communicated reports to appeal to investors/creditors, customers, regulators, and markets.[4]

Most models for the prediction of the deterioration or failure of individual banks assign important weights to equity. Equity's main function is to be readily available to absorb unexpected and/or uncontrollable losses (see Chapter 3). If a bank's equity is set by regulatory authorities at a minimum level without reference to risks on the assets side, the relationship is known as the 'gearing ratio'. In contrast, the risk-adjusted equity is linked to the bank's estimated risk exposures: the higher the risk, the higher the level of minimum equity required – as per the BCBS's capital adequacy recommendations of 2002/2003. What is intriguing is that the simple gearing ratio has yielded better predictions of bank defaults over the short and medium term than has the more sophisticated risk-adjusted equity calculations.[5]

Management enjoys some discretion in presenting the conditions of its enterprise in the best possible light. This is often done by massaging figures: certain costs, liabilities or losses are unaccounted for, and intrinsic values or profits are exaggerated. One eloquent example is that of pro forma earnings which are unaudited; they exclude gains, losses or expenses deemed to be non-recurring. Widely publicized pro forma earnings have served to entice credulous investors. To illustrate, the one hundred companies that make up the NASDAQ 100 reported to the SEC losses of US$82.3 billion over the first three-quarters of the year 2001, while their 'window-dressed' pro forma earnings were declared in the media to amount to US$19.1 billion – a difference of US$101.4 billion.[6]

A wide range of business expenses considered normal under GAAP – such as those related to restructuring – are often excluded by pro forma forecasts. In comparison, all gains – such as those from asset sales – are included. The SEC alerted investors that

'pro forma' financial results aren't prepared using GAAP, and they may not convey a true and accurate picture of a company's financial well-being. They often highlight only positive information. And because 'pro forma' information doesn't have to follow established accounting rules, it can be very difficult to compare a company's 'pro forma' financial information either to prior periods or to other companies'.[7]

It is also odd to note that US corporations whose shares are publicly traded produce two sets of books for two governmental entities. They report their book earnings to the US Securities and Exchange Commission (SEC) using GAAP methodology, while they follow different intricate calculations for their reporting to the US Internal Revenue Service (IRS). In the latter case, they reduce their taxable income by such practices as treating stock options and 'monthly income preferred shares' as deductible expenses. The difference between the higher book income reported to SEC and the lower IRS's reported income rose dramatically in the 1990s.[8]

7.2 Macro-level crisis indicators

Governmental agencies, international organizations, central banks, financial institutions, think tanks and academic researchers have used various indicators and models to (i) explain past and recent developments in business cycles, financial turbulences or country risks; (ii) assess current risks and returns for investors; and (iii) forecast likely future developments in national economies.

7.2.1 Country indicators

Quantitative economic factors often used to assess country risk comprise the relative importance of public and private debt, budget deficits, exchange rates, current account deficits, monetary growth and other financial variables.[9] Such variables would be insufficient to evaluate current and prospective conditions in unstable economies and environments, and socio-political and security factors also have to be included.[10]

External funders are concerned primarily with the timely recuperation of their principal and the full payment of financial charges. For this purpose, analysts have developed, on the basis of historical experience, benchmarks for capital-importing economies, calculated for both recent and prospective periods. The selected indicators shown in Table 7.1 are often used as leading benchmarks of investment-grade economies.[11] The quantitative indicators in Table 7.1 have to be complemented with an analysis of qualitative factors relating, *inter alia*, to domestic stability, the regulatory environment, the judicial system, governance, regional stability and peaceful relations.

Indicators of soundness or vulnerabilities of an economy and its financial sector are being developed and refined continuously. The IMF has identified a number of key quantitative variables that can serve to measure the evolution in the solidity of the financial sector. They comprise primarily a core set of five categories of variables: capital adequacy, asset quality, earnings and profitability, liquidity, and sensitivity to market risk. Supplementary variables to the core set shed additional light on the financial sector's evolution. These variables are defined in Table 7.2.

Currently available quantitative data, however, suffer from several shortcomings. These include: lumped items, non-reported factors, different definitions across countries (and sometimes across sectors within a single country), and imperfect measurement of risk (for example,

Table 7.1 Indicators used as leading benchmarks of investment-grade economies

Growth of exports	Stronger than growth in imports
Current account deficit/GDP	Less than 2 per cent
External debt/GDP	Less than 50 per cent
Debt servicing requirements	Less than 20 per cent of export revenues
Short-term debt/Total debt	Less than 25 per cent
Short term debt/foreign exchange reserves	Less than 100 per cent
Foreign exchange reserves/imports	More than 3 months' of import coverage
Budget deficit/GDP	Less than 3 per cent
Exchange rate competitiveness *vis-à-vis* the currencies of major markets	Not overvalued
Domestic investment/GDP	More than 20 per cent
National savings/GDP	More than 20 per cent
Inflation rate	Less than double digits and not rising

Source: see note 11.

Table 7.2   Financial soundness indicators (FSI)

Core set
Deposit-taking institutions:

Capital adequacy	Regulatory capital to risk-weighted assets
	Regulatory Tier I capital to risk-weighted assets
Asset quality	Non-performing loans to total gross loans
	Non-performing loans net of provisions to capital
	Sectoral distribution of loans to total loans
	Large exposures to capital
Earnings and profitability	Return on assets
	Return on equity
	Interest margin to gross income
	Non-interest expenses to gross income
Liquidity	Liquid assets to total assets (liquid assets ratio)
	Liquid assets to short-term liabilities
Sensitivity to market risk	Duration of assets
	Duration of liabilities
	Net open position in foreign exchange to capital

Encouraged set

Deposit-taking institutions:	Capital to assets
	Geographical distribution of loans to total loans
	Gross asset position in financial derivatives to capital
	Trading income to total income
	Personnel expenses to non-interest expenses
	Spread between reference lending and deposit rates
	Spread between highest and lowest interbank rate
	Customer deposits to total (non-interbank) loans
	Foreign currency-denominated loans to total loans
	Foreign currency-denominated liabilities to total liabilities
	Net open position in equities to capital
Market liquidity:	Average bid–ask spread in the securities market[1]
	Average daily turnover ratio in the securities market[1]
Non-bank financial institutions:	Assets to total financial system assets
	Assets to GDP
Corporate sector:	Total debt to equity
	Return on equity
	Earnings to interest and principal expenses
	Corporate net foreign exchange exposure to equity
	Number of applications for protection from creditors

cont. overleaf

Table 7.2   Financial soundness indicators (FSI)   *cont.*

Households:	Household debt to GDP
	Household debt service and principal payments to income
Real estate markets:	Real estate prices
	Residential real estate loans to total loans
	Commercial real estate loans to total loans

Note: 1. Or in other markets that are most relevant to bank liquidity, such as foreign exchange markets.
Source: R. Sean Craig, 'Role of Financial Soundness Indicators in Surveillance: Data Sources, Uses and Limitations', IMF Paper presented at the BIS Conference on Enhancing the Uses of Central Bank Statistics, Basel, 21 August 2002, p. 4.

when non-performing loans are accounted for at the sole discretion of banks). Moreover, qualitative factors (such as governance) need to be taken into consideration properly if a realistic appreciation of the financial sector's solidity is to be made. The IMF, through its *FSI Compliation Guide*, has been working on improving the conceptual and statistical foundations of the financial soundness indicators. Widespread use and dissemination of uniform standards across countries could help individual countries to better ascertain their own vulnerability (for domestic reasons and/or for significant linkages to other countries), and would enable them to enhance their preparedness in rapidly fending off crises.[12]

7.2.2   Bubbles and stocks

Financial bubbles are reckoned to be precursors of financial crises, and have an impact on the real economy. Nevertheless, the identification and measurement of these phenomena – with respect to timing, amplitude and severity cannot be ascertained *ex ante* with any precision. Some researchers have nevertheless come up with lead indicators for the build-up of financial bubbles. Notable among such indicators are: (i) a rise of the ratio of credit/GNP; (ii) an acceleration of 'price increases' in certain categories of assets (such as real estate properties or traded shares) which inflate collateral values of bank credit; and (iii) a substantial increase in the ratio of construction (or investment)/GNP.[13] The simultaneous occurrence of these three changes augur a higher (than normal) risk level in the economy, although these signals do not provide an exact measure of the *severity* or *timing* of prognosticated turbulence. A large variance in the above-mentioned indicators, with reference to historical averages, can therefore be the harbinger of a crisis.[14]

Monetary policy cannot be unconcerned about an excessive expansion of credit that fuels an asset price bubble. That could prove too costly for stability and sustained growth in the financial sector, and in the real economy (see Chapter 5, section 5.8).

For indicators of variations in the price level of assets, analysts often use changes in the ratio of 'prices of common stocks (P) to their past 12 month-earnings (E)' – in addition to changes in the price levels on residential property and/or commercial property. The P/E ratio is widely used, where P is generally reckoned to be equal to the discounted present value of the future cash flow investors expect to derive from holding the stock. The discount rate applied is that of the rate of return expected by the said investors (or the cost of equity). Viewed over time, companies with a steadily increasing P/E are expected by the investment community to grow and have higher earnings in the future, and conversely for a declining P/E.

Behavioural finance integrates non-rational (or not fully rational) factors in its models, to explain stock markets' fluctuations.[15] A non-rational market euphoria about the earnings outlook for the technology, media and telecommunications (TMT) group of companies can be illustrated by the strongly inflated P/E in the year 2000, peaking in March of that year at a P/E of 70, while other stocks peaked at 21 – compared with an average P/E of 13 for both groups of stocks over the period of January 1973 to December 1998.[16]

Instead of using the conventional P/E ratio calculated from earnings over only the previous year, analysts find it more judicious to calculate a less volatile measure of earnings. One such measure is the exponential trend for earnings that links the 'change in corporate earnings' to the size of the economy.[17]

In so far as relatively high stock prices do not reflect realistically the earning capacity of a wide spectrum of companies – though this is difficult to judge *ex ante* – a bubble situation exists in the stock market. It is equally difficult to forecast directional changes in recurrent financial bubbles or business cycles.[18] Investors' behaviour cannot be interpreted solely by reference to purely rational criteria, since psychological factors of euphoria or gloom are part of human nature and have had an impact on the 'mispricing' of assets[19].

Furthermore, stock price movements are reckoned to have reflected in the last couple of decades, and in several economic sectors, investors' sentiment *vis-à-vis* discrepancies between published 'accounting earnings', and the related projections made earlier by financial analysts. The latter, however, are not necessarily well informed or are not always free from bias. Moreover, most of these analysts' expectations are primarily focused on short term shareholder value (based on stock price movement and dividends), in lieu of long-term shareholder value creation. With a high proportion of stocks locked into passive pension funds, short term stock traders could influence corporate valuation. In these circumstances, the financial community needs to de-emphasize single measures, such as P/E. It pays all parties concerned to examine various drivers of company performance more objectively – while checking and controlling dubious accounting practices that circumvent economic reality by creating fictional results.[20]

To the extent that *earnings* can be window-dressed, some rigorous analysts may feel more confident with the use of *cash flows* in their evaluation of the situation of an enterprise. Indeed, in the calculation of earnings, the deduction of expenses (such as restructuring charges, the depreciation of assets, the amortization of capitalized expenses, imputed losses and so on) could be included or deferred to given periods of time – at the discretion of management to suit their needs. Disclosures about the methods of calculating earnings and on their composition are needed to avoid erroneous interpretations.

A widespread tendency to manipulate financial markets – for example, by using flawed accounts – could thus have macroeconomic effects. In particular it could (i) stir-up bubbles; (ii) shatter investors' confidence; and (iii) impinge adversely on the whole financial sector, and eventually on the real economy.

One cannot attribute swings in financial markets' solely to the credulity of retail investors, however. Professional investors have also been involved in this turbulence. They have often relied on, or been influenced by, the opinion of other so-called 'well-informed analysts' – since no single person can research perfectly a country, an industry, or even a company. Extrapolations, intuitive interpretations, group-thinking and conventional behaviour have involved the 'experts' as well – both during the phase of the build-up of the bubble and in the aftermath of its bursting. This even applies to managers of university endowments – who are normally chosen from among the finest scholars and successful business leaders. Rational investors cannot examine all the relevant macro and micro information, and often have to wrestle with hard-to-interpret evidence – such as the impact of technological innovation on future earnings. In such difficult situations, many resort to gut feelings, vague comparisons with past events, or market psychology.[21]

Some economists and policy-makers consider that a tax on traded securities could moderate 'excessive trading', and the occurrence of financial bubbles. John Maynard Keynes recommended a turnover tax for stock market transactions after the stock market crash of 1929, to stem speculative trading and to encourage investors to hold their assets for longer periods. James Tobin recommended a tax on foreign currency transactions in 1971 after the breakdown of the Bretton Woods system of pegged exchange rates. Although aimed at curbing swings in the valuation of financial assets, such levies present quite a few challenges. Among the most notable are: (a) the need for an effective global application of the levy to avoid offshore trading; (b) assessing an optimal size for the levy after taking into consideration the potential adverse impact on liquidity and an associated increase in volatility; and (c) increased costs for arbitrageurs whose activity is to correct the mispricing of financial assets by bringing them back to fundamentals.[22]

7.3   Regulatory cycles

The global financial landscape is changing continuously. Intermediaries have expanded their activities through new and more complex products and services, and extended their reach to span many national economies. Sizeable financial conglomerates have thus emerged, giving rise to important cross-border implications in business strategies, risk management and public policy. The unrestricted opening up of financial markets has the opportunity to enhance global growth, as well the potential to exacerbate turbulence, amplify financial cycles and raise the frequency of financial bubbles or crises.

The foregoing analysis has probed select aspects of financial instability – national and transnational – and examined desirable avenues to address them. The latter are premised on the principles of open markets and the competitive behaviour of firms operating within appropriate regulatory frameworks. Such markets are generally deemed to be more conducive to efficiency, longer-term stability and general welfare enhancement over the long term – subject to safeguards against abuses of market power, and adequate protection for the weaker segments of society. Figure 7.1 summarises several important and desirable characteristics of an 'optimally' advanced financial market. They cover five areas in particular: macroeconomic conditions; regulation and supervision; institutional frameworks; market infrastructure; the solidity of individual financial institutions; and governance.

Financial crises have differed with respect to origins, severity, geographic spread, timing, duration, impact, recurrence, principal actors, the relative importance of key determinants, and many other factors.

- Wide spectrum of financial products and services to cater for varied and changing needs

- Large financial resources, varied negotiable instruments, numerous customers, and liquid markets

- Several sophisticated and diverse financial institutions

- Timely diffusion of honest, accurate, transparent, and meaningful key data

- Efficient, safe, and solid financial intermediaries/payment and settlement infrastructures

- Ready access to managerial and technical talents at reasonable cost

- Adequate and reliable safety nets

- Sound corporate governance

- Effective regulatory–supervisory systems

- Competitive tax system

- Macroeconomic and financial stability

- Open economy, free entry, vigorous competition and level playing field

- Representative government, respect for property rights, rule of law and fair judicial system

Figure 7.1   An advanced financial market's key characteristics

Empirically-based explanatory models can be constructed and tested: they essentially help us to understand past events. Their use in forecasting is often constrained by imprecise measures, obsolete or erroneous data, and too many simplifying assumptions – such as the assumption of *rational behaviour*. Several observed economic phenomena show that economic agents have had complex reactions, where psycho-social factors

– such as the herd instinct – can be important sources of destabilization for the financial system and the real economy. Cognitive psychology should therefore help in shedding some light on the reasons behind the behaviour of economic agents in real life.[23]

The range of statistical–mathematical tools at the disposal of economists and other social scientists is expanding and evolving continuously. This is contributing towards improvement in the quality of their analyses. Nevertheless, a sole reliance on mathematical models built on lessons of past events and based on selected simplified assumptions can induce delusions of safety and rigour. Accordingly, no matter how sophisticated these models are, their assumptions should be re-examined continuously for their relevance, as warranted by the continuously changing environment. Models should then be used as aids to, rather than substitutes for, judgement.

Crisis prevention or moderation can be rendered more effective through the greater disclosure of honest and reliable statistical and accounting information – in addition to the enforcement of internationally accepted best standards, with respect to market efficiency, prudence, and codes of good 'governance' at both the micro and macro levels. Numerous and often repetitive failings of governments or institutions to ensure appropriate disclosure represent blatant violations of the fundamental principles of appropriate governance. These principles call in particular for accountability and transparency of policies and practices, respect for laws and regulations and a fair independent judicial system, as well as the control and repression of corruption or abuses. The observance of standards of best practices and of governance have proved to be essential prerequisites for efficiency, growth and progress.[24]

Financial markets are characteristically dynamic: new financial products and instruments are being developed continuously, and cross-border financial flows are broadening. Continuous improvements are needed in the fields of:

- the measurement and evaluation of costs, risks and returns pertaining to increasingly complex financial products and services;
- the disclosure of reliable, pertinent and accurate information to enable markets and the general public to reach sounder appraisals; and
- the enforcement of accountability rules and codes of integrity.

To render standards and codes universal, their development cannot be left solely to the forums of industrial countries (G-7 or G-10). Emerging and developing economies which have in the past generally been excluded from the process of preparing standards and codes – though they are expected to comply with these – need to be involved in their development and assessment, if efficient global enforcement is to be reached. Furthermore, appropriate incentives (for example, through reduced risk premiums and the readier availability of financing) could clearly be linked to the observance of such standards and codes.

Various institutions or organizations have been created with the objective of safeguarding economic–financial stability at national, regional or global levels. Their activities have addressed specific aspects of stability and/or focused on particular categories of economic actors – with several lacunae or overlaps. Their policies or recommendations have not always been credible, coherent and mutually reinforcing. To enhance the satisfaction of public interest, further effective co-ordination is needed. The Financial Stability Forum was set up for this purpose. Whether differing regulatory approaches should be deemed a welcome diversity in a complex environment remains a moot point. One can nevertheless see advantages in frameworks or regulations that can accommodate local conditions – compared to 'one-size-fits-all' methods.

The ebb and flow of economic activity is a constant feature of society, and students of economic fluctuations have found some regularity in the peaks and troughs of business cycles. The whole cycle from peak to peak (or trough to trough) would span some eight to ten years. Within these time horizons, researchers could also identify shorter, three-year cycles. Longer swings – called secular cycles – would cover periods of around half a century. The basic factor in such rhythmic economic fluctuations is psychology. As stated by an economic historian:

> The first and most important [factor] was personal – the optimism, self-confidence, and forgetfulness of the farmer, manufacturer, banker, trader, and investor. The desire of these men was to obtain as much income as possible. In dark days they might become very pessimistic, condemn themselves for their recent follies, make vows of caution, and resolve never again to let themselves be caught in the trap of a trade boom. But after a while, when demand began to expand and prices crept up from their low optimism, the vows were forgotten; or if the older men remembered them a new generation has entered the field eager to buy its own experience. Improving trade eventually begat over-optimism, which begat the conditions that led to depression, which begat pessimism, whose child was over-pessimism, which is where we began to trace the cycle.[25]

One can also observe that the public authorities have resorted recurrently to certain corrective measures – each more or less important – after events of bust, slump, stagnation, depression or debacle. Thus the regulatory framework itself – with its rules and their enforcement – has been changed (amended, overhauled or reformed) in the aftermath of the problems encountered by the national economy or by important economic sectors of it.

To explain the dynamics of the financial sector's regulation in modern times, a paradigm of crisis control cycles (CCC) is proposed in Figure 7.2, where:

- C1 = phase of a *poorly* – that is, loosely, heavily or wrongly – *regulated* financial sector, subject to turbulence and crises;
- C2 = phase of *improved* regulations of the financial sector – although still subject to moral hazard and some dysfunction;
- C3 = phase of a reasonably *efficient* financial sector – with appropriately designed regulations/safety nets, integrating market discipline;
- O = targeted *optimal* conditions comprising a mix of safety, stability, efficiency, competition, innovation and sustainable growth;
- B = eventuality of market *breakdowns*, brought on by business cycles, bubbles, fundamental imbalances, socio-economic shocks, important mutations and so on; and
- A–B = time span (n years) of a full regulatory cycle before its overhaul.

The CCC paradigm is derived from the gist of analyses in previous chapters, and is based on the following reasoning:

First, banks are inherently more vulnerable to risks than other businesses because (i) their core business consists of deposit liabilities, largely payable on demand (or at very short notice) and at face value, while their assets are largely composed of risky non-liquid loans and securities; (ii) they are intertwined through interbank deposits, counter-party relations, joint lending and participation in payments systems, which make them easily exposed to contagion; and (iii) a hitherto soundly and safely operated bank can readily be hurt by external shocks. The demise of one or a few banks can, therefore, promptly spread to other financial intermediaries and gravely hurt the national economy – possibly spilling over to regional economies and beyond.

Second, depositors and other creditors to, and investors in, banks often encounter certain disadvantages *vis-à-vis* financial intermediaries, notably (i) asymmetry of knowledge (that is, opaque, windowdressed or

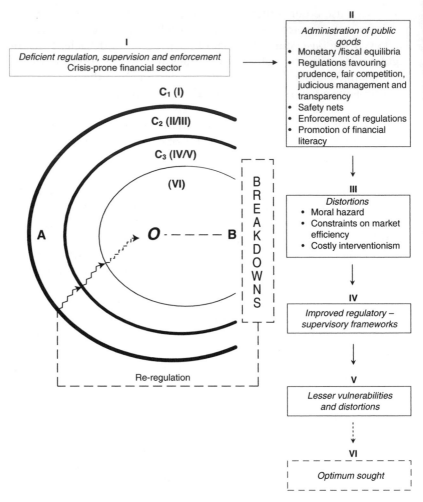

Figure 7.2   The dynamics of regulating the financial sector: a paradigm of 'crisis control cycles'

aggregated information); (ii) management's possible non-observance of depositors and investors legitimate rights; and (iii) unfavourable terms obtained by customers (because of the intermediaries' greater market power). Indeed, depositors and other creditors/investors cannot quickly access meaningful information on their bank's exposures, and cannot therefore assess the risk/return profile of their bank properly. The absence of such knowledge precludes individual depositors from the timely transfer of their funds elsewhere if the risk is too high for their liking. Such a situation could have deleterious consequences.

Third, the above-mentioned vulnerabilities, and the information problems encountered by depositors and other creditors of a bank, are sources of uncertainty. Should they perceive a problem – real or imagined – affecting their bank, their suspicion could lead to a run to withdraw deposits. Other catalysts for crisis arise from catastrophic losses of capital by banks (for example, due to severe problems affecting assets, or liquidity and currencies). Contagious behaviour could create logjams in the financial system – leading up in extreme cases to its paralysis. The end result could well be a generalized panic and an economic crisis, with its attendant trail of socio-political upheavals.

Fourth, market forces do not provide on their own the needed processes or mechanisms to promote efficiency, prudence and fairness – as well as to correct excesses and stabilize relations. The exploitation of customers and other stakeholders, and market volatility or failures have impelled the public authorities to design and enforce appropriate regulatory frameworks. The latter cover prudential requirements, honesty and transparency of information, competitive efficiency, safety nets, effective supervision, and appropriate sanctions. To increase the chances of enacting and implementing welfare-enhancing regulatory reforms in a market economy, a 'positive' political economy approach calls for satisfying and balancing of competing private interest groups.[26]

Fifth, regulation has costs (direct and indirect) and expected benefits. All parties in the financial sector generally seek to minimize the former and maximize the latter. Ill-designed regulatory frameworks are a potential source of moral hazard. They would thus impose financial and administrative costs, generate distortions in market discipline, allow undue forbearance, favour unwarranted interventionism, and constrain competition and innovation. Rules and standards should therefore be ameliorated continuously to serve customers' needs and to continue to foster efficiency and innovation in response to changing circumstances. What is needed is *better* regulation and supervision, in lieu of *more* regulation, that takes into account the self-interested reactions of market participants – through a better alignment of private incentives and public welfare.[27]

Sixth, optimal regulatory frameworks for the financial sector create a propitious environment of efficiency, innovation and growth–thanks to attractive incentives for prudence and dissuasive sanctions for laxity or abuse. A judicious risk management process for financial institutions (see the one proposed in Figure 7.3) calls on management to retain those risks in which it has a competitive advantage. The other risks would then be hedged, insured or transferred. This process comprises principally the identification, measurement, forecasting, pricing, control and evaluation of risks.

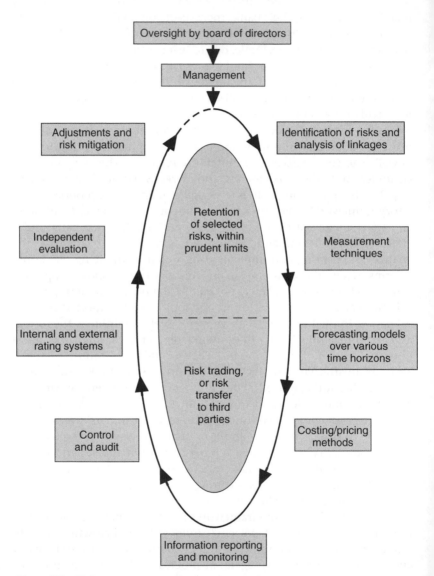

Figure 7.3   Risk management process

Seventh, uncertainty is a basic and perennial feature of life. Preparedness to confront future problems should help executives, policy-makers and regulators in protecting and strengthening the resilience of institutions and economies. Market breakdowns, bubbles and swings, or important mutations, could render irrelevant and or inappropriate certain risk management strategies that rest on assumptions derived from obsolete or fragmentary evidence. A dynamic environment would therefore require periodically novel approaches to, and judicious reforms of, regulatory frameworks – guided by the goal of optimality.

7.4 Concluding remarks

There are several objectives in instituting and developing high-quality regulatory frameworks for the benefit of a modern economy. They can be summarized in four long-term fundamental points: safety, stability, efficiency and sustainable growth. To achieve such objectives, policy-makers need to recognize that regulation should (a) be adapted and refined continuously to meet changes in socio-economic conditions; (b) maximize net benefits over and above the direct costs borne by the regulated institution and other costs borne by the economy; (c) include appropriate incentives to motivate all parties concerned to behave productively and prudently – abiding by recognized principles of governance; and (d) avoid over-regulation that numbs market signals, stifles innovation, and thwarts market efficiency.

The cumulative learning process from past mishaps or blunders could well enable policy-makers and regulators to design, over the medium-to-longer term, more effective and less costly frameworks – guided by the above-mentioned goals. Turbulence and crises encountered in an improperly regulated phase would thus moderate, as lessons are drawn from past experiences, and as pertinent safeguards are built, refined and enforced effectively.

Diversity of regulatory approaches – for example, those existing in large economies such as the USA or the EU – could be envisaged flexibly as a potential source of positive competition, so long as the choice of regulatory regimes does not favour laxity, forbearance, regulatory gaps or discrimination among sectors, or segments of these sectors. A global super-regulator is, furthermore, politically unrealistic, while an approved set of fundamental principles and standards, in which all economies recognize a mutual interest, is more viable and productive in an increasingly more complex and volatile global financial sector.

The general manager of the BIS acknowledges the guidance role for the few advanced economies in setting global 'standards that can be agreed by supervisors in the most advanced jurisdictions, whose broader adoption is encouraged by peer pressure and market forces'.[28]

Governmental policies and regulations can have an impact on the performance of individual banks and the financial system at large. Thus macroeconomic imbalances – such as large budgetary deficits leading to excessive monetary creation or unsustainable foreign borrowing in addition to burdensome constraints on business activity, would hurt economic growth and stability. Banks and their customers would then suffer from unsound governmental policies. Empirical evidence accumulated by a large body of research shows the positive correlation between high-quality financial regulation and supervision, genuine corporate governance, and sound macroeconomic policies. Together, they can moderate financial–economic instability and promote long-term growth.[29]

Increasing interconnectedness among financial markets and institutions world-wide is a fundamental feature of the contemporary world economy at the beginning of the twenty-first century. Such a situation offers potential benefits for fructifying opportunities and creating values, if resources are allocated judiciously and risks properly managed. The transnational free flow of funds can also be a source of volatility and instability to risk-exposed financial institutions (for example, for reasons of mismatched maturities and/or currency exposures). Such institutions are vulnerable to shocks or contagion leading to depositor runs or unexpected transfers, a phenomenon that can create havoc, and bring ruin to the financial sector and the real economy. To avoid such an eventuality, governmental agencies have been created to regulate and protect.

Concerned with enhancing financial stability, policy-makers have to calibrate the trade-off between competition and safety. Their objective is to favour productive competition while containing (by appropriate incentives or sanctions) unwarranted risk-taking, and preventing abuse of power by managers. The legal infrastructure should then include effective means for implementing good corporate governance and market discipline. The latter necessitate adequate disclosure and transparency, especially from large, complex financial conglomerates whose systemic risk is likely to be particularly high. With proper transparency and communication, depositors, lenders, borrowers and investors would then be in a position to make sound decisions, and so would regulators and policy-makers.[30]

Though a few economically powerful countries have taken a leadership role in setting regulatory frameworks aimed at crisis prevention and crisis management, communication and co-operation among all countries should enhance the prospects of global financial stability in an interdependent world where unsuspected catastrophes with contagious impact remain a basic feature of life. Accordingly, the readiness of public and private decision-makers to co-operate in tackling the roots as well as the aftermath of crises is crucial to global prosperity.

So-called stable conditions can prove to be ephemeral, since imponderable and unpredictable shocks are bound to break out in future periods in an increasingly complex, and often unwieldy world. Wise leaders of the private and public sectors are recognized in due course for their preparedness with crisis scenarios, contingency plans and back-up arrangements, and for their capacity to cope innovatively with problems as they arise. Techniques of crisis management at the macro or micro levels need continuously to be tested, re-evaluated, updated, refined and enriched by novel experiences and groundbreaking research. Decision-makers braced up in readiness to face hazards and to seize opportunities are better-placed to perform. Their success hinges on their capacity to learn from past blunders, mishaps or crises, and to remain ever vigilant – especially in periods of prosperity which generate euphoria, characterized by a propensity for insouciance and oblivion of risk.

Notes and References

1 Introduction: Risks and Protagonists

1. See J. Downes and J. E. Goodman, *Dictionary of Finance and Investment Terms*, (New York: Barrons, 1991), p. 380. Technically, one can calculate the mean of an asset's yields obtaining over a series of identical periods. The average of the squared deviations from the same mean – called variance – is positive. The value of the variance becomes larger, as the deviations increase in size. The square root of the variance – called standard deviation (σ) – is used as an indicator of volatility or risk of the asset in question.
2. For a pioneering work on the subject, see Frank H. Knight, *Risk, Uncertainty, and Profit*, Midway Reprint edition, (University Press of Chicago, 1985).
3. For useful references, see for example: Charles P. Kindleberger, *A Financial History of Western Europe*, 2nd edn, (Oxford University Press, 1993); Eugen N. White, ed. *Stock Market Crashes and Speculative Manias*, (Edward Elgar: Brook Field, VT, 1996); Benton E. Gup, *Bank Failures in the Major Trading Countries of the World*, (Greenwood Publishing Group, USA, 1998); and R. Glenn Hubbard, *Financial Markets and Financial Crises*, (University of Chicago Press, 1991).
4. See World Bank, *Finance for Growth – Policy Choices in a Volatile World*, (Oxford University Press, 2001), pp. 80–1.
5. For a summary of major international financial crises, see M. D. Bordo and A. P. Murshid, 'Are Financial Crises Becoming More Contagious? What is the Historical Evidence on Contagion?', in S. Claessens and K. J. Forbes (eds) *International Financial Contagion*, Kluwer, (Boston: 2001), pp. 367–403.
6. See J. Aziz, F. Caramazza and R. Salgado, 'Currency Crises: In Search of Common Elements', in International Monetary Fund (IMF), *World Economic Outlook Supporting Studies*, (Washington, DC: IMF, 2000), pp. 86–128.
7. See, for example, Group of Thirty, *Global Institutions, National Supervision and Systemic Risk*, Group of Thirty Study Report, (Washington, DC: 1997) and Olivier de Bandt and Philip Hartman, 'Systemic Risk in Banking: A Survey' in Charles Goodhart and Gerhard Illing (eds), *Financial Crises, Contagion, and the Lender of Last Resort*, (Oxford University Press, 2002), pp. 249–97.
8. See Group of Ten, *Report on Consolidation in the Financial Sector*, (Basel: Bank of International Settlements [BIS], January 2001), pp. 126–7.
9. For a central banker inside story, see Ruth de Krivoy, *Collapse – The Venezuelan Banking Crisis of '94*, (Washington, DC: Group of Thirty, 2000).
10. See Federal Deposit Insurance Corporation, *Country Risk Management*, (Washington, DC: FDIC, 11 March 2002).
11. Federal Deposit Insurance Corporation, *An Examination of the Banking Crises of the 1980s and Early 1990s*, Vol. i, (Washington, DC: FDIC, December 1997), p. 204.

12. The current account records a country's balance-of-trade on visible goods and its invisible services (such as banking, insurance, transport, transfers) *vis-à-vis* the outside world. The capital account records all long- and short-term capital flows.

13. See, for example, Guillermo Ortiz, Governor, Banco de Mexico, 'Recent Emerging Market Crises – What Have We Learned?', Per Jacobson Lecture, Basel, 7 July 2002.

14. Cited by Morris Goldstein, Graciela L. Kaminsky and Carmen M. Reinhart, *Assessing Financial Vulnerability – An Early Warning System for Emerging Markets.* (Washington, DC: Institute of International Economics, June 2000), pp. 6–8.

15. Gauged by the standard deviation of price/yield changes at fixed intervals in a given period: volatility is *low* if changes are clustered near their mean and *high* if widely dispersed.

16. See, for example, *World Development Report 1999/2000*, (World Bank/Oxford University Press, 2000), p. 75.

17. See OECD Observer, *Economic Survey of the Euro Area, 2002*, Paris, July 2002.

18. *World Development Report*, as note 16, pp. 46–63.

19. See, for example, George G. Kaufman, 'Banking and Currency Crises and Systemic Risk: Lessons from Recent Events', *Economic Perspectives*, (Chicago: Federal Reserve Bank of Chicago, 3rd quarter 2000), pp. 9–28; Frederik S. Mishkin, 'Securing a Safety Net Against Economic Free Fall', in *Financial Times – Mastering Risk* (London: 6 June 2000), pp. 6–7; and Bank for International Settlements, *10th Annual Report*, (Basel, 5 June 2000), p. 49.

20. See Glenn Hoggarth, Ricardo Reis and Victoria Saporta, 'Costs of Banking System Instability: Some Empirical Evidence', *Journal of Banking and Finance*, May 2002, pp. 825–55.

21. Ross Levine, 'International Financial Liberalization and Economic Growth', *Review of International Economics*, September 2000.

22. See also Thorsten Beck, Asli Demirgüç-Kunt, Ross Levine and Vojislav Maksimovic, *Financial Structure and Economic Development: Firm, Industry and Country Evidence*, mimeo, (World Bank, November 2002).

23. For a succinct summary, see United States General Accounting Office (GAO), *Multilateral Development Banks – Profiles of Selected Multilateral Development Banks*, (Washington, DC: GAO, May 2001).

24 See IMF, *World Economic Outlook – Trade and Finance*, (Washington, DC: IMF, September 2002), pp. 131–8.

25. See, for example, Derek H. Aldcroft, 'The Twentieth Century International Debt Problem in Historical Perspective', *The Journal of European Economic History*, (Bank of Rome, Spring 2001), pp. 173–202.

26. Maurice H. Hartigan, *The RMA Journal*, (Philadelphia: The Risk Management Association, July/August 2002), p. 6.

2 Challenges of Corporate Governance

1. See, for example, Section on Business Law in American Bar Association, Committee of Corporate Laws, *Corporate Director's Guidebook*, 3rd edn, 2001, p. 4, cited by Carolyn Brancato, The Conference Board, Testimony before the Senate Finance Committee, Washington, DC, 18 April 2002.

2. See David Gale, 'How to Create Truly Independent Boards', *The Wall Street Journal Europe*, 16–18 August 2002, p. A6.
3. Robert F. Felton and Mark Watson, 'Change Across the Board', *McKinsey Quarterly*, no. 4, New York, 2002, pp. 31–45.
4. See, for example, 'Corporate Governance – Is Germany's Model Finding Its Level?', *Financial Times*, 5 September 2002, p. 8.
5. See, for example, International Corporate Governance Network (ICGN), *Statement on Global Implementation of ICGN Share Voting Principles*, (New York: ICGN, 14 July 2000) (www.icgn.org).
6. Among the sizeable corporations which came prominently to the attention of the general public in the USA and Europe in 2001–02, one can cite ABB, Global Crossing, Energis, Lucent Technologies, Enron, WorldCom, Tyco and Quest Communication – to mention only a few.
7. See John H. Biggs, CEO of TIAA-CREF, Testimony before the US Senate Finance Committee, Washington, DC, 18 April 2002. TIAA-CREF is the largest private pension system in the world (managing about US$275 billion in assets in 2002).
8. Percy Barnevik left the ABB chairmanship on 23 November 2001 while taking 'responsibility for the less good performance of ABB in recent years': www.news.bbc.co.uk.
9. See Dan Bilefsky and Goran Mijuk, 'Model No More: ABB Caps Disastrous Week With Loss', *The Wall Street Journal Europe*, 25–27 October 2002, pp. A1 and A6.
10. ABB press release, Zurich, 21 October 2002.
11. See 'Barnevik's Disgrace Has Greater Impact than His Preaching', and 'Former ABB Executives Will Repay €92.2 million', *The Wall Street Journal Europe*, 8 and 11 March 2002, respectively. Also, 'Former ABB Bosses Face Criminal Investigation', from Swiss Radio International, 20 June 2001: www.swissinfo.ch.
12. See www.thecorporatelibrary.com.
13. GE Press releases: *Welch and GE Board to Modify Agreement*; *Jack Welch's Wall Street Journal Op/Ed*; *Statement from Jeff Immelt, GE Chairman and CEO*; and *GE Statement on SEC's request*, all dated 16 September 2002. Also Reuters article by Deepa Babington, 16 September 2002.
14. See, for example, 'The Lessons of Jack Welch's Outrageous Employment Contract', *The Economist*, 21 September 2002, p. 70; and 'Editorial – Courtside Tickets for Life', *New York Times*, 21 August 2002.
15. See Lucian A. Bebchuk, Jesse M. Fried and David I. Walker, *Executive Compensation in America: Optimal Contracting or Extraction of Rents?*, Harvard Law School, 2002.
16. See, for example, 'SEC Censures 2 Fund Managers for Inflating Stock Portfolios', *International Herald Tribune*, 13 August 2001, p. 9.
17. See 'More Wall Street Firms Targeted in IPO Probe', *The Wall Street Journal Europe*, 25 April 2002, pp. A1–A2.
18. See 'CSFB Fined' and 'Initial Public Offerings: Crime and Punishment', *The Economist*, 15 December 2001, and 26 January 2002 respectively.
19. SEC, *Commission Approves Rules to Address Analysts Conflicts*, (Washington, DC: SEC, 8 May 2002).

20. See, for example, Martin D. Weiss, *Crisis of Confidence on Wall Street – Brokerage Firm Abuses and the Worst Offenders*, (Washington, DC: National Press Club, 19 June 2002).
21. See, for example, 'Analyst Struggle to Repair their Damaged Reputation', *Financial Times*, 18–19 May 2002, p. 24.
22. 'Merrill's CEO Takes on a Crisis', and 'Merrill to Pay $100 Million in Deal with Prosecutors' in *The Wall Street Journal Europe*, 30 April 2002, p. M5, and 22 May 2002, p. A1 and A14, respectively.
23. See 'Class Notices', filed by Cohen, Milstein, Hausfeld and Toll, P.L.L.C., New York, 28 May and 11 June 2002, respectively.
24. Office of New York State Attorney General Eliot Spitzer, 'Spitzer, Merrill Lynch Reach Unprecented Agreement to Reform Investment Practices – Merrill Lynch to Pay $100 Million Penalty', Press release, 21 May 2002.
25. Testimony of Jack B. Grubman, US House Committee on Financial Services, *Hearing Regarding WorldCom*, Washington, DC, 8 July 2002.
26. 'New York Attorney General Targets Ebbers' and Others' IPO Profits', *Associated Press*, 30 September 2002.
27. See 'Jack Grubman's Platinum Parachute', Editorial, *The Washington Times*, 23 August 2002.
28. House Committee on Financial Services, *Oxley Releases New Citigroup Information: Millions of Gains by WorldCom Insiders*, Washington, DC, 30 August 2002.
29. See, for example, 'Initial Public Offerings – Did Wall Street Firms Bribe Bosses with Shares?', *The Economist*, 7 September 2002, p. 78.
30. Testimony of John C. Coffee – Professor of Law at Columbia University, before the US Senate Committee on Banking, Housing, and Urban Affairs, *Public Company Accounting Reform and Investor Act of 2002*, Washington, DC, 5 March 2002.
31. Press release by the SEC and the New York State Attorney General (20 December 2002, 3 p.); also 'The Wall Street Settlement-Unclean Slate', *The Economist*, 4 January 2003, p. 59; and US Senate Committee on Commerce, Science and Technology, *Hearing on Corporate Governance*, 'Testimony of Eliot Spitzer', Washington DC, 26 June 2002, 14 p.
32. See, for example, 'Conflicts of Interest in Finance', *The Economist*, 24 August 2002, pp. 12 and 53–5.
33. Goldman Sachs chairman, Henry M. Paulson, Press release, New York, 5 June 2002.
34. Press release dated 6 June 2002. Also 'Big Board Drafts a Plan to Restore Public Trust', *International Herald Tribune*, Paris, 3 June 2002, p. 9.
35. See, for example, 'A Premium for Good Governance', *The McKinsey Quarterly*, New York, 2002, no. 3, pp. 20–7.
36. See Report of the Comptroller General of the United States (David M. Walker) to the US Senate's Chairman of the Committee on Banking, Housing, and Urban Affairs (Paul S. Sarbanes), *Accounting Profession: Oversight, Auditor Independence, and Financial Reporting Issues*, (Washington, DC: US General Accounting Office, 3 May 2002).
37. See, for example, 'Wall Street Governance – Regulate Thyself', *The Economist*, 12 October 2002, p. 76.

38. See, for example, 'A Theory of Financial Exchange Organisation', *Journal of Law & Economics*, The University of Chicago, October 2000, pp. 437–71. See also US General Accounting Office, *Securities Markets – Competition and Multiple Regulators Heighten Concerns about Self-Regulation*, (Washington, DC, May 2002).
39. See 'Reforming Corporate Governance – In Search of Honesty', *The Economist*, 17 August 2002, pp. 49–51.
40. See, for example, 'European Securities Watchdogs Are Toothless', *The Wall Street Journal Europe*, 16–18 August 2002, pp. A1 and A8.

3 Prudential Regulatory Norms

1. See, for example, Martin Blåvarg and Patrick Nimander, 'Inter-bank Exposures and Systemic Risk', *Sveriges Riksbank Economic Review*, Stockholm, 2002, 2nd quarter, pp. 19–45.
2. Ibid., pp. 23–4.
3. See, for example, Sonja Daltung, 'The Relationship Between Price Stability and Financial Stability', *Sveriges Riksbank Economic Review*, Stockholm, 2001, 4th quarter, pp. 5–37.
4. See Charles Calomiris and Gary Gorton, 'The Origins of Banking Panics: Models, Facts, and Bank Regulation', in Glenn Hubbard (ed.), *Financial Markets and Financial Crises*, (University of Chicago Press, 1991), pp. 109–73.
5. See, for example, Anthony M. Santomero, president, Federal Reserve Bank of Philadelphia, 'Does Bank Regulation Help Bank Customers?', *Business Review*, Federal Reserve Bank of Philadelphia, 2002, 2nd quarter, pp. 1–6.
6. Originally sponsored by the G-10, the BCBS comprises in 2003, Belgium, Canada, France, Germany, Italy, Japan, Luxembourg*, the Netherlands, Spain*, Sweden, Switzerland*, United Kingdom and the USA (*subsequently became full members).
7. See Financial Stability Forum, *Issues Paper of the Task Force on Implementation of Standards*, Basel, 15 March 2000; also, Swiss Federal Banking Commission, *Management Report 2000*, Berne, pp. 170–5.
8. See, for example, Kate Langdon, 'Implementing International Standards for Stronger Financial Systems', *BIS Quarterly Review*, (Basel: Bank for International Settlements, March 2001), pp. 46–53.
9. See 'FSAP Provides a Framework for Identifying Financial Sector Vulnerabilities in Countries', *IMF Survey*, (Washington, DC: IMF, 5 March 2001), pp. 76–7.
10. The G-7 is an economic grouping of seven industrialized nations whose aim is to co-ordinate monetary, financial and fiscal policies to promote a more stable world economic system. It comprises: France, Germany, Japan, the United Kingdom, and the USA (Group of Five), plus Canada and Italy.
11. See Proceedings of the G-24 Workshop on *Coherence or Dissonance in the International Institutional Framework: A Shifting Paradigm*, held on 29–30 September 2000, (Vienna: The OPEC Fund for International Development, August 2001). The Intergovernmental Group of 24 on International Monetary Affairs (G-24) was established in 1971 to represent the interests of the developing countries in negotiations regarding international monetary matters.

12. 'Interview: Andrew Crockett', *The Financial Regulator*, vol. 6, no. 4, March 2002, p. 19.
13. See, for example, ECB, 'International Supervisory Co-operation', *Monthly Bulletin*, (Frankfurt: ECB, May 2002), pp. 55–66; also Shelagh Heffernan, *Modern Banking in Theory and Practice*, Chichester, England: John Wiley, 1996), pp. 271–2.
14. See, for example, National Bank of Belgium, *The Oversight Responsibilities of Central Banks According to the Core Principles for Systemically Important Payment Systems*, (Brussels, 2002), pp. 81–95.
15. See Zuhayr Mikdashi, (ed.), *Financial Intermediation in the 21st Century*, (Basingstoke: Palgrave/Macmillan, 2001), pp. 282 ff.; Gabriele Galati, 'Settlement Risk in Foreign Exchange Markets and CLS Bank', *BIS Quarterly Review*, Basel, December 2002, pp. 55–65; and ECB, 'CLS – Purpose, Concept and Implications', *Monthly Bulletin*, (Frankfurt: ECB, January 2003), pp. 53–66.
16. The BIS is the world's oldest international financial organization and meeting place, set up by central banks in 1930 to facilitate German reparations after the First World War. It currently performs the functions of promoter of central bank co-operation and provider of certain financial facilities. Its membership is selective and comprises the principal central banks of the world.
17. See 'Foreign Exchange: The Long, Dark Shadow of Herstatt', *The Economist*, 14, April 2001, pp. 78–9; and European Central Bank, *Annual Report 2001*, Frankfurt, pp. 128–9.
18. See ECB, 'The Role of the Eurosystem in Payment and Clearing Systems', *Monthly Bulletin*, Frankfurt, April 2002, pp. 47–59.
19. See, for example, US General Accounting Office, *Payment Systems – Central Bank Roles Vary, but Goals Are the Same*, Washington, DC, February 2002; and 'RTGS plus Successfully Established, *Deutsche Bundesbank Monthly Report*, Frankfurt, April 2002, pp. 57–70.
20. See, for example, A. Enge and B. Bakke, 'Risk in the Norwegian Settlement System 1995–2000', *Economic Bulletin* (Oslo: Norges Bank, April 2001), pp. 20–7; and 'Real-time Gross Settlement in Japan: An Evaluation of the First Six Months', *Quarterly Bulletin*, Bank of Japan, November 2001, pp. 132–49.
21. Blåvarg and Nimander, 'Inter-bank Exposures', p. 39 (see note 1 above).
22. See US General Accounting Office, *Information Systems – Opportunities Exist to Strengthen SEC's Oversight Capacity and Security*, Washington, DC, July 2001.
23. See, for example, Joseph E. Stiglitz, 'Principles of Financial Regulation: A Dynamic Portfolio Approach', *The World Bank Research Observer*, Spring 2001, pp. 1–18.
24. This point is developed by Alan Morrison (Oxford University) and Lucy White (Harvard Business School) in 'Crises and Capital Requirements in Banking', Working Paper, Oxford, February 2002.
25. See, for example, Ralph C. Kumball, 'Failures in Risk Management', *New England Economic Review*, Boston, Mass., January/February 2000, pp. 3–12.
26. More generally, the duration (or the average time of payment) on various categories of assets should reasonably match those of liabilities. This, along with hedging, will reduce the chance that adverse movements in interest rates lead to large losses.

27. See 'Credit Institutions' Capital Viewed from a Business and a Regulatory Perspective', *Monthly Report*, (Frankfurt: Deutsche Bundesbank, January 2002), pp. 39–57.
28. See, for example, 'Mortgage-lending Agencies in America', *The Economist*, 21 July 2001, pp. 61–2; 'Japan May Open Financial Sector', *Financial Times*, 2 August 2001, p. 4; and US General Accounting Office, *Federal Home Loan Bank System – Establishment of a New Capital Structure*, Washington, DC, 20 July 2001.
29. The OECD (Organization for Economic Co-operation and Development) at that time was a group of 24 countries. In 2003, they numbered 29 – mainly industrial, developed and market-orientated economies.
30. See Martin N. Baily, Diana Farell and Susan Leend, 'Hot Money', *McKinsey Quarterly*, New York, 2000, no. 2, pp. 108–19.
31. See, for example, P. Artzner, F. Delbaen, J.-M. Eber and D. Heath, 'Coherent Measures of Risk', *Mathematical Finance*, vol. 9, no. 3, 1999, pp. 203–28.
32. See, for example, William C. Hunter and Stephen D. Smith (eds), 'Risk Management in the Global Economy: Measurement, Management and Macroeconomic Implications, *Journal of Banking & Finance*, Special issue, vol. 26, 2002, pp. 303–74.
33. See, for example, I. Fender, M. S. Bibson and P. C. Mosset, 'An International Survey of Stress Tests', *Current Issues in Economics and Finance*, Federal Reserve Bank of New York, November 2001.
34. See, for example, Patricia Jackson, 'Bank Capital Standards: The New Basel Accord', *Quarterly Bulletin*, Bank of England, Spring 2001, pp. 55–63.
35. See, for example, Kathleen Beans, 'Regulators & Bankers Disagree on Proposed Disclosure Rules', *The RMA Journal*, (Philadelphia: The Risk management Association), September 2002, pp. 48–50.
36. See H. Benink and C. Wihlborg, 'The New Basel Capital Accord: Making it Effective with Stronger Market Discipline', *European Financial Management*, March 2002, pp. 103–15.
37. See, for example, Credit Suisse Group, *Annual Report 2001*, Zurich, pp. 42–63.
38. See BIS, 'The New Basel Accord: Comments Received on the Second Consultative Package', 21 August 2001.
39. See 'Credit-rating Agencies: New Interests, New Conflicts', *The Economist*, 14 April, 2001, pp. 72 and 77.
40. Leo O'Neil – president, Standard & Poor's (New York), *The Economist*, 2 February 2002, p. 18.
41. See Swiss Federal Banking Commission, *Management Report 2001*, Berne, pp. 252–6.
42. See 'The Evolution of Accounting Standards for Credit Institutions', *Deutsche Bundesbank Monthly Report*, Frankfurt, June 2002, pp. 39–54.
43. Ibid., p. 51.
44. See, for example, E. I. Altman, A. Resti and A. Sironi, *The Link between Default and Recovery Rates: Effects on the Procyclicality of Regulatory Capital Ratios*, BIS Working Papers, Basel, July 2002.
45. See, for example, Andrew Crockett, 'Market Discipline and Financial Stability', *Journal of Banking & Finance*, March 2002, pp. 977–87.
46. See, for example, Svein Gjerdrem, Governor, 'Is the Financial System Stable?', *Economic Bulletin*, Norges Bank, December 2001, pp. 127–33.

47. US Comptroller of the Currency, John D. Hawke, Jr, Press release, Washington, DC, 4 March 2002.

48. For example, Alan D. Morrison, *The Economics of Capital Regulation in Financial Conglomerates*, Working Paper, Oxford University, September 2002.

49. See Viral Acharya, Iftekhar Hasan and Anthony Saunders, *Should Banks Be Diversified? Evidence from Individual Bank Loan Portfolios*, BIS Working Paper, Basel, September 2002.

50. See, for example, 'Credit Institutions' Capital Viewed from a Business and a Regulatory Perspective', Deutsche Bundesbank (see note 27 above), pp. 37–57.

51. See, for example, Andrew Logan, *The United Kingdom's Small Banks' Crisis of the Early 1990s: What Were the Leading Indicators of Failure?*, Bank of England, Working Paper No. 139, London, July 2001.

52. Ibid.

53. To be contrasted with 'fair value', (i) which is equivalent to the market price under normal conditions, or (ii) in the absence of such a price, by the present value of expected cash flows.

54. See Jeremy Taylor, 'A Unified Approach to Credit Limit Setting', *The RMA Journal*, (Philadelphia: The Risk Management Association, July/August 2002), pp. 56–61 and 72.

55. See Jason Kofman, 'Capitalizing on Capital', *ERisk White Paper Series*, October 2001, New York.

56. See, for example, Joseph W. May, 'Watch Out for Those Collateral Constraints', *The RMA Journal*, Philadelphia: The Risk Management Association, June 2002, pp. 52–3.

57. See Dietrich Domanski and Uwe Neumann, 'Collateral in Wholesale Financial Markets', *BIS Quarterly Review*, Basel, September 2001, pp. 57–64.

58. See Ralph C. Kimball, 'Perils and Pitfalls in Risk Management', *Regional Review*, The Federal Reserve Bank of Boston, 2nd quarter, 2000, p. 5.

59. John D. Hawke, Jr, Comptroller of the Currency, *The Road to Basel II: Good Intentions and Imposing Challenges*, Washington, DC, 6 June 2002.

60. Ibid.

61. See, for example, Kostas Tsatsaronis, 'Special Feature: Hedge Funds', *BIS Quarterly Review*, Basel, November 2000, pp. 61–71.

62. US General Accounting Office, *Long Term Capital Management*, Washington, DC, October 1999, p. 12.

63. For more details, see: SFBC, *Jahresbericht* 1995, pp. 27 ff; and SFBC, *Bulletin* 30/1996.

64. Swiss Federal Banking Commission, as note 41 above, pp. 182 and 187.

65. See FSF, *Report of the Working Group on Highly Leveraged Institutions*, Basel, 5 April 2000.

66. For an investigative article, see Michael Schroeder and Greg Ip, 'Enron Spotlights a Gap in Laws: Energy Firm Lobbied Hard to Limit Oversight of Its Trading Operations', *The Wall Street Journal Europe*, 14–15 December 2001, pp. 11 and 16.

67. See, for example, William Poole, president and CEO of the Federal Reserve Bank of St. Louis, 'Financial Stability', *Review*, Federal Reserve Bank of St. Louis, September/October 2002, pp. 1–7.

4   Effective Supervision and Enforcement

1. For a comparative analysis of supervisory principles, see BCBS, *Core Principles – Cross Sectoral Comparison*, BIS, Basel, November 2001.
2. See BCBS, *Internal Audit in Banks and the Supervisor's Relationship with Auditors*, August 2001; also BCBS, *Internal Audit in Banks and the Supervisor's Relationship with Auditors: A Survey*, BIS, Basel, August 2002.
3. Several well established banks have been involved in various aspects of money laundering. For example – in relation to accepting illegal funds siphoned out by the family of the former military ruler of Nigeria Sani Abacha, estimated at US$2.2 billion, which found refuge mostly in British and Swiss banks – the Credit Suisse Group was fined in 2002 for negligence by Swiss regulators CHF 750 000 + 50 000 for administrative costs: I'*AGEFI*, Lausanne, 29 November 2002, p. 12.
4. Bank of England, *Report of the Board of Banking Supervision Inquiry into the Circumstances of the Collapse of Barings*, London, July 1995.
5. See 'AIB Chief Faces His Equivalent of Barings' Leeson', *Financial Times*, 24 February 2002, p. 16; also 'Allfirst's Foreign-exchange Losses', *The Economist*, 23 March 2002, p. 72.
6. BCBS, *The Relationship between Banking Supervisors and Banks' External Auditors*, BIS, Bank for International Settlements, Basel, January 2002.
7. See, for example, 'The Gaps in GAAP', *The Banker*, London, March 2002, pp. 20–1.
8. See, for example, 'CSFB Executives Were Directors of Enron Entity', *The Wall Street Journal Europe*, 8 April 2002, pp. M1–M5.
9. Senator Carl Levin, 'Senate Subcommittee Report Charges U.S. Financial Institutions with Aiding Enron Deceptions', Press Release, Washington, DC, 2 January 2003 (http://levin.senate.gov).
10. Remarks of Joseph F. Berardino, managing partner CEO, Andersen, US House of Representatives, Committee on Financial Services, 12 December 2001.
11. Ibid.
12. Filed at the US District Court, Southern District of Texas, 7 March 2002.
13. See Mark Kessel, 'Training Auditing Watchdogs to Bark', *Financial Times*, 21 December 2001, p. 12.
14. 'Auditors Still Offer Nonaudit Services', *The Wall Street Journal Europe*, 4 April 2002, pp. M1–M6.
15. See speech by Don Powell, chairman of the Federal Deposit Insurance Corporation (FDIC), Washington, DC, Press release, 11 March 2002.
16. See J. Carvana, A. Crockett, D. Flint, T. Haris and T. Jones, *Enron et al: Market Forces in Disarray*, Group of Thirty, Washington, DC, 2002, 54 p.
17. See, for example, 'SEC Censures 2 Fund Managers for Inflating Stock Portfolios', *International Herald Tribune*, 13 August 2001, p. 9.
18. See the World Bank, *World Development Report 2002*, Washington, DC, pp. 80–2.
19. See, for example, 'On-site Examination Policy in Fiscal 2001', *Quarterly Bulletin*, (Tokyo: Bank of Japan, May 2001), pp. 147–51; Bank of Japan, *Annual Review 2002*, (Tokyo, 2002), pp. 28–38; Japanese Bankers Association, *The Banking System in Japan*, (Tokyo, March 2001), pp. 1–12;

and 'Japan's Recent Monetary and Structural Policy Initiatives' in International Monetary Fund, *World Economic Outlook*, (Washington, DC: IMF, May 2001), pp. 19–20.

20. See 'Japanese Banks' Bad Loans', *The Economist*, 14 July 2001, p. 74.

21. See, for example, 'Turkey Must at Last Embark on Banking Reform', *Financial Times*, 28 June 2001.

22. See 'Regulators Delay Provisioning Rules', *Bangkok Post Business*, 9 January 2002, p. 1.

23. See, for example, Stuart I. Greenbaum and Anjan V. Thakor, *Contemporary Financial Intermediation*, (Orlando, Fl: Dryden Press, 1995), p. 66.

24. *An Examination of the Banking Crises of the 1980s and Early 1990s*, (as in note 11 of Chapter 1), p. 208.

25. See 'Bank Scandal Cost French Taxpayers over euro 11 bn', *Financial Times*, 8 June 2001, p. 3.

26. Financial Service Agency, quoted by Japanese Bankers Association, see note 16 above, pp. 10 and 13.

27. See, for example, BIS, *72nd Annual Report*, Basel, 8 July 2002, pp. 133–6.

28. Ref. 'Japan's Nonperforming Loan Problem', *Quarterly Bulletin*, Bank of Japan, Tokyo, November 2002, p. 97–108.

29. Anil K. Kashyap, 'Sorting out Japan's financial crisis', *Economic Perspectives*, Federal Reserve Bank of Chicago, 2002, 4th quarter p. 42–55.

30. See 'Discussants Weigh Impact of Foreign Participation in Financial Systems of Developing Countries', *IMF Survey* (Washington, DC: IMF, 21 May 2001), pp. 173–5; and J. S. Crystal, B. G Dages and L. S. Goldberg, 'Has Foreign Bank Entry Led to Sounder Banks in Latin America?,' *Current Issues in Economics and Finance*, Federal Reserve Bank of New York, January 2002.

31. See C. W. Calomiris and R. E. Litan, 'Financial Regulation in a Global Marketplace', *Brookings – Wharton Papers on Financial Services*, Washington, DC, 2000, pp. 283–339.

32. Swiss Federal Banking Commission, *Rapport de gestion 2000*, Berne, pp. 185–6 and 194–6.

33. Institute of International Bankers, *Global Survey 2002 – Regulatory and Market Developments, Banking – Securities – Insurance*, New York, September 2002.

34. In general, Tier 1 capital is the sum of a banking institution's common stockholders' equity (as defined in the agencies' regulatory capital standards), non-cumulative perpetual preferred stock, and minority interests in consolidated subsidiaries, less goodwill and other intangible assets (other than limited amounts of servicing assets and purchased credit card relationships), and less disallowed deferred tax assets and disallowed credit-enhancing interest-only strips.

35. Federal Financial Institution Examination Council, *Bank Reports – Proposed Collection of Data on Subprime Consumer Lending Programs*. Washington, DC, 28 July 2002.

36. See R. A. Gilbert, A. P. Meyer and M. D. Vaughan, 'Could a CAMELS Downgrade Model Improve Off-Site Surveillance?, *Review*, Federal Reserve Bank of St. Louis, January/February 2002, pp. 47–63; and BCBS, *Supervisory Guidance on Dealing with Weak Banks*, BIS, March 2002.

37. *World Development Report 2002*, (see note 18 above) pp. 79–84.

38. One senior bank supervisor's rule-of-thumb is 'any bank which has doubled its loans book in three years will fail during the next three years'; see John Hawkins and Philip Turner, 'International Financial Reform: Regulatory and Other Issues', in S. Claessens and K. J. Forbes (eds), *International Financial Contagion,* (Boston: Kluwer, 2001), pp. 431–60.

39. For a survey of such models, see Ranjana Sahajwala and Paul Van den Bergh, *Supervisory Risk Assessment and Early Warning Systems,* (Basel: BIS, December 2000).

40. See, for example, J. W. Gunther, M. E. Levonian and R. R. Moore, 'Can the Stock Market Tell Bank Supervisors Anything They Don't Already Know?', *Economic and Financial Review,* Federal Reserve Bank of Dallas, 2001, 2nd quarter, pp. 2–9.

41. Ancient Roman adage: *'Who will police the policemen'*?

42. See, for example, J. McAndrews and C. Stefanandis, 'The Consolidation of European Stock Exchanges', *Current Issues,* Federal Reserve Bank of New York, June 2002.

43. Calomiris and Litan, as note 31 above, pp. 301–2.

44. Ibid.; see also *World Development Report 2002,* as in note 18 above, p. 79–84.

45. Statement before the New York State Department of Banking, 15 October 2001.

46. John D. Hawke, Jr, Comptroller of the Currency, 'Fee Disparity Problem Must be Fixed', Washington, DC, 9 May 2002.

47. See Donald E. Powell, chairman of FDIC, *Why Regulatory Restructuring? Why Now?,* Washington, DC, 16 October 2002.

48. See, for example, Andrew Crockett, BIS, *Issues in Global Financial Supervision,* 36th South East Asian Central Banks' Governors' Conference, Singapore, 1 June 2002.

49. John D. Hawke, Jr, Comptroller of the Currency, 'Fee Disparity Problem Must be Fixed', Washington, DC, 9 May 2002.

50. See US General Accounting Office, *Bank Regulation – Analysis of the Failure of Superior Bank,* (Thomas J. McCool), Washington, DC, 7 February 2002.

51. Prepared statement of Jeffrey Rush, Inspector General of the Department of the Treasury, Testimony, *Hearing on Analysis of the Failure of Superior Bank,* FSB, Illinois, US Senate Committee on Banking, Housing, and Urban Affairs, Washington, DC, 7 February 2002.

52. Statement of Gaston L. Gianni, Inspector General, FDIC, 7 February 2002, – prepared for the above-mentioned Hearing, (see note 51 above).

53. Ibid.

54. See, for example, Pierluigi Ciocca, 'Supervision: One or More Institutions', *Economic Bulletin,* Bank of Italy, Rome, October 2001, pp. 113–16.

55. Board of Governors of the Federal Reserve System, *Improving Public Disclosure in Banking,* Study Group on Disclosure, Washington, DC, March 2000.

56. See, for example, Patrick Donnelly, 'What Every Audit Committee Member Should Know', *The RMA Journal,* (Philadelphia: The Risk Management Association, September 2001), pp. 48–51.

57. See 'When the Numbers Don't Add Up', *The Economist,* 9 February 2002, pp. 62–4.

58. See, for example, Claudio Borio and Philip Lowe, 'To Provision or Not to Provision', *BIS Quarterly Review,* September 2001, pp. 35–48.

59. See, for example, 'Accounting – Shining a Light on Company Accounts', *The Economist*, 18 August 2001, pp. 55–6.
60. See, for example, 'Wall Street Banks Draw Up Code of Conduct for Analysts', *Financial Times*, 21 May 2001, p. 1.
61. See, for example, Charles W. Calomiris and Joseph R. Mason, 'Contagion Bank Failures During the Great Depression: The June 1932 Chicago Banking Panic', *American Economic Review*, December 1997, pp. 863–8; and Diane S. Docking, Mark Hirschey and Elaine Jones, 'Information and Contagion Effects of Bank Loan-Loss Announcements', *Journal of Financial Economics*, February 1997, pp. 219–39.
62. See, for example, Andrew Crockett, BIS, *Market Discipline and Financial Stability*, Banks and Systemic Risk Conference, Bank of England, London, 23–25 May 2001.
63. See Robert M. Hunt, 'What's in the File? The Economics and Law of Consumer Credit Bureaus [*sic*]', *Business Review*, Federal Reserve Bank of Philadelphia, 2nd quarter, 2002, pp. 17–24.
64. See, for example, *World Development Report 2002*, as note 18 above, pp. 94–6.
65. See FDIC, Press release, 5 October 2001, *Syndicated Banks Loans in 2001*.
66. See, for example, 'Investment Banking under Fire – Capitulate or Die', *The Economist*, 5 October 2002, pp. 79–80; and 'Prosecutors in France Get Tough with Bankers', *The Wall Street Journal Europe*, 13 February 2002, pp. A1 and A8.
67. 'Whistleblowing – Peep and Weep' and 'Christine Casey: Whistleblower', *The Economist*, 12 January 2002, and 18 January 2003, pp. 61–2. and p. 66, respectively.
68. See 'FDIC Chairman Appoints Contrell L. Webster as Agency's Ombudsman', Press release, (Washington, DC: FDIC, 28 June 2002).
69. Financial Ombudsman Service, *Annual Review*, 13 June 2002.
70. See, for example, Swiss Banking Ombudsman, *Annual Report 2001*, Basel, 2002.
71. Bert Ely's testimony, 'The Failure of Superior Bank, FSB', Hearing of the Senate Committee on Banking, Housing, and Urban Affairs, Washington, DC, 11 September 2001.
72. Ibid.; also Bert Ely, 'Regulatory Moral Hazard: The Real Moral Hazard in Federal Deposit Insurance', *The Independent Review*, Oakland, Calif., 1999, pp. 241–54.

5 Financial Safety Nets

1. For a brief synopsis of recent crisis situations that had a potential of systemic problems, see Arturo Estrella, 'Dealing with Financial Instability: The Central Bank's Tool Kit', *Sveriges Riksbank Economic Review*, Stockholm, 2001, 2nd quarter, pp. 34–49.
2. See Bank for International Settlements, *10th Annual Report*, Basel, 5 June 2000, p. 139.
3. See FSCS, *Annual Report and Accounts: 2001/02*, London, pp. 6–7; and Suzanne McCarthy, chief executive, FSCS, 'Key Elements of a Continuous Improvement Process', International Conference on Deposit Insurance, Basel, 24 October 2001.
4. See *Finance for Growth* (see note 4 of Chapter 1), p. 106.

5. John D. Hawke, Jr, US Comptroller of the Currency, 'Remarks Before the New York State Department of Banking', 15 October 2001.
6. See Eugene White, *Deposit Insurance*, World Bank Policy Research Working Paper, Washington, DC, November 1995.
7. Ibid.
8. Reserve Bank of New Zealand: www.rbnz.govt.nz.
9. See *Finance for Growth: Policy Choices in a Volatile World*, (Oxford University Press, 2001), p. 13; Luc Laeven, *Pricing Deposit Insurance*, World Bank Policy Research Working Paper, July 2002; J. R. Barth, G. Caprio and R. Levine, *Bank Regulation and Supervision: What Works Best*, World Bank Policy Research Working Paper, December 2001; and Eugene White, *Deposit Insurance* (see Note 6 above).
10. See, for example, 'Depositor Protection and Investor Compensation in Germany', *Deutsche Bundesbank Monthly Report*, Frankfurt, July 2000, pp. 29–45.
11. See *Viewpoints of the FDIC and Select Industry Experts on Deposit Insurance Reform* (hereafter *Deposit Insurance Reform*), Hearing before the Subcommittee on Financial Institutions and Consumer Credit of the Committee on Financial Services, US House of Representatives, 17 October 2001, (Washington, DC: US Government Printing Office, 2001), p. 3.
12. See Luis Javier Garcia Macarron, director general, Sociedad Gestora de Los Fondos de Garantía de Depositos en Entidades de Credito, *Premium Assessment*, International Conference on Deposit Insurance, BIS, 24 October 2001.
13. Maxine Waters in: *Deposit Insurance Reform* (see note 11 above), p. 13.
14. Statement of Donald E. Powell, chairman of FDIC, in: *Deposit Insurance Reform* (see note 11 above), pp. 30–44.
15. See, for example, Kenneth H. Thomas, University of Pennsylvania's Wharton School, testimony in *Deposit Insurance Reform* (see note 11 above), pp. 67–96.
16. Ibid., pp. 83–4.
17. Blåvarg and Nimander (as note 1, page 203), p. 23.
18. *World Development Report 1999/2000*, (see note 16 of Chapter 1), p. 76.
19. Lars Frisell and Martin Noréus, 'Consolidation in the Swedish Banking Sector: A Central Bank Perspective', *Sveriges Riksbank Economic Review*, Stockholm, 2002, 3rd quarter, pp. 20–38.
20. Group of Ten, *Report on Consolidation in the Financial Sector*, BIS, January 2001.
21. Frisell and Noréus, as note 19 above.
22. K. H. Thomas' Testimony (see note 15 above), p. 75.
23. See, for example, Michael Wolgast, 'M&As in the Financial Industry – A Matter of Concern for Bank Supervisors?', *Bulletin*, (Frankfurt: Deutsche Bank Research, 5 June 2001), pp. 25–34.
24. See *World Development Report 2002*, p. 88 (see note 18, p. 206).
25. See Lisa M. De Ferrari and David E. Palmer, 'Supervision of Large Complex Banking Organizations', *Federal Reserve Bulletin*, Washington, DC, February 2001, pp. 47–57.
26. This is the case with the supervisory authorities in Switzerland; *L'AGEFI*, Lausanne, 27 April 2001, p. 3.
27. See CDIC, *Annual Report 2000/2001*, pp. 5–8.

28. FDIC, Rosalind L. Bennett, 'Failure Resolution and Asset Liquidation: Results of an International Survey of Deposit Insurers', *FDIC Banking Review*, Washington, DC, vol. 14, no. 1, 2001, pp. 1–28.
29. See, for example, A. George Kaufman and Steven A. Seeling, 'Post-resolution Treatment of Depositors at Failed Banks: Systemic Risk, and Too Big to Fail', *Economic Perspectives*, 2002, 2nd quarter, pp. 27–41.
30. See, for example, Timothy Curry and Lynn Shibut, 'The Cost of the Savings and Loan Crisis: Truth and Consequences', *FDIC Banking Review*, Washington, DC, 2000, vol. 13, no. 2, pp. 26–35.
31. See RBA Holding, *Poursuite de l'évolution stratégique sur un fondement solide*, Berne, April 2002.
32. For further details, see Joseph Yung, *From Schweizrische Kreditanstalt to Credit Suisse Group – The History of a Bank, Credit Suisse Group.* (Zurich: NZZ Verlag, 2000), pp. 257–63.
33. See John S. Jordan, 'Depositor Discipline at Failing Banks', *New England Economic Review*, Federal Reserve Bank of Boston, March/April 2000, pp. 15–28.
34. See, for example, R. D. Eisenbeis and L. D. Wall, 'Reforming Deposit Insurance and FDICIA', *Economic Review*, Federal Reserve Bank of Atlanta, 2002, 1st quarter, pp. 1–16.
35. See Japanese Bankers' Association, *Japanese Banks 2001*, May 2001, p. 14; and Bank of Japan, *Annual Review 2001*, Tokyo, 2001, p. 77.
36. See Japanese Bankers' Association, *Japanese Banks 2002*, Tokyo, 2002, p. 13.
37. See, for example, FDIC, *Deposit Insurance Options Paper*, Washington, DC, August 2000.
38. For a succinct review of the literature on this subject, see, for example, João A. C. Santos, *Bank Capital Regulation in Contemporary Banking Theory: A Review of the Literature* (Basel: BIS, September 2000).
39. See FDIC, *Annual Report 2000*, Washington, DC, pp. 2–12.
40. See Ron Feldman and Mark Levonian, 'Market Data and Bank Supervision: The Transition to Practical Use', *The Region*, Federal Reserve Bank of Minneapolis, September 2001, pp. 11–13 and 46–53.
41. See Eugène Fama, 'Efficient Capital Markets: A Review of Theory and Empirical Work', *Journal of Finance*, May 1970.
42. See FDIC, *Financial Education in Underserved Communities*, Press release, Washington, DC, 13 June 2002.
43. See *FDIC's 'Money Smart' Financial Education Program to Aid Victims of Predatory Lending in East Palo Alto and Menlo Park*, FDIC Press release, Washington, DC, 28 August 2002.
44. See, for example, FSCS, *Annual Report 2001/02*; and FSA, *Annual Report*, 2001/02.
45. Kaufman and Seeling, (see note 29 above).
46. See Institute of International Bankers, *Global Survey 2002 – Regulatory and Market Developments, Banking – Securities – Insurance*, New York, September 2002, pp. 25–6; 'Argentina's Economy – Defaulter of Last Resort', *The Economist*, 8 March 2003, pp. 54 and 55.
47. See Marco del Negro and Stephen J. Kay, 'Global Banks, Local Crises: Bad News from Argentina', *Economic Review*, Federal Reserve Bank of Atlanta, 2002, 3rd quarter, pp. 89–106.

48. See *Convention relative à la protection des déposants en cas de liquidation forcée d'une banque*, dated 1 July 1993.

49. Swiss Federal Ministry of Finance, *Assainissement et liquidation de banques, protection des déposants*, October 2000.

50. See *Finance for Growth*, (see note 4 of Chapter 1), pp. 13–14, and 104–19.

51. *World Development Report 2002*, (see note 18, p. 206), p. 80.

52. See also Financial Stability Forum (FSF), *Guidance for Developing Effective Deposit Insurance Systems*, Basel, September 2001; and G. Garcia, *Protecting Bank Deposits*, (Washington, DC: IMF, July 1997).

53. See US General Accounting Office, *Securities Investor Protection – Steps Needed to Better Disclose SPIC Policies to Investors*, Washington, DC, May 2002; and 'Millions in US Believe Their Losses Will Be Covered', *Financial Times*, London, 2 August 2001, p. 5.

54. Hans-Jörg Rudloff, cited in 'Investment Banks – Living in Leaner Times', *The Economist*, 4 August 2001, pp. 57–8.

55. See, for example, 'Hard Sell', *Financial Times*, 2 August 2001, p. 10.

56. See, for example, 'Women Robbing Women: A New Pyramid Scheme Has Cost Thousands of British Women Their Hard-earned Savings', *Newsweek*, 13 August 2001, p. 48.

57. See, for example, 'Our Columnist Confesses His Sin', *The Wall Street Journal Europe*, 10–11 August 2001, p. 9.

58. See William R. White, *Recent Initiatives to Improve the Regulation and Supervision of Private Capital Flows*, (Basel: BIS, October 2000).

59. GAO, *Securities Investor Protection – Steps Needed to Better Disclose SIPC Policies to Investors*, Washington, DC, May 2001, p. 69.

60. SIPC, *Annual Report 2000*; and Media Center (www.sipc.org).

61. See, 'Unit Trust of India – To the Rescue, Once More', *The Economist*, 7 September 2002, p. 79.

62. See, for example, C. Enoch, G. Garcia and V. Sundararajan, 'Recapitalizing Banks with Public Funds', *IMF Staff Papers*, vol. 48, issue 1, Washington, DC, 2001, pp. 58–110.

63. See E. Barandiaran and L. Hernández, *Origins and Resolution of a Banking Crisis: Chile 1982–86*, Central Bank of Chile, December 1999, Working Paper No. 57.

64. 'More Bubble and Squeak', *The Economist*, 20 April 2002, p. 80; and 'Central Bank They Deserve', *Financial Times*, 18–19 May 2002, p. 6.

65. Alan Greenspan, *The Challenge of Central Banking in a Democratic Society*, (Washington, DC: American Enterprise Institute for Public Policy Research), 5 December 1996.

66. See, for example, Philip Lowe, 'Maintaining Financial Stability: Possible Policy Options', *Sveriges Riksbank Economic Review*, Stockholm, 2001, 2nd quarter, pp. 25–33.

67. See National Bank of Belgium, *Financial Stability Review*, Brussels, 2002, issue no. 1, p. 5.

68. See, for example, Claudio Borio and Philip Lowe, *Asset Prices, Financial and Monetary Stability: Exploring the Nexus*, Basel: BIS Working Papers, July 2002.

69. Alan Greenspan, *Economic Volatility Symposium*, sponsored by the Federal Reserve Bank of Kansas City, 30 August 2002.

70. See 'To Burst or Not to Burst', *The Economist*, 7 September 2002, p. 80.

71. *The Economist*, 21 September 2002, p. 18.

72. See Groupe Caisse des Dépôts, 'Political Risk: A Component of Country Risk', *Lettre Economique de la CDC*, Paris, April 2002, pp. 4–6.
73. For calculation of premiums, see, for example: ERG, *Swiss Export Risk Guarantee Agency*, (Zurich: ERG, April 2002).
74. See MIGA, *Annual Reports*.
75. See 'Lloyd's to Offer Companies War Protection', *Financial Times*, 28 May 2001, p. 6.
76. See, for example, 'Terrorism and Insurance – Risk's New Dimension', *The Economist*, 29 September 2001, p. 82; and 'Terrorist Insurance', *The Economist*, 12 January 2002, p. 72.
77. See, for example, US General Accounting Office, *Disaster Assistance*, Washington, DC, August 2001.
78. *IMF Survey*, Washington, DC, 12 November 2001, p. 334.
79. See, for example, Ron J. Feldman, 'Mortgage Rates, Homeownership Rates, and Government-Sponsored Enterprises', *The Region*, Federal Reserve Bank of Minneapolis, Annual Report 2001, vol. 16, no. 1, pp. 5–23.
80. See William Poole (see note 67 of Chapter 3) *Review*, Federal Reserve Bank of St. Louis, September/October 2002, pp. 1–7.
81. See Bert Ely, *The Federal Financial Sector Safety Net: An Overview of the Issues*, (Washington, DC: The Financial Services Roundtable, March 2001). The Financing Corporation was established by Congress in 1987 to recapitalize the insolvent Federal Savings and Loan Insurance Corporation by raising private funds through bonds issues, to be reimbursed by the FHLB System and deposit insurance premiums.
82. GAO, *Government-Sponsored Enterprises – The Government Exposure to Risks*, Washington, DC, August 1990, p. 143.
83. James A. Brickley and Peter C. Meyers, presidents and CEOs of Federal Farm Credit Banks Funding Corporations, and of the Farm Credit Council, respectively, (see preceeding note for source).
84. FHLB, for example, issues short-term securities (360 days or less) exempt from state and local income tax for domestic investors. The FHLB system is the largest issuer of these notes (US$978 billion in 2001).
85. See W. S. Frame and L. D. Wall, 'Financing Housing through Government-Sponsored Enterprises' and 'Fannie Mae's and Freddie Mac's Voluntary Initiatives: Lessons from Banking', *Economic Review*, Federal Reserve Bank of Atlanta, 2002, 1st quarter, pp. 29–59; and 'Fannie Mae and Freddie Mac – Mortgage Myopia', *The Economist*, 20 July 2002, pp. 62–3.
86. See 'Spanish Saving Banks', *The Economist*, 11 May 2002, pp. 76 and 78.
87. See 'The Riksbanks's Opinion on the Report "Public Administration of Banks in Distress" ', *Sveriges Riksbank Economic Review*, Stockholm, 2000, 1st quarter, p. 70.

6   In Search of Financial Stability

1. See, for example, David D. Driscoll, *The IMF and the World Bank – How Do They Differ?*, (Washington, DC: IMF), August 1996.
2. See, for example, 'Cross-border Capital Movements and the Role of the International Monetary Fund', *Deutsche Bundesbank Monthly Report*, Frankfurt, July 2001, pp. 15–30.

3. See Guillermo Ortiz, governor, Banco de Mexico, *Recent Emerging Market Crises – What We Learned?*, Per Jacobson Lecture, Basel, 7 July 2002.
4. Independent Evaluation Office (IEO) of the IMF, *Statement*, 7 February 2002. David Goldsbrough, Kevin Barnes, Isabelle Mateos y Lago, and Tsidi Tsikata, 'Prolonged Use of IMF Loans – How Much of a Problem Is It?' *Finance & Development*, IMF, Washington, DC, December 2002, pp. 34–7.
5. The IMF supports low-income countries – defined to comprise those with a GDP per capita of less than US$885 (77 countries in 2001) – through the Poverty Reduction and Growth Facility, established in 1999. Annual charges are 0.5 per cent, and repayments are made semi-annually, beginning at five-and-a-half years until the tenth year after the disbursement. The maximum a country can borrow under this facility is generally 140 per cent of its IMF quota. See IMF Factsheet, The IMF's *Poverty Reduction Facility*, Washington, DC, March 2001.
6. See, for example, M. Ahmed, T. Lane and M. Schulze-Ghattas, 'Refocusing IMF Conditionality', *Finance & Development* (Washington, DC: IMF, December 2001), pp. 40–3.
7. Guillermo Ortiz, see note 3 above.
8. See, for example, 'The IMF and the World Bank – Bribing Allies', *The Economist*, 29 September 2001, p. 85.
9. In May 2003, one Special Drawing Right (SDR) was equal to about US$1.43. The SDR is an international reserve asset, created by the IMF to meet the need to supplement global liquidity. It is potentially a claim on the freely usable currencies of IMF members. Its value is based on four currencies used in international transactions (US dollar, 45 per cent; euro, 29 per cent; Japanese yen 15 per cent; and pound sterling, 11 per cent).
10. IMF, *Annual Report 2001*, p. 63.
11. 'Le Monde sans Michel', *The Economist*, 13 November 1999, pp. 89–90.
12. See, for example, Stanley Fischer's interview in: *IMF Survey*, Washington, DC, 3 September 2001, p. 278.
13. US General Accounting Office, *Mexico's Financial Crisis – Origins, Awareness, Assistance and Initial Efforts to Recover*, Washington, DC, February 1996.
14. *IMF Survey*, Washington, DC, 27 February 1995, p. 53.
15. For a detailed analysis, see Michael Bowe and James W. Dean, *Has the Market Solved the Sovereign-Debt Crisis?*, Princeton Studies in International Finance, Princeton University, NJ, August 1997.
16. See *An Examination of the Banking Crises of the 1980s and Early 1990s*, p. 209, (see note 11 of Chapter 1) .
17. IMF Public Information Notice, 'IMF concludes Article IV Consultation with Ecuador', 7 September 2000.
18. See, for example, US General Accounting Office, *International Financial Crises, Efforts to Anticipate, Avoid and Resolve Sovereign Crises*, Washington, DC, 7 July 1997.
19. See Charles W. Calomiris, Columbia University, 'The IMF's Imprudent Role as Lender of Last Resort', *The Cato Journal*, vol. 17, no. 3, 1998.
20. See Xiaoming Alan Zhang, *Testing for 'Moral Hazard' in Emerging Market Lending*, (Washington, DC: Institute of International Finance, August 1999).
21. See Timothy Lane and Steven Phillips, *Moral Hazard – Does IMF Financing Encourage Imprudence by Borrowers and Lenders?*, (Washington, DC: IMF, March 2002).

22. See Kenneth S. Rogoff, 'Moral Hazard in IMF Loans – How Big a Concern?', *Finance & Development*, (Washington, DC: IMF, September 2002), pp. 56–7.
23. See, for example, Corrine Ho, 'A Survey of the Institutional and Operational Aspects of Modern-day Currency Boards', *BIS Working Papers*, March 2002.
24. See, for example, W. C. Gruben and J. H. Welch, 'Banking Currency Crisis Recovery: Brazil's Turnaround of 1999', *Economic & Financial Review*, 2001, 4th quarter, Federal Reserve Bank of Dallas, pp. 12–23.
25. See also Anne Krueger, first deputy managing director, IMF, 'Crisis Prevention and Resolution: Lessons from Argentina', National Bureau of Economic Research, *Conference on the Argentina Crisis*, Cambridge, Mass., 17 July 2002.
26. M. Quispe-Agnoli and S. Kay, 'Argentina: The End of Convertibility', *EconSouth*, Federal Reserve Bank of Atlanta, 2002, 1st quarter, pp. 14–19.
27. See Emanuele Baldacci, Luiz de Mello and Gabriela Inchauste, 'Financial Crises, Poverty, and Income Distribution'; and Martin Ravallion, 'An Automatic Safety Net?', in *Finance & Development*, (Washington, DC: IMF, June 2002), pp. 21–3, and 24–7 respectively.
28. OECD, *Agricultural Policies in OECD Countries – Monitoring and Evaluation 2002, Highlights*, Paris p. 51; also cited by Hans Peter Lankes, 'Market Access for Developing Countries', *Finance & Development*, (Washington, DC: IMF, September 2002), pp. 8–13.
29. See, for example, 'Argentina joins Brazil in WTO appeal vs. US agricultural subsidies', Reuters Press release, 23 May 2002.
30. US Mission, Geneva, *Administration Unveils Comprehensive US Trade Proposal to Expand American Farmers' Access to Overseas Markets*, Press release, 25 July 2002; also *Le Temps*, Geneva, 7 September 2002, p. 28.
31. Created in the mid-1980s to promote free and fair trading in agricultural products, with 17 producing member countries: Argentina, Australia, Bolivia, Brazil, Canada, Chile, Colombia, Costa Rica, Guatemala, Indonesia, Malaysia, New Zealand, Paraguay, The Philippines, South Africa, Thailand and Uruguay.
32. 'US Farm bill called "immoral" ', *International Herald Tribune*, 16 May 2002, p. 13.
33. In his opening remarks at the International Conference on Poverty Reduction Strategies, Washington, DC, 14 January 2002. For a detailed study, see the study prepared by the staff of the IMF and the World Bank under the direction of Timothy Geithner and Gobind Nankani, *Market Access for Developing Country Exports – Selected Issues*, Washington, DC, 26 September 2002.
34. See Timothy Lane and Steven Phillips, 'Does the IMF Financing Result in Moral Hazard?', IMF Working Paper 2000/168.
35. Michael Mussa, *Argentina and the Fund: From Triumph to Tragedy*. (Washington, DC: Institute for International Economics, 25 March 2002), p. 3; also analyses and data by several specialists are available in *Argentina's Economic Meltdown: Causes and Remedies*, Hearings before the Subcommittee on International Monetary Policy and Trade of the Committee on Financial Services, US House of Representatives, 6 February and 5 March 2002, Washington, DC.
36. 'Public's View Sought on Study of Fiscal Adjustment in IMF Programs', *IMF Survey*, Washington, DC, 8 April 2002, p. 100; and IMF's Independent Evaluation Office, *Fiscal Adjustment in IMF-Supported Programs*, 28 March 2003, Washington, DC.

37. Horst Köhler, 'Reform of the International Financial Architecture: A Work in Progress', *Central Bank Governors' Symposium*, Bank of England, London, 5 July 2002 (bold text in the original).
38. See, for example, the book by the World Bank's former chief economist, Joseph Stiglitz, *Globalization and Its Discontents*, (New York: W. W. Norton June 2002).
39. IMF's economic counsellor and director of research, Kenneth Rogoff, 'An Open Letter', *IMF Survey*, Washington, DC, 8 July 2002, pp. 209–11.
40. This extreme position was taken by B. T. Johnson and B. D. Schaefer, *The International Monetary Fund: Outdated, Ineffective, and Unnecessary*, (Washington, DC: The Heritage Foundation, 6 May 1997).
41. See Thomas C. Dawson, director of the IMF External Relations Department, 'The Way Ahead', *Far Eastern Economic Review*, Hong Kong, 25 July 2002.
42. An ex-governor of the Central Bank of Venezuela recommends notably, sound public policies, transparency, effective prudential regulation, and debtor/creditor cost sharing: Ruth de Krivoy, 'Financial Crises and the Private Sector: Reducing Moral Hazard', Proceedings of a Workshop of the G-24, held in New York, 6–7 September 2002, published by the OPEC Fund, Vienna, August 2002, pp. 169–89.
43. Mostly through the Poverty Reduction and Growth Facility.
44. John B. Taylor, under-secretary for international affairs, Department of the Treasury, *Hearings on 'Argentina's Economic Crisis'*, US Senate Committee on Banking, Housing and Urban Affairs, Subcommittee on International Trade and Finance, Washington, DC, 28 February 2002.
45. Andrew Berg and Catherine Patillo, 'The Challenge of Predicting Economic Crises', *International Monetary Fund*, Washington, DC, July 2000.
46. Aziz et al., (see note 6 in Chapter 1).
47. Staffan Viotti, 'Dealing with Banking Crises – Proposal for a New Regulatory Framework', *Sveriges Riksbank Economic Review*, Stockholm, 2002, 3rd quarter, p. 30.
48. See 'Early Warning Systems: Fad or Reality', *IMF Survey*, Washington DC, 12 November 2001, pp. 347–8.
49. R. Dornbusch, Y. C. Park and S. Claessens, 'Contagion: How It Spreads and How It Can Be Stopped', *World Bank Research Observer*, Washington DC, 2000.
50. Thomas D. Willet, 'International Financial Markets as Sources of Crises or Discipline: The Too Much, Too Late Hypothesis', *Essays in International Finance*, (Princeton, NJ: Princeton University, May 2000).
51. IMF, *External Evaluation of IMF Surveillance*, Report of a group of independent experts, Washington, DC, p. 56, cited by Goldstein, p. 7,(note 14 of Chapter 1).
52. See, for example, 'Indonesia and the IMF – Twisting in the Wind', *The Economist*, 21 April, 2001, p. 80.
53. Ibid., p. 110.
54. IMF, *Survey Supplement*, Washington, DC, September 2001, pp. 7–8.
55. IMF, *Annual Report 2002*, Washington, DC, p. 29.
56. See also Hawkins and Turner, (see note 38 of Chapter 4).
57. Marten Blix, Joachim Wadefjord, Ulrika Wienecke and Martin Adahl, 'How Good is the Forecasting Performance of Major Institutions', *Sveriges Riksbank Economic Review*, Stockholm, 2001, 3rd quarter, pp. 38–68.

58. See, for example, Paolo Presenti and Cédric Tille, 'The Economics of Currency Crisis and Contagion: An Introduction', *Economic Policy Review*, Federal Reserve Bank of New York, September 2000, pp. 3–16.

59. Trond Eklund, Kari Larsen and Eivind Berhardsen, 'Model for Analysing Credit Risk in the Enterprise Sector', *Economic Bulletin*, Norges Bank, Oslo, October 2001, p. 104.

60. See, for example, 'The Role of the International Monetary Fund in a Changing Global Economic Environment', *Monthly Report*, Frankfurt: Deutsche Bundesbank, September 2000), pp. 15–43.

61. Horst Köhler, Statement to the International Monetary and Financial Committee, Washington, DC, 29 April 2001.

62. Adam Lerrick, 'Sovereign Debt Crises – It's a Repeat Game', *Euromoney*, London, March 2001, pp. 102–5.

63. European Central Bank, *Annual Report 2000*, Frankfurt, May 2001, p. 105.

64. For details, see 'Recent Developments in International Co-operation', *Monthly Bulletin*, European Central Bank, February 2002, pp. 53–65.

65. Stanley Fischer, *On the Need for an International Lender of Last Resort*, Essays in International Economics, Princeton University, November 2000; and 'Fisher Outlines Role for the IMF's Improved Contingent Credit Lines Facility', *IMF Survey*, 11 December 2000, pp. 389–90.

66. See 'Reserves Should Be Adequate to Reflect Increase in Capital Account Flows, Need for Crisis Prevention', *IMF Survey*, Washington, DC, 19 February 2001, pp. 66–8.

67. Köhler, 5 July 2002, See note 61 above.

68. The FSF comprises currently representatives from the G-7 (Canada, France, Germany, Italy, Japan, United Kingdom, and the USA) to which have been added four countries (Australia, Hong Kong, the Netherlands and Singapore) and five organizations (BCBS, BIS, IOSCO, OECD, and the World Bank).

69. See Sophie Béranger-Lachand and Christian Eugène, 'Le Club de Paris: Un Rôle Toujours Central', *Bulletin de la Banque de France*, Paris, no. 81, September 2000; see also www.clubdeparis.org.

70. See *The Riksbank's Opinion* (see note 87 of Chapter 5), pp. 70–85.

71. Requiring the approval of three-fifths of the members and 85 per cent of the total voting power.

72. See 'Modified Sovereign Debt Proposal', *IMF Survey*, Washington, DC, 8 April 2002, pp. 98–100; and Ann O. Krueger, *A New Approach to Sovereign Debt Restructuring*, (Washington, DC: IMF, April 2002).

73. IMF's International Monetary and Financial Committee, 'IMFC communique–Ministers press for progress on global trade talks', in: *IMF Survey*, Washington, DC, 21 April 2003, pp. 99–102.

74. See, for example, *The Resolution of International Financial Crises: Private Finance, Public Funds*, Joint working paper, Bank of Canada/Bank of England, 2001.

75. See Barry Eichengreen and Michael Mussa, 'Capital Account Liberalization and the IMF', *Finance & Development*, (Washington, DC: IMF, December 1998), vol. 35, no. 4.

76. See also *Deutsche Bundesbank Monthly Report*, July 2001.

77. See also Lee Hsein Loong, *Post Crisis Asia: The Way Forward*, (Washington, DC: Group of Thirty, 2001).

78. See, for example, Stanley Fischer *et al.*, *Should the IMF Pursue Capital Account Convertibility?* (Princeton, NJ: Princeton University, International Finance Section, May 1998); and Benu Schneider, *Issues in Capital Account Convertibility in Developing Countries*, Overseas Development Institute, London, June 2000.

79. See IMF, *World Economic Outlook*, Washington, DC, October 2001, pp. 145–73.

80. 'Monetary Policy Report to the Congress – 27 February 2002', *Federal Reserve Bulletin*, Washington DC, March 2002, p. 165.

81. Banks raise funds through repurchase operations or 'repos'. A repo is a liquidity-providing contract between the seller of that security in need of liquidity and the buyer of that security, whereby the seller agrees to repurchase the security in the future at an agreed price, and at a stated time.

82. Federal Reserve, New York State Banking Department, Office of the Comptroller of the Currency, and the Securities and Exchange Commission, *Summary of 'Lessons Learned' and Implications for Business Continuity*, Federal Reserve Bank of New York, 13 February 2002.

83. BIS, *72nd Annual Report*, Basel, 8 July 2002, p. 154.

84. Robert P. Hartwig, *The Long Shadow of September 11: Terrorism and Its Impacts on Insurance and Reinsurance Markets*, (New York: Insurance Information Institute, March 2002), www.iii.org.

85. Ref. Jason Bram, James Orr, and Carol Rapaport, 'Measuring the Effects of the September 11 Attack on New York City', *The Economic Effects of September 11*, Special Issue, Federal Reserve Bank of New York, November 2002, p. 5–20.

86. The bank (or security firm) obtains liquidity through selling its security to a counterparty (here the Federal Reserve), with the commitment to buy it back at a future agreed date (see footnote 81 above).

87. The Federal Reserve continued to credit the accounts of banks for deposited cheques, although cheques normally shipped by air could not be presented for settlement to the banks of cheque writers, because of the grounding of aeroplanes in the USA.

88. See S. P. Coleman, 'The Evolution of the Federal Reserve's Intraday Credit Policies', *Federal Reserve Bulletin*, Washington, DC, February 2002, pp. 67–84; and 'Monetary Policy Report to the Congress – 27 February 2002', p. 142.

89. See *IMF Survey*, Washington, DC, 17 September 2001, p. 293.

90. ECB, *Annual Report 2001*, Frankfurt, p. 80.

91. Dated 6 November 2002.

92. See, for example, 'G-7 Promises to Boost Growth in the World Economy', *Financial Times*, 8 October 2001, p. 7.

93. FSA, *Annual Report 2001/02*, p. 7.

94. See 'AIG Urges an End to War Insurance for US Airlines', *The Wall Street Journal Europe*, 27 February 2002, p. A5; and 'Airline Insurance', *The Economist*, 23 March 2002, p. 71–2.

95. See, for example, 'Nobody Looking at the Road', *The Economist*, 1 December 2001, pp. 45–6; and 'The Wrong Sort of Stimulus', *Financial Times*, 21 December 2001, p. 14.

96. The Federal Reserve Board, FDIC, Comptroller of the Currency, and the Office of Thrift Supervision, *Press releases*, 11, 13 and 14 September 2001.

97. See, for example, IMF, *The Global Economy After September 11*, Washington, DC, December 2001.

7 Overview and Conclusion: Regulatory Progress

1. See Edward Altman, *Corporate Financial Distress and Bankruptcy – A Complete Guide to Predicting and Avoiding Distress and Profiting from Bankruptcy*, 2nd edn (New York: John Wiley, 1993). [First published in 1968].
2. See A. Gilbert, A. P. Meyer and M. D. Vaughan, 'Could a CAMELS Downgrade Model Improve Off-Site Surveillance?', *Review*, Federal Reserve Bank of St. Louis, January/February 2002, pp. 47–63.
3. For example, Gertjan W. Vlieghe, *Indicators of Fragility in the UK Corporate Sector*, Bank of England, London, December 2001; and Trond Eklund, Kari Larsen and Eivind Berhardsen, 'Model for Analysing Credit Risk in the Enterprise Sector', *Economic Bulletin*, Norges Bank, Oslo, October 2001, pp. 99–106.
4. Logan, p. 22 (see note 51 of Chapter 3).
5. Arturo Estrella, Sangkyun Park and Stavros Persitiani, 'Capital Ratios as Predictors of Bank Failure', *Economic Policy Review*, Federal Reserve Bank of New York, July 2000, pp. 33–52; and Robert Bichsel and Jürg Blum, 'Gearing Ratios – A Survey', *Quarterly Bulletin*, (Zurich: Swiss National Bank, September 2001), pp. 48–58.
6. 2002 SmartStockInvestor.com.
7. See 'Pro Forma Forecasts Are Ill-Defined', *The Wall Street Journal Europe*, 28 May 2002, pp. M1, M6; and 'SEC Cautions Companies, Alerts Investors to Potential Danger of "Pro Forma" Financials', Press releases, 4 December 2001.
8. I. Carnahan and J. Novack, 'Two Birds, One Stone', *Forbes Global*, 4 March 2002, p. 23.
9. See, for example, Peter Stalder, 'An Economic Macro-economic Model for Switzerland', *Bulletin Trimestriel*, (Zurich: Swiss National Bank, June 2001), pp. 63–93.
10. This is provided, for example, by Lehman Brothers Eurasia Group in New York. It produces on a monthly basis for several emerging economies a stability index that provides a composite measure for a country's capacity to withstand political, economic, security and social shocks.
11. Adapted from a presentation by Claude Poppe, Citigroup, 'Crisis Prevention and Management', at the University of Lausanne's Graduate School of Management and Economics, 29 October 2002.
12. See Craig (see source of Table 7.2)
13. On the role of real estate booms in provoking financial crises, see Philip Lowe (note 66 of Chapter 5); and Richard J. Herring and Susan M. Wachter, *Real Estate Booms and Banking Busts – An International Perspective* (Washington, DC: Group of Thirty, 1999).
14. See also D. Barton, R. Newell and G. Wilson, 'Preparing for a Financial Crisis', *The McKinsey Quarterly*, 2002 Special edition, New York, pp. 79–87.

15. See, for example, Nicholas Barberis and Richard Thaler, *A Survey of Behavioural Finance*, National Bureau of Economic Research), Working Paper No. 9222, Cambridge, Mass., September 2002.
16. European Central Bank, 'Recent Stock Price Developments in the High Technology Sector', *Monthly Bulletin*, February 2002, p. 45.
17. See C. J. Neely, 'How Expensive Are Stocks?', *Monetary Trends*, Federal Reserve Bank of St. Louis, June 2002, p. 1.
18. For a review of directional changes models, see Marco Del Negro, 'Turn, Turn, Turn: Predicting Turning Points in Economic Activity', *Economic Review*, Federal Bank of Atlanta, 2001, 2nd quarter, pp. 1–12.
19. See, for example, David Hirshleifer, 'Investor Psychology and Asset Pricing', *The Journal of Finance*, August 2001, pp. 1533–97.
20. See, for example, Douglas Flint, 'Banker's View', *Enron et al*, p. 31–41 (full reference in note 16 of Chapter 4).
21. See, for example, Robert J. Shiller, 'Bubbles, Human Judgement, and Expert Opinion', *Financial Analysis Journal*, Charlotteville, Virginia, May/June 2002, pp. 18–26.
22. See, for example, Franck A. Schmid, 'The Tobin Tax', *International Economic Trends*, The Federal Reserve Bank of St. Louis, November 2001, p. 1.
23. See, for example, Henriëtte Prast and Marc de Vor, 'News Filtering, Financial Instability and the Euro', in *Marrying the Macro- and Micro-Prudential Dimensions of Financial Stability*, BIS, March 2001, pp. 301–9.
24. For references, see, for example, a series of articles on 'Taking the Offensive Against Corruption', *Finance & Development*, (Washington, DC: IMF, June 2000), pp. 2–21. For additional information on bribery in business sectors, and factors influencing corruption in various countries, see documents of *Transparency International*, www.transparency org.
25. Herbert Heaton, *Economic History of Europe*, (New York: Harper & Brothers, 1948), p. 654.
26. See, for example, Randall S. Kroszner and Philip E. Strahan, *Obstacles to Optimal Policy: The Interplay of Politics and Economics in Shaping Bank Supervision and Regulation Reforms*, (Cambridge, Mass.: National Bureau of Economic Research, March 2000).
27. See, for example, Anthony M. Santomero, 'Does Bank Regulatory Help Bank Customers?', *Business Review*, Federal Reserve Bank of Philadelphia, 2002, 2nd quarter, pp. 1–6.
28. See Andrew Crockett, *Issues in Global Financial Supervision*, BIS, 1 June 2001.
29. See BIS, *72nd Annual Report*, Basel, 8 July 2002, pp. 126–7; Alan Greenspan, 'Cyclicality and Banking Regulation', *Conference on Bank Structure and Competition*, Federal Reserve Bank of Chicago, 10 May 2002; and William R. White, *What Have We Learned From Recent Financial Crises and Policy Responses?*, BIS Working Paper no. 84, Basel, January 2000.
30. See, for example, Richard A. Brealy et al., *Financial Stability and Central Banks – A Global Perspective*, Bank of England Central Bank Governors' Symposium Series, (London: Routledge, 2001).

Select Bibliography

Note: In addition to sources cited in the text, the following biographical list offers a few recent references of pertinence to the subject matter of this book.

* * *

Agenor, Pierre-Richard, *Capital-market Imperfections and the Macroeconomic Dynamics of Small Indebted Economies*, Princeton Studies in International Finance No. 82 (Princeton, NJ: Princeton University Press, 1997).

Ariyoshi, Akira; Canale-Kriljenko, Jorge Ivan; Habermeier, Karl; Kirilenko, Andrei; Laurens, Bernard; Otker-Robbe, Inci. *Capital Controls: Country Experiences with their Use and Liberalization* (Washington, D.C.: International Monetary Fund, 2000) (Occasional paper/IMF; No. 190, 123 Seiten).

Auerbach, Alan J., Hermann, Heinz (eds), *Ageing, Financial Markets and Monetary Policy* (Berlin: Springer, 2002 348 Seiten) Papers presented at a joint conference on May 4 and 5 held by the Bundesbank and the Burch Center of the University of California, Berkeley.

Beim, David O. and Calomiris, Charles W., *Emerging Financial Markets* (Boston, Mass.: McGraw-Hill, 2001).

Benink, Harald A. (ed.), *Coping with Financial Fragility and Systemic Risk* (Boston, Mass.: Kluwer, 1995). (Financial and monetary policy studies; vol. 30). Parts of the book are reproduced from the *Journal of Financial Services Research*, vol. 9, nos. 3–4, 1995.)

BIS, *International Financial Markets and the Implications for Monetary and Financial Stability*, (BIS conference papers, Vol. 8) (Basel: Bank for International Settlements, 2000).

Bordo, Michael D., Mizrach, Bruce and Schwartz, Anna J., *Real versus Pseudo-International Systemic Risk: Some Lessons from History* (Working paper NBER; No. 5371) (Cambridge, Mass.: National Bureau of Economic Research, 1995).

Boughton, James M., *Different Strokes?: Common and Uncommon Responses to Financial Crises* (Washington, DC: International Monetary Fund, 2001).

Brealey, Richard A. [et al.], *Financial Stability and Central Banks: A Global Perspective* (London: Routledge, 2001).

Caouette, John B., Altman, Edward I. and Narayanan, Paul, *Managing Credit Risk: The Next Great Financial Challenge* (New York: John, Wiley, 1998).

Carmichael, Jeffrey and Pomerleano, Michael, *The Development and Regulation of Non-bank Financial Institutions* (Washington, DC: World Bank, 2002).

Chakravorti, Sujit, *Analysis of Systemic Risk in the Payments System*, Working paper, Federal Reserve Bank of Dallas, Financial Industry Studies (Dallas, Tx: Federal Reserve Bank of Dallas, 1996), pp. 2–96.

Chorafas, Dimitris N., *New Regulation of the Financial Industry* (London: Macmillan, 1999).

Chordia, Tarun, Sarkar, Asani and Subrahmanyam, Avanidhar, *Common Determinants of Bond and Stock Market Liquidity: The Impact of Financial Crises,*

Monetary Policy, and Mutual Funds Flows (New York: Federal Reserve Bank of New York, 2001).

Claessens, Stijn, Djankov, Simeon and Mody, Ashoka (eds), *Resolution of Financial Distress: An International Perspective on the Design of Bankruptcy Laws* (Washington, DC: World Bank, 2001).

Claessens, Stijn, Klingebiel, Daniela and Laeven, Luc, *Financial Restructuring in Banking and Corporate Sector Crises: What Policies to Pursue?* (Cambridge, Mass: National Bureau of Economic Research, 2001).

Daniel, Betty C. and Bailey Jones, John, *Financial Liberalization and Banking Crises in Emerging Economies* (San Francisco: Federal Reserve Bank of San Francisco, 2001).

De Bandt, Olivier and Hartmann, Philipp, *Systemic Risk: A Survey*, Working paper series, ECB, No. 35 (Frankfurt: European Central Bank, 2000).

Dekle Robert and Kletzer, Kenneth M., *Domestic Bank Regulation and Financial Crises: Theory and Empirical Evidence from East Asia* (Washington, DC: International Monetary Fund, 2001).

Dow, James, *What Is Systemic Risk?: Moral Hazard, Initial Shocks and Propagation*, IMES discussion paper series, Bank of Japan; 2000-E-17 (Tokyo: Bank of Japan, Institute for Monetary and Economic studies, 2000).

Durbin, Erik and Tat-Chee Ng, David, *Uncovering Country Risk in Emerging Market Bond Prices*, International finance discussion papers, Board of Governors of the Federal Reserve System, No. 639 (Washington, DC: Board of Governors of the Federal Reserve System, 1999).

Eichengreen, Barry and Bordo, Michael D., *Crises Now and Then: What Lessons from the Last Era of Financial Globalization?* (Cambridge, Mass: National Bureau of Economic Research, 2002).

Folkerts-Landau, David, Garber, Peter M. and Schoenmaker, Dirk, *The Reform of Wholesale Payment Systems and its Impact on Financial Markets* (Washington, DC: Group of Thirty, 1996). Washington DC: Group of Thirty, 1996/Working paper, Nr. 96/37, 48 Seiten.

Freixas, Xavier and Rochet, Jean-Charles, *Microeconomics of Banking*, 2nd edn. (Cambridge, Mass: MIT Press, 1998).

Freixas, Xavier, Parigi, B. B. and Rochet, Jean-Charles, *Systemic Risk, Interbank Relations and Liquidity Provision by the Central Bank*, DNB staff reports No. 47/2000 (Amsterdam: Nederlandsche Bank, 2000).

Frowen, S. F., Pringle, Robert and Benedict, Weller (eds), *Risk Management for Central Bankers* (London: Central Banking Publications, 2000).

Goodhart, Charles; Hartmann, Philipp; Llewellyn, David; Rojas-Súarez, Liliana, Weisbrod, Steven; *Financial Regulation: Why How and Where Now?* (Foreword by Eddie George, Governor of the Bank of England) Published in association with the Bank of England, London, 1998, 251 seiten.

Global Institutions, National Supervision and Systemic Risk: A Study Group Report (Washington, DC: Group of Thirty, 1997).

Global Financial Stability Report: Market Developments and Issues, World economic and financial surveys, September 2002 (Washington, DC: International Monetary Fund, 2002).

Hellwig, Martin, *Systemic Aspects of Risk Management in Banking and Finance*, WWZ discussion paper: No. 9519 (Basel: Wirtschaftswissenschaftliches Zentrum der Universität Basel, 1995).

Hernandez, Leonardo and Schmidt-Hebbel, Klaus, (eds), *Banking, Financial Integration and International Crisis*, Series on central banking, analysis and economic policies, Vol. III (Santiago, Chile: Central Bank of Chile, 2002).

Herring, Richard J. and Litan, Robert E., *Financial Regulation in the Global Economy* (Washington, DC: Brookings Institution, 1995).

Hull, Leslie, *Foreign-owned Banks: Implications for New Zealand's Financial Stability* (Discussion paper series, Reserve Bank of New Zealand, DP 2002/05) (Wellington: Reserve Bank of New Zealand, 2002).

Ishii, Shogo, (authored by a staff team led by Shogo Ishii and Karl Habermeier, with Jorge Ivan Canales-Kriljenko and others), *Capital Account Liberalization and Financial Sector Stability*, Occasional paper, IMF; No. 211 (Washington. DC, International Monetary Fund, 2002).

Jahjah, Samir, *Financial Stability and Fiscal Crises in a Monetary Union* (Washington, DC: International Monetary Fund, 2001).

Jonung, Lars, *EMU and the Euro, the First 10 Years: Challenges to the Sustainability and Price Stability of the Euro Area: What does History Tell Us?* (Economic papers, European Commission, No. 165) (Brussels: European Commission, Directorate-General for Economic and Financial Affairs, 2002).

Kaufman, George G. (ed.), *Banking, Financial Markets, and Systemic Risk* (Greenwich, Conn.: JAI Press, 1995). (Research in financial services, private and public policy, Vol. 7); papers presented at a conference in Washington, DC on 2 December, 1994.)

Kaufman, George G., *Banking and Currency Crises and Systemic Sisk: A Taxonomy and Review*, DNB staff reports No. 48/2000 (Amsterdam: Nederlandsche Bank, 2000).

Khambata, Dara, *The Practice of Multinational Banking: Macro-policy Issues and Key International Concepts*, 2nd edn (Westport, Conn.: Quorum Books, 1996).

Large, Andrew, *The Future of Global Financial Regulation* (Occasional papers, Group of Thirty, No. 57) (Washington, DC: Group of Thirty, 1998).

Lipsey, Robert E., *Foreign Direct Investors in Three Financial Crises* (Cambridge, Mass.: National Bureau of Economic Research, 2001).

Littlejohn, George and Fry, Adrian, *Systemic Risk Facing the World's Financial Institutions* (London: Financial Times, 1996).

Mishkin, Frederic S., *Financial Policies and the Prevention of Financial Crises in Emerging Market Countries* (Cambridge, Mass.: National Bureau of Economic Research, 2001).

Omotunde, E. G. Johnson (ed.), *Financial Risks, Stability, and Globalization: Papers Presented at the Eight Seminars on Central Banking*, Washington, DC, 5–8 June 2000, (Washington, DC: International Monetary Fund, 2002).

Pauses, Theodor, *Banking Crises and Public Policy in a World of Open Markets: How Should the International Financial System Be Reformed?* (Stockholm: Sveriges Riksbank, 2001).

Quintyn, Marc and Taylor, Michael W., *Regulatory and Supervisory Independence and Financial Stability*, Working paper, IMF, No. 02/46 (Washington, DC: International Monetary Fund, 2002).

Razin, Assaf and Sadka, Efraim, *Country Risk and Capital Flow Reversals* (Working paper series, NBER, No. 8171) (Cambridge, Mass.: National Bureau of Economic Research, 2001).

Reynoso, Alejandro, *Can Subsidiaries of Foreign Banks Contribute to the Stability of the Forex Market in Merging Economies?: A Look at Some Evidence from the Mexican Financial System* (Cambridge, Mass.: National Bureau of Economic Research, 2002).

Reuven, Glick, Moreno, Ramon and Spiegel, Mark M. (eds) *Financial Crises in Emerging Markets* (Cambridge University Press, 2001).

Risk Measurement and Systemic Risk, proceedings of a joint central bank research conference held on 16–17 November 1995 at the Board of Governors of the Federal Reserve System in Washington, DC (Washington, DC: Board of Governors of the Federal Reserve System, 1996).

Schachter, Barry (ed.), *Derivatives, Regulation and Banking*, (Advances in finance, investment and banking Vol. 3,376 Seiten) Elsevier, Lausanne 1997. (Advances in finance, investment and banking, Vol. 3.)

Stone, Mark R. and Weeks, Melvyn, *Systemic Financial Crises, Balance Sheets, and Model Uncertainty* (Washington, DC: International Monetary Fund, 2001).

Sundararajan, V., *et al.*, *Financial Soundness Indicators: Analytical Aspects and Country Practices*, Occasional paper, IMF, No. 212, (Washington, DC: International Monetary Fund, 2002).

Yamazaki, Akira, *Foreign Exchange Netting and Systemic Risk*, Discussion paper series, Bank of Japan IMES, No. 96-E-23 (Tokyo: Bank of Japan, Institute for Monetary and Economic Studies, 1996).

Index

225